PUERTO RICAN AMERICANS

ETHNIC GROUPS IN AMERICAN LIFE SERIES

Milton M. Gordon, *editor*

PUERTO RICAN

JOSEPH P. FITZPATRICK
Fordham University

AMERICANS

The

Meaning of

Migration to

the Mainland

PRENTICE-HALL, INC., ENGLEWOOD CLIFFS, NEW JERSEY

PUERTO RICAN AMERICANS

*The
Meaning of
Migration to
the Mainland*   FITZPATRICK

P: 13–740100–0   C: 13–740118–3

Library of Congress Catalog Card No.: 74–150712

Current printing (last digit):

10 9 8 7 6 5 4 3 2 1

Printed in the United States of America

PRENTICE-HALL INTERNATIONAL, INC., *London*
PRENTICE-HALL OF AUSTRALIA PTY. LTD., *Sydney*
PRENTICE-HALL OF CANADA LTD., *Toronto*
PRENTICE-HALL OF INDIA PRIVATE LTD., *New Delhi*
PRENTICE-HALL OF JAPAN, INC., *Tokyo*

This book is dedicated, con mucho cariño,
to the thousands of Puerto Ricans
who helped me write it.

Foreword

The problem of how people of diverse racial, religious, and nationality backgrounds can live together peaceably and creatively within the same national society is one of the most crucial issues facing mankind, second in importance only to the overriding problem of international war itself. Indeed, these two problem areas, while not identical, are, from the viewpoint of recurring social processes of group interaction, interrelated at many points. The United States of America, as the classic example of a highly industrialized nation made up of people of diverse ethnic origins, constitutes, both in its history and its current situation, a huge living laboratory for the serious study of various underlying patterns of ethnic interaction—patterns which produced in this country both corroding failure (particularly with respect to the treatment of racial minorities) and certain modified successes which, however, have by no means been free of a residue of unfulfilled personal hopes, psychological scars, and unjustified hardships for those who were not born with the majority sociological characteristics of being white, Protestant, and of Anglo-Saxon cultural origins.

The explosion in the 1960's of the Negro's or black American's anger and growing revolt against centuries of white prejudice and discrimination have shocked the nation out of an attitude of mass complacency with regard to ethnic group relations. Now, not only social scientists, academic liberals, and well-meaning humanitarians, many of whom had waged valiant battles against racism before, but also millions of other Americans in all walks of life are becoming aware that to devalue another human being simply on the grounds of his race, religion, or national origins, and to act accordingly, is to strike at the very core of his personality and to create a living legacy of personal hatred and social disorganization. All the great religious and ethical traditions have spoken out prophetically against ethnic prejudice (however weak their followers have been in implementation). Now it has become increasingly clear that sheer self-interest and the desire to preserve a viable nation sternly countenance the conclusion that prejudice and discrimination are dubious luxuries which Americans can no longer afford.

We have spoken of the social scientific knowledge to be derived (and, hopefully, to be creatively used) from intensive study of American ethnic groups. There is another reason to commend such focused scientific attention. The history and the decisive contributions of the various racial, religious, and national origins groups to the warp and woof of American life is not a story that, to say the least, has been overly told in American publication or pedagogy. The important pioneer studies on the Negro of E. Franklin Frazier, John Hope Franklin, and Gunnar Myrdal, and on the white immigrant of Marcus Hansen, Oscar Handlin, and John Higham, all stem from either the present generation or the one immediately preceding it. In the main, American minority ethnic groups have been, by patronizing omission, long deprived of their past in America and of a rightful pride in the nature of their role in the making and shaping of the American nation. It is time for a systematic overview, group by group, of this long neglected portion of the American experience, one that on the one hand avoids filiopietistic banalities and, on the other, does justice to the real and complex nature of the American multiethnic experience.

A final and equally compelling reason for instituting a series of studies of America's ethnic groups at this time is that more adequate theoretical tools for carrying out the respective analyses are currently at hand. In my book, *Assimilation in American Life*, published in 1964, I presented a multidimensional approach to the conceptualization of that omnibus term "assimilation" and endeavored to factor it into its various component processes, at the same time offering certain hypotheses concerning the ways in which these processes were related to each other. Such an approach appears to facilitate dealing with the considerable complexity inherent in the functioning of a pluralistic society. Furthermore, studies of social stratification or social class which have burgeoned to become such an important part of American sociology in the past few decades have made it abundantly clear that the dynamics of ethnic group life, both internally and externally, constantly involve the interplay of class and ethnic considerations. And, lastly, the passage of time, producing a third generation of native-born children of native-born parents even among those ethnic groups who appeared in large numbers in the last great peak of emigration to America in the early part of the twentieth century, has emphasized the need for considering generational change and the sociological and social psychological processes peculiar to each successive generation of ethnic Americans.

For all these reasons, I am proud to function in the capacity of general editor of a series of books which will attempt to provide the

American public with a descriptive and analytic overview of its ethnic heritage in the third quarter of the twentieth century from the viewpoint of relevant social science. Each book on a particular ethnic group (and we include the white Protestants as such a sociologically definable entity) is written by an expert in the field of intergroup relations and the social life of the group about which he writes, and in many cases the author derives ethnically himself from that group. It is my hope that the publication of this series will aid substantially in the process of enabling Americans to understand more fully what it means to live in a multi-ethnic society and, concomitantly, what we must do in the future to eliminate the corrosive and devastating phenomena of prejudice and discrimination and to ensure that a pluralistic society can at the same time fulfill its promised destiny of being truly "one nation indivisible."

MILTON M. GORDON

Preface

A book about the Puerto Ricans in mainland United States, with a special focus on those in New York City, is very risky but also is very necessary. It is risky because the Puerto Rican community is in a state of turbulent change in a city and a nation which are also in a state of turbulent change. So many different currents of change affect Puerto Ricans at the present time that it is foolhardy to attempt to describe this group adequately or put them into focus. Nor is it possible to point out clearly any one direction in which the Puerto Rican community is moving in its adjustment to life on the mainland. Its directions are often in conflict, and no single leader or movement has given sharp definition to one direction as dominant over others. It is not even possible to give an accurate statistical description of the Puerto Ricans, since the detailed data of the 1970 census will not be available until 1972.

Despite these risks, I found it necessary to write this book. What is most needed at this moment of the Puerto Rican experience, both for Puerto Ricans and other mainland Americans, is *perspective*: a sense of the meaning of the migration for everyone involved in that migration, for the new-comers as well as the residents of the cities and neighborhoods to which the Puerto Ricans come. Perspective is what this book seeks to provide. If it enables Puerto Ricans and other mainland Americans to live together by helping them understand the difficult process of adjustment they both must face, it will have achieved its purpose.

JOSEPH P. FITZPATRICK

Contents

CHAPTER FIVE

CHAPTER SIX

CHAPTER SEVEN

CHAPTER EIGHT

List of Tables and Figures

This book is a study of the latest of the great migrations to a city that has been made great by migrations; it concerns the experience of Puerto Ricans in New York. The study is not descriptive; the Puerto Ricans are fortunate in having had an abundance of able chroniclers to record the progress of their migration to New York.[1] Neither is it an attempt at a definitive study, which cannot yet be written, since the eventual pattern by which the Puerto Ricans will establish themselves in the city will not become clear for another generation. This book is what I would call an interpretative essay, an effort, at this point in the migration, to examine the meaning of the migration as a profound human experience for both the Puerto Ricans involved in it and the New Yorkers who react to it in a variety of ways, ranging from extreme hostility to extreme romantic enthusiasm.

It is my conviction that the meaning of the Puerto Rican migration can be initially understood only by perceiving it as a continuation of the experience New York City has always had with newcomers. It is not new or unusual that the Puerto Ricans should be coming to New York City in large numbers; rather, it would be unusual if the city did not have them or millions of other strangers in her midst. The presence of the stranger has given New York many of its unique characteristics. In coming to the city, the Puerto Ricans face an experience that is neither new nor unusual. They inherit the role of strangers, and

Old Experience, New Style

[1]The first book about the Puerto Rican migration was Lawrence Chenault, *The Puerto Rican Migrant in New York City* (New York: Columbia University Press, 1938). This was based on data from the early 1930's and is an excellent description of the Puerto Rican community. The next extensive study was C. Wright Mills, Clarence Senior, and Rose Goldsen, *Puerto Rican Journey* (New York: Harper & Row, Publishers, 1950). It is unfortunate that this excellent survey of the situation in the late 1940's has not been updated. *The Puerto Rican Study, 1953–57. A Report on the Education and Adjustment of Puerto Rican Pupils in the Public Schools of the City of New York*, J. Cayce Morrison, Director, Board of Education, New York City, was concentrated on educational problems, but provided extensive information about many aspects of the Puerto Rican community in the mid-1950's. Elena Padilla published an anthropological study of a small Puerto Rican barrio, *Up From Puerto Rico* (New York: Columbia University Press, 1958). Dan Wakefield's *Island in the City* (Boston: Houghton Mifflin Company, 1959) is an excellent journalistic account of the East Harlem Puerto Rican Community in the late 1950's. Christopher Rand's *The Puerto Ricans* (New York: Ox-

relive that painful but exciting drama of adjustment, the source of suffering and challenge out of which the strangers have consistently emerged as a new and greater people.

However, this perception of the significance of the migration in the context of the city's history is not sufficient. There are new dimensions to this migration, as there are new dimensions in the city's life. The Puerto Ricans have come for the most part in the first great airborne migration of people from abroad; they are decidedly newcomers of the aviation age. A Puerto Rican can travel from San Juan to New York in less time than a New Yorker could travel from Coney Island to Times Square a century ago. They are the first group to come in large numbers from a different cultural background but who are, nevertheless, citizens of the United States. They are the first group of newcomers who bring a cultural practice of widespread intermingling and intermarriage of peoples of many different colors. They are the first group of predominantly Catholic migrants not accompanied by a native clergy. Numerous characteristics of the Puerto Ricans make their migration unique.

Finally, they come to New York City at a time when many aspects of the city make their experience different. Change has always been part of the city's life, but change today is more rapid and extensive than ever before. Communication through radio and television has created a context in which people are in immediate contact, and in which news in all its visual detail is available in the home of a Puerto Rican migrant at the moment of its happening. In a world of telephones, people in Brooklyn and the Bronx can be neighbors more intimately than people separated by a city block could have been a century ago. The city is older, and much of its real estate is being replaced on an enormous scale. The Puerto Ricans come when more than a million Blacks are citizens of the city. They have lived through the days when the civil rights movement was

---

ford University Press, Inc., 1958), is also a journalistic account. Oscar Handlin presented a more careful historical analysis of the progress of the Puerto Ricans in *The Newcomers* (Cambridge, Mass.: Harvard University Press, 1959). Nathan Glazer and Daniel P. Moynihan included an important chapter on the New York Puerto Ricans in *Beyond the Melting Pot* (Cambridge, Mass.: Harvard-M.I.T. Press, 1963). The Introduction to the 2nd Edition, 1970, provides some comments on the contemporary scene. Patricia Cayo Sexton has done the most recent study of the Puerto Rican community in *Spanish Harlem: Anatomy of Poverty* (New York: Harper & Row, Publishers, 1966). Clarence Senior has published a succession of informative booklets with extensive information about the Puerto Ricans in New York. The first, *Strangers and Neighbors: The Story of Our Puerto Rican Citizens*, was published by the Anti-Defamation League of B'nai B'rith in 1952. This was republished in 1961 as *Strangers Then Neighbors: From Pilgrims to Puerto Ricans*, and was revised as a substantial paperback, *The Puerto Ricans: Strangers—Then Neighbors* (Chicago: Quadrangle Books, 1965). There is an abundance of more specialized material which will be noted at appropriate places in the following chapters.

at its peak, as white and Black dedicated themselves to the achievement of racial integration. They have seen the development of the Black Power movement, and their own experience has been seriously affected by it. They come when automation is creating a new kind of economy, and jobs which once were the great channels of immigrant advancement are being eliminated by the hundreds of thousands. They come when the City and Federal Governments provide a range of public services, from public housing to welfare, which did not exist half a century ago. Thus, the coming of the Puerto Ricans is not just a repetition of the past, because the past no longer exists, and no people exactly like the Puerto Ricans have ever come before. Any interpretation of the meaning of the migration in the perspective of earlier migrations must be related to the unique characteristics of the Puerto Rican people and of New York City in the third quarter of the twentieth century.

The focus of the present study is the quest of the Puerto Ricans for identity. This is the feature of their migration which they share most intimately with all other immigrant groups, and yet it is the aspect in which their experience both on the Island before they come, and in New York, is unique. Puerto Ricans on the Island are passing through a difficult period of distress. The question of identity, the question of "Who are we?" is critical. Therefore, the secure sense of identity—a deep-rootedness in a culture and tradition of long standing which most earlier immigrant groups had before they came—is being lost on the Island. From many points of view, Puerto Ricans on the Island have already been uprooted even before they come to the mainland. Second, after they arrive, they face a set of circumstances which make the quest for identity much more difficult for them than it was for earlier groups. Initial dispersal over wide areas, continued relocation, and the policy of integration in public housing make it more difficult for Puerto Ricans to establish or retain stable and strong Puerto Rican neighborhoods. The need of the great majority who are Catholics to adjust to integrated parishes, rather than having Puerto Rican parishes, largely eliminates the parish as the focus of identity, a role it played for almost all other Catholic immigrant groups. The facility of low cost travel back to Puerto Rico may make it easier to retain identity with the Island rather than establish a strong identity as a migrant people in New York. Finally, the variety of color among the Puerto Ricans, which may enable them to make a singular contribution to mainland cities, also complicates the problem of identity in the presence of mainland discrimination.

Therefore, the quest for identity among the Puerto Ricans will be the replaying of a familiar basic theme, but with significant variations. These variations make the adjustment of Puerto Ricans to New York a new human experience which may give us new insights into the process of migration, adjustment, and identification, and which should enable us to define more clearly the process of the assimilation of newcomers to the city's life.

THE BASIC THEME

I indicated above that one cannot understand the meaning of the Puerto Rican migration unless it is perceived as the continuation of the history of great migrations which constitute the essence of the way of life of New York City. Puerto Ricans have suffered greatly in New York, and New York has likewise suffered in their coming. Exploitation, discrimination, hostility, and distress are not new. In fact, difficult as life is in New York for many of the Puerto Ricans, it cannot compare in suffering with the experience of immigrants of a century ago. But New York has always been a troubled city, sometimes a violent one, because the city has always insisted on accepting the newcomers, on enabling them to become part of her own life. The pain of the newcomers, as well as that of the older residents, has a great meaning when seen in the perspective of the creative achievement to which the city has always been dedicated. No human achievement is gained without a price in effort and suffering, and the creation of what may be the greatest city man has ever built will certainly involve enormous human cost. Even more significant, however, is the kind of city that New York is. In a century and a half it has absorbed millions of immigrants from dozens of cultural backgrounds as different as that of Iroquois Indians from Russian emigrés. To cope with this variety and achieve a common life, provide advancement, and create an educational, economic, and political system which would enable the immigrants to develop themselves and participate actively in the city's life, is little less than a social miracle. The fact that it was attended by suffering and sometimes violence is not the mystery; the mystery is that it was done at all.

This experience did not occur only once; it has been a continuing event. Now, however, the Puerto Ricans are among the people sharing in it. New York is again remaking itself, physically and socially. Together with millions of other residents of a variety of backgrounds, it now numbers 1,400,000 Blacks among its citizens (making it the city with the largest Negro population in the world) and an estimated 800,000 Puerto Ricans (making it the city with the largest population of Puerto Ricans in the world). The process of receiving the newcomers continues. This time the creative effort is particularly difficult, since it involves integration of Blacks into the life of the City. But the same process of upheaval, distress, and rapid change will be part of the life of the citizens today as it was in generations past.

From this point of view, the distress of the city at the present time, particularly the difficulties which Puerto Ricans must face, is not a sign of decay or deterioration. It is part of the human effort and suffering involved in the continuing creative achievement of New York City. In this historical perspective the migration has a very positive meaning.

I have often been struck by the resistance to this point of view regularly found among both New Yorkers and Puerto Ricans. Many New York residents consider it unrealistic and overoptimistic. They are convinced that the city has reached a critical moment, quite unlike anything that has happened before; that disorder, violence, and fear of personal attack are signs of widespread social disorganization rather than pains of creative growth. This conviction of decay can easily be turned into an accusation against Blacks and Puerto Ricans as the responsible parties. More will be said about this issue later on. It is sufficient to note here that this conviction of a decaying city is not new; it appears at every difficult moment of the city's history, and lamentations about the decline of the city are not as serious today as they were in previous generations.

The resistance of many Puerto Ricans to the optimistic point of view takes a different form. They are generally appalled at the extent and intensity of suffering which they see their people facing in New York. Understandably, they attribute the problem not to the Puerto Rican people, but to the city. They project into a judgment on New York the same judgment they make about the consequences of rapid industrialization and commercialization on the Island. They see New York as the most evident example not only of what is right in an advanced technological age, but also of all that is wrong with it. It is impersonal, materialistic, secular, and it makes particularly difficult the kind of human relationships which characterized the culture of Puerto Rico. This point of view does not perceive the city in decay, but rather sees it as too highly developed along technological and commercial lines to permit the human kind of existence to which Puerto Ricans are adapted.

The objective of the present book is not to refute these points of view. I do not think they can be convincingly refuted, any more than I believe that my own point of view can be convincingly established. All three viewpoints deal with prophecy, an estimate of the nature of present conditions in terms of their future consequences. History will prove which, if any, view was correct. The present book is an attempt to seek the meaning of the Puerto Rican migration in the only sources from which we can seek the meaning of any migrations to New York, that is, in the meaning that migrations have had in the past. In this sense, we are not dealing with prophecy. We live in the consequences of the previous experience of the city, and we know that what thousands of knowledgeable people considered to be signs of decay and deterioration were actually the pains of creative growth. In that perspective, as we see repeated the experience of the past, the optimistic interpretation is reasonable. The sufferings of the Puerto Ricans today can be seen as the pains of a creative growth toward the future. Their problem of identity is the problem of becoming New Yorkers, of establishing themselves confidently and securely as part of the great tradition and social process which has issued in the life of the world's greatest city.

THE PUERTO RICANS

It is not easy to find the meaning of the migration in the other two dimensions mentioned above—the unique characteristics of the Puerto Ricans and the new characteristics of New York City. The Puerto Ricans are different from any group that has come before, and the character of their migration is unique in many ways. Their quest for identity is not simply a repetition of the older experiences.

The crucial point is the problem of what specific identity the Puerto Ricans will eventually have as they become New Yorkers, and what specific problems of assimilation they will face. A history of Puerto Rican migrations is not very helpful. They have migrated before, to Hawaii and to South America, but never in numbers comparable with the migration to New York, and there is little in either experience which helps us to perceive the meaning of the present one.

However, the peculiar problem of identity with which the Puerto Ricans have been struggling for the past generation on the Island can be helpful here. There suddenly appeared an interesting convergence of United States citizenship (which enables them to move freely to the mainland), a new political status (they are neither independent nor a State, but a Free Associated State), rapid economic development (of which Puerto Rico is the most impressive example in the world), and changing religious conditions (they have been strongly influenced by American Catholicism at a time when all of North America suddenly awakened to the importance of Catholicism in the Latin World). These and a number of other experiences have propelled the people of the Island at a disturbing pace into a significant but uncertain role in the rapid developments of the world today. What and who the Puerto Ricans are must be related to all of this, because their efforts to clarify their identity for themselves are taking place in this troublesome context.

The struggle for identity in New York, the emergence of the Puerto Ricans as a specific kind of New Yorkers, will be related to these experiences which have shaken the Island and have created the challenge out of which they must make of themselves, in one sense, a new people. While this takes place in the world from which they come, the identity which they will seek to preserve in New York (and which they will eventually succeed in preserving) will be deeply affected by it.

THE CITY OF NEW YORK

Finally there is the new dimension in the experience of newcomers which has developed out of changes in the city of New York. The coming of the Puerto Ricans represents not only a new people facing an old experience, but a new people facing an old experience in a new city. There is no way of telling at present what effect changes in the city will have on the assimilation of the Puerto Ricans. At least it may be said that the experience of migration and assimilation will be deeply affected by the nature of the urban way of life which is emerging in the modern complicated city. Consequently, an interpretation of the experience of the Puerto Ricans will depend on one's interpretation of the nature of the modern city, whether one views the city as an approach to Orwell's *1984* or Huxley's *Brave New World*, or as a creative leap to a much higher level of human achievement. The difficulties of the migration will be seen either as part of the effort of Puerto Ricans to share the unfolding history of a much greater and richer world, or as another manifestation of man's struggle with the destructive environment of the modern city.

The problem of identity will also be interpreted in the context of either of these views. Scholars who accept the optimistic view will perceive the struggle for identity as part of that distressing human experience which always attends the efforts of men to break through a limited, traditional world in order to become part of a larger, more expansive way of life. Those who accept the pessimistic view will perceive it as the effort of the Puerto Ricans to preserve the values of the past and protect themselves against the destructive anonymity of the present.

IDENTITY

The central concept with which we will be dealing is that of identity, those points of reference whereby persons (or a group) define themselves in relation to the world and to other people: an awareness of persons (or a group) of who they are and where they belong. In the extensive literature about migrations, identity is singled out as the central problem of people who have been uprooted from their way of life and are seeking to establish themselves anew. As Will Herberg expresses it, as with individuals, so with groups, the basic question of existence which must be answered is "Who am I?" Uprooting is simply the loss of those perceptions of values and points of reference by which a person defines his relationships to others. The problem of adaptation to a new way of life, the process of assimilation or integration (whichever it may be called), involves developing a new set of reference points which enable the person or group to define who they are, what they are, and where they belong. This is the problem of identity.

A number of significant books in recent years have analyzed this problem and clarified many of its aspects. From Will Herberg's provocative analysis[2] to Milton Gordon's work,[3] the quest for identity as the central problem of immigrants is unfolded in abundant detail.

Therefore, a study of the experience of Puerto Ricans in New York has the benefit of an extensively developed theory with which to start. At the same time, in view of the unusual character of this migration, a study of the Puerto Ricans promises to provide new insights, as well as a testing of theory which will enable it to be modified, sharpened, and made more comprehensive.

The second chapter of the book will offer a brief historical sketch of Puerto Rico and of the Puerto Rican migration in order to provide some helpful reference points for the larger study. The third chapter will attempt to record as completely as possible the present state of the theory of assimilation, particularly in terms of community and identity. The following chapters will then examine those areas in the Puerto Rican experience in which the problem of identity is most acute: (a) the background of uncertainty on the Island; (b) the difficulty of achieving solidarity as a Puerto Rican community in New York; (c) the difficult problem of identification on the basis of race and color; (d) the problem of religion as related to Puerto Rican identity; (e) a series of particularly troublesome problems in education, public welfare, mental illness, and drug abuse; and (f) the problem of commitment to the mainland in view of the possibility of ready return to the Island.

What is the value of such a study? In the presence of a great human experience—and the migration of Puerto Ricans to New York is a great human experience for both Puerto Ricans and New Yorkers—man's basic

---

[2]Will Herberg, *Protestant, Catholic, Jew* (Garden City, N.Y.: Doubleday & Company, Inc., 1955).

[3]Milton Gordon, *Assimilation in American Life* (New York: Oxford University Press, Inc., 1963).

effort is to understand it, because in such an understanding man comes to understand himself; the range of human knowledge is expanded.

Migration and assimilation are processes which regularly involve unrest, conflict, and hostility. The more man understands them, the more capable he is likely to be of resolving the conflict, moderating the hostility, and enabling the assimilation to take place more peacefully. This would be especially true of the Puerto Rican situation in New York. A clearer understanding of the process through which they are passing would enable them and other New Yorkers to prevent social conflict from arising, to reduce it when it does occur, and to make a creative adjustment to their new way of life. Furthermore, migration, displacement, expulsion, flight, and the pursuit of a better life are commonplace experiences in the modern world. Insights into the nature of migration and assimilation and the development of more reliable theory concerning these human processes would enable men to be of assistance to the increasing millions who experience the problems of uprooting and the formation of a new life in a new land.

According to the 1960 census, almost 900,000 Puerto Ricans were living in the mainland United States in that year. The great majority of these (about 615,000, close to 70 per cent) had been born in Puerto Rico and had migrated to the mainland; about 275,000, close to 30 per cent, had been born on the mainland to Puerto Rican parents. In 1950, 80 per cent of the Puerto Rican mainland population lived in New York City; by 1960, the percentage had declined to 70 per cent (see Table 2–1).

This represents a substantial movement of people. Actually, since Puerto Ricans are citizens of the United States, their migration to the mainland is part of the general movement of U.S. citizens from one part of the country to another. In terms of internal migration, the movement of the Puerto Ricans is relatively small. However, they come from a cultural background quite different from that of the mainland, so in this sense they are "newcomers," living as "strangers in our midst," and their experience resembles that of earlier immigrants who came from foreign lands. From this viewpoint they are a cultural minority of considerable size.

Dynamics of Migration

Puerto Ricans had been known in the United States during the nineteenth century, generally as men of some importance who distinguished themselves in some way by their achievements.[1] However, it was the movement of large numbers of poor Puerto Ricans that gave the character to the Puerto Rican population of more recent years. This movement began in 1898 after the annexation of Puerto Rico to the United States following the Spanish-American War. By 1910, 1,513 Puerto Ricans were living on the mainland, more than one-third of them in New York City. A considerable number were at-

[1]Many were political exiles working from a base in New York for the independence of the Island. Prominent among them were Ramon E. Betances, an early and vigorous leader of the independence movement. Working with Betances in New York, was Eugenio Maria de Hostos. Lola Rodriquez de Tio, author of the national hymn of Puerto Rico, *La Borinqueña*, frequently spent time in the city. Francisco Gonzalez Marin Shaw (Pachin Marin), who had founded his revolutionary newspaper, *El Postillon*, in Puerto Rico, came to New York, where he continued to publish it after it had been suppressed on the Island. Sotero Figueroa, Luis Muñoz Rivera, father of Luis Muñoz Marin, and Santiago Iglesias, founder of the Socialist Party in Puerto Rico, also spent time in New York. It was a colorful, militant group, many of whom were disappointed when the United States annexed the Island in 1898 instead of granting it the independence for which many of them had struggled.

TABLE 2–1

PERSONS OF PUERTO RICAN ORIGIN IN
COTERMINOUS UNITED STATES AND NEW YORK CITY:
1920 TO 1960

Nativity and Year	United States		New York City	
	Number	% Increase	Number	% of Total
Puerto Rican birth				
1960	615,384	172.2	429,710	69.8
1950	226,110	223.2	187,420	82.9
1940	69,967	32.6	61,463	87.8
1930	52,774	346.8	—[a]	—[a]
1910	1,513	—[a]	554	36.6
Puerto Rican parentage[b]				
1960	272,278	261.8	182,864	67.2
1950	75,265	—[a]	58,460	77.7

SOURCE: U.S. Bureau of the Census, *U.S. Census of Population, 1960. Subject Reports. Puerto Ricans in the United States.* Final Report. PC(2)-1D (Washington, D.C.: U.S. Government Printing Office, 1963), Table A, p. viii.

[a]Not available.

[b]Born in the United States.

tracted to the mainland during World War I because jobs were plentiful; still more continued to come during the prosperous days of the 1920's. They numbered close to 53,000 on the mainland in 1930. The trend reversed during the early days of the depression in the early 1930's, and was beginning to increase again when the outbreak of World War II, the involvement of the United States in the war, and the activity of submarine warfare in the Caribbean cut off practically all movement between 1940 and 1945. After the end of World War II, movement to the mainland increased steadily until it reached its peak in the early 1950's (see Table 2–2).

It is important to note one characteristic of these figures. The intensity of migration has always been calculated by taking the difference between number of persons arriving on the mainland from Puerto Rico and number departing for Puerto Rico. The difference, indicating either a net flow to the mainland or back to the Island, has been used as an index of migration. There are difficulties in this method. There is no way of telling the characteristics of the persons traveling, how many are Puerto Ricans coming to the mainland for the first time, how many are coming

TABLE 2–2

PUERTO RICO PASSENGER TRAFFIC FOR
FISCAL YEARS 1940–1969 (NUMBER OF PERSONS)

Fiscal Years	Departures	Arrivals	Net Balance
1940	24,932	23,924	− 1,008
1941	30,916	30,416	− 500
1942	29,480	28,552	− 928
1943	19,367	16,766	− 2,601
1944	27,586	19,498	− 8,088
1945	33,740	22,737	− 11,003
1946	70,618	45,997	− 24,621
1947	136,259	101,115	− 35,144
1948	132,523	104,492	− 28,031
1949	157,338	124,252	− 33,086
1950	170,727	136,572	− 34,155
1951	188,898	146,978	− 41,920
1952	258,884	197,226	− 61,658
1953	304,910	230,307	− 74,603
1954	303,007	258,798	− 44,209
1955	315,491	284,309	− 31,182
1956	380,950	319,303	− 61,647
1957	439,656	391,372	− 48,284
1958	467,987	442,031	− 25,956
1959	557,701	520,489	− 37,212
1960	666,756	643,014	− 23,742
1961	681,982	668,182	− 13,800
1962	807,549	796,186	− 11,363
1963	930,666	925,868	− 4,798
1964	1,076,403	1,072,037	− 4,366
1965	1,265,096	1,254,338	− 10,758
1966	1,475,228	1,445,139	− 30,089
1967	1,628,909	1,594,735	− 34,174
1968	1,858,151	1,839,470	− 18,681
1969	2,105,217	2,112,264	+ 7,047

SOURCE: Puerto Rico Planning Board.
These data are for fiscal years. The figures
change considerably if they are given according to calendar years.

with the intention of remaining, or how many are going back with the
intention of remaining on the Island. In years in which one or two
million persons traveled each way, the net figure may indicate a migration
to the mainland of only one or two thousand, whereas in actuality 22,000
new Puerto Ricans may have come to the mainland for the first time, and
20,000 may have returned permanently to the Island. Thus, concealed
beneath a figure of net out-migration of 2,000 may be a sizable new migra-

tion of more than 20,000 people. It also must be noted that, since the earliest years, travel back to the Island has been heavy.[2]

In 1968, H. C. Borton attempted to calculate the flow of Puerto Ricans coming to remain permanently on the mainland or returning to live permanently on the Island. He identifies his data as a "mixture of guesses (1951–1955), census data on residence (1956–1960) and sample survey results (1964–1967)," but the data (Table 2–3) give some indication of the magnitude of the flow in both directions.

TABLE 2–3

MIGRATORY FLOW FROM AND TO PUERTO RICO
(YEARS ENDING IN MARCH)

| | Annual Averages | | | | | | |
	1951–55	1956–60	1961–63	1964	1965	1966	1967
Emigration	60,000	55,400	38,000	43,000	66,000	79,600	76,700
Immigration	10,000	15,400	29,000	51,000	50,000	49,600	42,700
	−50,000	−40,000	−9,000	+8,000	−16,000	−30,000	−34,000

SOURCE: H. C. Borton, Jr., "The Employment Situation in Puerto Rico and Migratory Movements Between Puerto Rico and the United States," in *Summary of Proceedings: Workshop on "Employment Problems of Puerto Ricans,"* Center for the Study of the Unemployed, Graduate School of Social Work, New York University, 1968, Table V, p. 53.

FACTORS CONTRIBUTING
TO MIGRATION

A number of factors have contributed to the migration. *Population increase* on the Island has been one of them. Like most underdeveloped areas in 1898, Puerto Rico had a high birth rate and a high death rate, with a reasonably low rate of natural increase. As a result of improved medical services and hygiene, the death rate began to decline, and by 1950 reached a point lower than the death rate of mainland U.S.A. The birth rate continued at high levels, leading to an unusually rapid rate of population growth (Table 2–4).

This population increase took place in the presence of an underdeveloped economy, thus creating a strong *economic pressure* to seek relief

[2]The first study of migration back to the Island was published by José Hernandez Alvarez, *Return Migration to Puerto Rico*, Population Monograph Series, No. 1, Institute of International Studies (Berkeley, Calif.: University of California Press, 1967). The latest study of remigration is found in Eva E. Sandis, "Characteristics of Puerto Rican Migrants to, and from, the United States," *The International Migration Review*, IV (Spring, 1970), 22–43.

TABLE 2–4

ESTIMATED RATES OF NATURAL INCREASE,
PUERTO RICO, 1887–1969

Intercensal Interval or Year	Estimated Annual Birth Rate per 1,000	Estimated Annual Death Rate per 1,000	Estimated Rate of Natural Increase
1887–1899	45.7	31.4	14.3
1899–1910	40.5	25.3	15.2
1910–1920	40.4	24.0	16.4
1920–1930	39.3	22.1	17.2
1930–1935	39.0	20.1	18.9
1935–1940	40.2	19.2	21.0
1940–1945	40.6	15.7	24.9
1950	38.5	9.9	28.6
1955	35.2	7.2	28.0
1960	32.2	6.7	25.5
1965	30.1	6.7	23.4
1969 (provisional)	24.3	6.3	18.0

SOURCE: 1887–1945: H. Perloff, *Puerto Rico's Economic Future* (Chicago: University of Chicago Press, 1950), p. 197. 1950–1969: *Annual Vital Statistics Report*, Department of Health, Puerto Rico, 1969.

elsewhere. Per capita income in 1939–1940 was $121 (at 1964 prices).[3] The economy was based primarily on production of sugar, tobacco, and coffee, which required large amounts of labor for some months of the year and left the majority unemployed during the rest of the year. In 1946–1947, for example, the average months worked per worker in sugar was 8.7, in tobacco 5.0, and in coffee 6.8. The averages do not reveal the intensity of unemployment, however. In 1946–1947, out of 130,000 employes in sugar production, 30,000, almost 25 per cent, worked five months or less during the year. The situation was worse in tobacco and coffee.[4]

Finally, Puerto Ricans, being citizens, have no *legal or political* restrictions on migration. Therefore, by the end of World War II, all of the elements of a large mass migration were present: pressure from the Island, availability of employment on the mainland, a beachhead of relatives and friends on the mainland, freedom to move, and availability of cheap transportation. The great migration began. The migration has

[3]Office of the Commonwealth of Puerto Rico, 322 W. 45th Street, N.Y., N.Y., 10036, *A Summary in Facts and Figures*, 1964–65 edition, p. 10.
[4]Harvey S. Perloff, *Puerto Rico's Economic Future* (Chicago: University of Chicago Press, 1950), p. 146.

always followed economic trends on the mainland. When employment is up, the migration increases; when employment drops, it decreases. The importance of the economic regulator is obvious.[5]

Transportation has also been a major factor. Commercial air travel between the Island and the mainland developed rapidly after World War II. As travel increased, the rates for plane travel dropped. At the present time, a person can travel from Island to mainland for less than $50.00. Agencies even provide special credit arrangements—$5.00 down and easy payments per month bring a person to New York.

The Puerto Ricans, therefore, constitute the first airborne migration to the United States, making their experience in this regard different from that of earlier migrants. Travel conditions for earlier immigrants were often horrible. The Puerto Ricans have had little of this to face. Apart from the fear that may have attended the first long flight over the ocean, conditions of air travel have been generally excellent. The trip in the early two engine planes took eight hours; in the four engine propeller planes, it was six hours; now, in commercial jets, it is three hours and ten minutes.[6]

The great majority of Puerto Ricans have settled in New York. However, in recent years, they have been dispersing over a much wider area. The states and cities with largest populations are listed in Table 2–5.

THE CONTRACT
FARM WORKER PROGRAM

As early as 1940 Puerto Ricans had begun to enter the migrant farm labor stream along the East Coast. Employers came to Puerto Rico and

[5]Myths become associated with every migration, and the Puerto Ricans have theirs in abundance. One of the earliest was the myth that Congressman Vito Marcantonio, who was widely accused of Communist affiliations, was bringing the Puerto Ricans to New York and arranging to get them on public welfare in order to get their votes. It is surprising that such a belief—and it was widespread—could have developed. The numbers of Puerto Ricans in Marcantonio's district were never large enough to be politically significant. Furthermore, Puerto Ricans were hampered by a language problem that made it difficult for them to qualify for registration. Until 1964 they were required to pass a literacy test in English. Finally, even at best, Puerto Ricans have been rather slow to engage in political activity. Nevertheless, the myth of Puerto Rican support for Marcantonio was so strong that, in the mayoralty election of 1949, Mayor William F. O'Dwyer, running for reelection, created a "Mayor's Committee for Puerto Rican Affairs" to give the impression of great interest in the Puerto Rican community. Actually, it was not needed. In Manhattan, Marcantonio polled about 20 per cent of the total vote. In Marcantonio's district, then including the largest concentration of Puerto Ricans, less than 20 per cent of the entire population was Puerto Rican.

[6]Air travel has been impressively safe. The last fatal accident in Mainland-San Juan air travel occurred in 1952.

TABLE 2–5

PUERTO RICAN POPULATION BY STATES
AND SELECTED CITIES

California	28,108	New Jersey	55,351
Connecticut	15,247	Camden	3,759
Bridgeport	5,840	Hoboken	5,313
Hartford	2,307	Jersey City	7,427
New Haven	1,169	Newark	9,698
Waterbury	1,027	Patterson	5,123
		Passaic	1,713
Florida	19,535	Perth Amboy	2,718
Miami	6,547	Trenton	1,803
		New York	642,622
Hawaii	4,289	Buffalo	2,172
Honolulu	3,129	New York City	612,574
		Rochester	1,990
Illinois	36,081	Ohio	13,940
Chicago	32,371	Cleveland	4,116
Indiana	7,218	Lorain	3,799
East Chicago	2,889	Youngstown	1,814
Gary	2,946	Pennsylvania	21,206
		Bethlehem	1,145
Massachusetts	5,217	Philadelphia	14,424
Boston	995	Texas	6,050
Michigan	3,806	Wisconsin	3,574
Detroit	1,549	Milwaukee	2,820

SOURCE: U.S. Bureau of the Census, *U.S. Census of Population, 1960. Subject Reports. Puerto Ricans in the United States.* Final Report. PC(2)-1D (Washington, D.C.: U.S. Government Printing Office, 1963), Table 15, pp. 103–104.

hired Puerto Ricans, who have always had the reputation of being excellent farm laborers. This arrangement was attractive because the active employment seasons on the mainland coincided with dead seasons on the Island. In the early 1940's, a large percentage of Puerto Ricans in Puerto Rico were employed in the harvesting of sugar cane. The sugar cane season ends in about June or July, when harvesting on the mainland becomes most active. As a result, a Puerto Rican could work in the United States from July until the end of October or November, and be back in Puerto Rico for the beginning of the sugar cane season in January.

However, it is well known that workers in the uncontrolled migrant labor stream have been victims of unfavorable treatment, suffering, and injustice. Puerto Ricans who moved with the stream were no exception, and suffered the added handicaps of speaking a different language and of having to make the initial trip from Puerto Rico to the mainland, and of having to get back to the Island when work on the mainland was finished. Puerto Rican and mainland newspapers began to run stories of the evils of the migrant farm worker labor stream, and demanded that remedies be applied.

Two laws passed in Puerto Rico in 1947 and 1948 attempted to regulate the recruitment of farm laborers there. The laws required that any mainland farm employer wishing to recruit Puerto Ricans on the Island had to do so under the form of a labor contract approved by the Department of Labor of Puerto Rico. The contract provides a guarantee of employment for the Puerto Rican worker of 160 hours in a given month at a prevailing wage level identified in the contract. Provisions are made for transportation to and from the Island, suitable housing, food and medical care, insurance, and death benefits. The farm labor contracts gave to Puerto Rican farm laborers on the mainland a measure of protection which most American farm laborers, whether in the migrant stream or not, do not have. The Office of the Commonwealth of Puerto Rico, established on the mainland, had responsibility for supervising fulfillment of the contracts in the mainland states.

An average of 20,000 contract farm laborers have been coming to the mainland each year. They come for varying lengths of time and to a wide variety of places. They harvest sugar beets in Michigan, tobacco in Connecticut, garden crops in New Jersey, potatoes in Long Island, and a range of other crops from Massachusetts to Illinois.

The farm labor program has been important in a number of minor ways with reference to Puerto Rican migration. In some cases a contract farm laborer and his employer would come to know each other, and the Puerto Rican worker would either stay on in the United States after the contract expired, or return later without a contract as a permanent employee. In many other cases, the contract farm workers do not return to Puerto Rico, but simply stay on in the area where they were working or move to a nearby city and establish a permanent residence. Many of the original Puerto Rican communities, such as those in Camden or Trenton, New Jersey, Springfield, Massachusetts, Detroit, Michigan, and Rockland County or eastern Long Island, New York, began with small clusters of former contract workers who remained on the mainland. Once established, these clusters attracted relatives and friends directly from Puerto Rico, and the urban Puerto Rican communities in these cities began to develop.

Contract laborers sometimes break their contracts for a number of reasons. The only control the employer has over a contract worker is his arrangement to pay the return flight to Puerto Rico if the farm worker fulfills his contract. The Office of the Commonwealth estimates that 10 per cent of the contract farm workers remain on the mainland as permanent residents. Furthermore, the farm labor contract gives thousands of Puerto Ricans their first experience with the mainland. They come into contact with relatives or friends, explore the possibility of permanent employment, become familiar with cities or towns near the farms where they are working, and, as a result, are prepared to move to any of these places if occasion offers. The account of the Rios family, which Oscar Lewis studied in *La Vida*,[7] describes the continual movement of this group of Puerto Ricans from one job to another and from one state to another, with a few months of farm labor, a few months in New York, a period of work in Pennsylvania, and periodic visits to Puerto Rico to see relatives, to seek temporary jobs, or to make an attempt at permanent residence in a Puerto Rican city.

The Puerto Rican contract farm labor program has provided employment for thousands of Puerto Ricans, and, through its control over the contracts, the Puerto Rican Government has sought to prevent the kinds of gross injustices generally found in the lives of migrant farm workers. Complaints have always been raised about the program: the workers have complained about poor housing, failure to fulfill contract provisions for hours of work, poor food, or poor working conditions; employers have complained about workers walking out on contracts. But the program has succeeded in avoiding the serious problems which affect workers in the migrant farm labor stream in the United States.[8] This is partly due to the fact that the Puerto Rican contract farm laborers do not have the difficulty of caring for a family traveling with them. In addition, the timely intervention of the Puerto Rican Government can prevent a difficulty from becoming critical.

The young militant Puerto Ricans have begun to demonstrate against the program, mainly on the charge that it is another manifestation of colonialism and capitalistic exploitation. They attribute the seasonal unemployment in Puerto Rico to radical dislocations in the economic system, and they define the farm labor program as a convenient system of getting poor Puerto Ricans to perform essential farm labor at a

---

[7]Oscar Lewis, *La Vida: A Puerto Rican Family in the Culture of Poverty—San Juan and New York* (New York: Random House, Inc., 1965).

[8]In the summer of 1970 serious protest developed around the migrant workers not covered by contract. Charges were made that migrant workers were jailed without due process or legal counsel; complaints have been raised about the violation of civil rights and intimidation by employers. For newspaper reports of the complaints, see *The New York Times*, August 17, 1970, p. 1; August 19, 1970, p. 26; August 20, 1970, p. 23; August 23, 1970, p. 39; August 31, 1970, p. 32. A feature article on the plight of migrant workers appeared August 23, 1970, Sec. 4, p. 5.

cheap rate. As a result, they criticize the Government of Puerto Rico for maintaining a system of exploitation rather than correcting the more fundamental problem of unemployment on the Island. Demonstrations have been directed at the Office of the Commonwealth in New York City at a moment (Fall 1970) when a new regime is in the process of reorganizing the work of the Office. The new regime is work centered rather than social service centered. It remains to be seen how its policy will affect the employment situation among Puerto Ricans on the mainland, and what changes this will involve in the farm labor program.

The major difficulty surrounding the farm labor program has been the problems Puerto Ricans face when they seek to establish themselves permanently in small towns in farm areas. Complaints regularly arise from permanent residents even in the vicinity of contract farm labor camps. Small rural towns are not prepared to provide recreation or ordinary community services to a population of different language and ethnic background; color has also complicated the problem, since many Puerto Ricans are defined on the mainland as colored, and meet with concomitant prejudice. If a small community of Puerto Ricans begins to settle in or near a small town, tensions can develop quickly over problems of schooling, employment, recreation, public order, and, if unemployment strikes the newcomers, public welfare. Much of the effort of the Office of the Commonwealth is directed toward resolution of these local community tensions. The unpleasant experiences of Simplicio, described in Chapter 37 of *La Vida*, are a good example of the problems of a Puerto Rican trying to locate himself in a rural area not accustomed to permanent Puerto Rican residents. Nevertheless, the clusters of Puerto Ricans continue to develop, with the result that, even outside the large city concentrations, hundreds of small Puerto Rican communities exist on the margins of the farming areas. In comparison to the cities, however, the numbers of Puerto Ricans in these rural communities are very small.

The contract farm labor program has not completely corrected the problem of Puerto Rican workers in the regular migrant worker stream. Hundreds still follow the crops on their own and face the usual problems of migrant farm workers in this country. No one has any accurate estimate of their number. The Office of the Commonwealth developed a program in 1969, financed by the United States Department of Labor, which sought to identify Puerto Rican workers in the ordinary migrant worker stream, and to resettle them permanently in small communities in centers of permanent farm employment. The program was not very successful. The Office discovered that it required a much larger staff than they had anticipated, that the community problems mentioned above made resettlement difficult if not impossible, and that, when resettlement did prove possible, there was no way to guarantee that the Puerto Ricans would remain. The project was given up in the Fall of 1969.

The farm work experience, apart from attracting Puerto Ricans who later settled in the cities, has been marginal to the Puerto Rican experience in the United States. An insignificant part of the Puerto Rican population lives in rural nonfarm areas or on farms, while about 95 per cent live in urban areas (see Table 2–6). The population is almost perfectly divided between men and women, indicating that, by 1960, the migration was definitely a family affair, in the sense that an equal number of men and women migrate and either marry before they leave the Island or after they arrive on the mainland.

TABLE 2–6

PERSONS OF PUERTO RICAN BIRTH
AND PARENTAGE IN THE UNITED STATES,
RURAL AND URBAN, BY SEX, 1960

	Total	Urban	Rural Nonfarm	Farm
Total	892,513	859,247	30,464	2,802
P.R. birth	617,056	593,883	21,040	2,133
P.R. parentage	275,457	265,364	9,424	669
P.R. birth				
Male	307,408	292,233	13,484	1,691
Female	309,648	301,650	7,556	442
P.R. parentage				
Male	138,953	133,532	5,088	333
Female	136,504	131,832	4,336	336

SOURCE: U.S. Bureau of the Census, U.S. Census of Population, 1960. *Puerto Ricans in the United States,* PC (2)-10, Table 1.

This is a large migration. Like many earlier migrations, its heaviest impact has been on the City of New York. In perspective, however, it still cannot compare with earlier migrations to the city. In the period between 1845 and 1855, the population of New York City increased from 300,000 to 600,000, and one-third of all inhabitants in 1855 were poor Irish or German immigrants who had come to the City in the previous ten years.[9] If one-third of the almost eight million people in New York in 1960 were Puerto Ricans who had arrived in the previous ten years, the city would have experienced a problem similar to the one it suffered

[9]Robert Ernst, *Immigrant Life in New York City, 1825–63* (New York: Kings Crown Press, Columbia University, 1949), App. 3.

through a century earlier. Furthermore, when the Puerto Ricans arrived, the city had a large number of well organized institutions to care for a needy population, institutions which its experience with newcomers had taught it to develop. Most important, the City had behind it a century and a half of experience of dealing with newcomers, with the poor, with immigrants or migrants seeking a new life. From every point of view it would seem that this latest of the great migrations should not have been burdensome to the city, and the way of the Puerto Ricans should have been made smooth by so many millions who had traveled the same way before. Such, for a number of reasons, was not to be the case.

When a group of people migrate from one area to another, they are usually leaving what they have traditionally recognized as their way of life, their culture. This culture has expressed itself in a definite geographical area, in activities which enabled the people to gather their food, provide their clothing and shelter, protect themselves, marry and raise children, and cope with the meaning and mystery of existence. This human interaction which constitutes the daily life of men is their society. In the framework of culture and society, as a member of a social group interacting with others according to commonly accepted norms, man finds his identity, knows who he is, where he belongs, and what his life and actions mean.

The problem faced by people migrating from their home and moving into a different society with a different way of life is to find a new identity, to adjust themselves to new forms of social interactions, and assimilate a new way of life. This is called *cultural assimilation.* In order to understand it better, some detail must be added about "culture," "society," and "identity."

Identity: The Abiding Problem

CULTURE

Culture is the sum total of all the ways of believing, thinking, feeling, and behaving which makes up a person's way of life. Culture consists of things that make a man German rather than Irish, or Puerto Rican rather than Japanese. It is the expression in a variety of human forms of the meaning that things have for a person, the reason he is alive, where is he going, and how is he going to get there. It is the burning of paper by the Chinese before the shrine of his ancestors; the careful chaperoning of girls by the Puerto Ricans; the reverent response of the Hindu to anything he believes is holy; the sense of personal pride of the Latin; the preference for family members of the Oriental; and the preference for efficiency, regardless of family, of the Anglo-Saxon.

A given culture is one of many possible responses men find to meet the basic questions and challenges of existence: the way to gather, exchange, and prepare food, and to provide clothing and shelter; methods of protection against enemies in nature or in the form of other men; defining and maintaining relationships with other men; and fulfilling oneself as a man. The variety of alternatives for answering these basic questions and fulfilling basic needs is remarkable. The Papuans consider the pig as sacred, while the Hebrews were forbidden to eat the pig. Western cultures have recently come to consider the woman equal with the man; in the Orient, and in earlier centuries in the West, she was considered subordinate. Families in village India choose the marriage partner for sons and daughters; American boys and girls insist on choosing a marriage partner for themselves. In Africa, a man feels he is important only as a member of his family; in the United States, family is almost lost in the emphasis on the individual as unique and independent.

The important thing about culture in the present discussion is that, in expressing the meaning that life and human activity have for a man, it enables the man to define himself. Culture is the basis of group identity, and as such it becomes the basis for personal identity as well. In a very real sense a person's culture is himself. It expresses the way man defines his origin and his end, his relationship to nature, to other men, and to God. In terms of this complex of interrelated meanings and values a man knows who he is, who others are, and what other people think he is.

"To be a man" is an important consideration for any male individual. But what constitutes "being a man" in one society will be quite different from what constitutes it in another. In the culture of Puerto Rico, being a man means having a keen sense of one's inner worth as an individual, exercising authority firmly over wife and children in a home; receiving proper respect from people younger than oneself; manifesting fidelity to deep family loyalties and a preference of family over others; and demonstrating a mastery over those types of work which are a man's responsibility, whether the humble cutting of sugar cane or the skills of a lawyer or architect. When one has achieved these elements, he has the confidence of knowing that others acknowledge him as a man. He identifies himself as a man by reference to the values of his culture, the expectations of his fellows.

The same is true for the many other roles which people fulfill as members of a society, such as being a wife or mother, a good son or daughter, a loyal and devoted neighbor, or a trusted friend. If these definitions suddenly change, a crisis of identity immediately arises. If exercising authority and loyalty to and preference for family members becomes challenged as a fault, and no longer means "being a man," the complex of meanings is confused. People are no longer sure what or who they are.

This kind of a change of culture, which is really a change of meaning occurs most sharply and rapidly in the experience of migration. People move into a way of life different from their own. What was defined as good in the way of life left behind may be bad in the way of life to which they come. What was defined as vice may now be defined as virtue. Behavior, such as the firm exercise of authority, for which they were praised in their former environment, may now bring them ridicule. And loyalties, such as the preference for family and relatives, may be criticised as a form of corruption. This is not simply a difference of opinion or custom. It creates a serious problem of identity for newcomers to a culture. Asking them to adopt a new culture, a new way of life, is really asking them to become someone else. This process is the most difficult aspect of migration and cultural adaptation.

However, the problem of identity has another dimension. It is related to the sense of group solidarity in the acceptance of certain values, goals, or meanings. Granted that a way of life according to commonly accepted patterns of behavior gives people a sense of belonging, of unity, there are generally elements in a culture which, more than others, come to symbolize the group and its unity and solidarity. This might be nation-wide—a common dramatic experience such as the years of oppression by the English were to the Irish, or the concentration camps were to the Jews; it might be dedication to a common cause. This symbol may become the center around which group loyalties crystallize, and it thus creates a strong sense of identity. In the process of migration and integration into a new culture, the presence of some impressive symbol is thus important in the preservation of a sense of identity. This will be discussed at length later on.

SOCIETY

If culture consists of patterns of interaction, society is the actual interaction; it is the people acting according to commonly accepted values, norms, objectives, and meanings. Men's relationships tend to become structured, acting in a definite relationship to one another. Young boys become formally acknowledged as adults in some societies when they reach the age of twelve. In the United States, entrance into adulthood is generally delayed until after years of schooling. Therefore, in the structure of American society, there are large groups of young people who constitute a school population. They generally do not support themselves; they are not adults, but are preparing for adult life; they constitute a large, recognizable sector of United States society which is not present in other societies.

For our purposes the important characteristic of the society of the

United States is its stratification—the manner in which its members are ranked from high to low on a socioeconomic scale. There are upper class, middle class, and lower class, or what large numbers of Americans claim themselves to be, working class. There are also the white collar class and the blue collar class. One may become very specific and speak of the upper-upper class, the middle-upper class, the lower-upper class, and so on. What all these categories seek to express is the ranking of people in the United States as higher or lower according to a set of norms which are not too clearly defined. This constitutes the class structure of the society of the United States.

I mention this aspect of the social structure because, in the present discussion, the problem of class is the problem most closely related to the problem of identity. The United States is, by ideal and by expressed definition, an open class society with equal opportunity for everyone to advance to that position to which his ability and effort entitle him. The central value of the culture is the value of the individual and, unlike most other cultures, this culture set out to release the individual from all the bonds of class, family, or race which would hinder him from developing himself fully and reaching the level which he deserved. Therefore, ideally, the man on a high level of society whose ability or effort do not warrant that position should yield the position to others; the person on a lower level whose ability and effort entitle him to a high position should find the way to his advancement open. Problems of prejudice and discrimination have hindered fulfillment of this ideal, but to a surprising degree it has worked. As a result, one central characteristic of American society is the phenomenon of upward mobility, of advancement through education, business success, and political power to social and economic positions higher than the ones at which one began.

The ideals of opportunity, upward mobility, personal fulfillment, and advancement are central to American culture. The interaction of the members of American society is constantly related to the effort of men to find their place in the range of positions. As a result, the problem of status becomes a preoccupation of Americans of all kinds and all backgrounds.

In more traditional societies, an individual's status was more inflexibly fixed. These were generally societies with two classes, a higher class who possessed the wealth, exercised the power, and enjoyed the prestige, and another class who were poor and did most of the manual or menial work. People were born into their class, and had no expectation of changing it. A poor farmer in Puerto Rico, for example, was in the same social position that his father and grandfather had occupied, and expected that his son and grandson would occupy this position. In this situation there was a stability to a person's status. An individual had no difficulty knowing where he belonged, what was his status, and how he was related to other people; life was consistent and secure.

When people from this kind of background enter an open class society with upward mobility, the lack of a defined status is troublesome. It is one of the most difficult aspects of the uprooting, and it is directly related to the problem of identity.

On this level, the problem of identity goes beyond acceptance by a person of a particular set of values or meanings. It involves the social interaction in which a person becomes aware that he is accepted by others as an equal in the acting out of these values or in expressing those meanings. It involves participation in that social interaction which touches such intimate aspects of human life as companionship, recreation, family relationships, courtship, and marriage. This means involvement in the social group which is expressing the culture in forms of social interaction, and is a much more difficult dimension of identity than that of cultural identity. It is referred to by contemporary writers as *social assimilation*, in contrast to cultural assimilation.

IDENTITY AND COMMUNITY

In a social setting, group identity normally exists where there is the experience of *community*. Community is the expression in social interaction of the common values and norms which bind a people together.

In his text on sociology, Timasheff[1] defines community as a group in which the value of a person in himself and as a person is previous to the achievement of any objective or the fulfillment of any function. He distinguishes it from association, which is a social group in which achievement of an objective or fulfillment of a function is prior to the value of the individual in himself. No matter how honorable a person is, if he cannot play basketball, he cannot be put on the team, whereas the member of a family is accepted for what he is regardless of his achievement.

What Timasheff is emphasizing is a social situation in which fulfillment of the person's life as a person is preeminent, and in which those satisfactions of life which are most deeply human are realized. This is the experience of community, within which the person is known, accepted, and esteemed for what he is, who he is and what he is being preeminent

---

[1]Nicholas S. Timasheff, Paul W. Facey, and John C. Schlereth, *General Sociology* (Milwaukee: The Bruce Publishing Co., 1959), Chap. 2 and 5.

over what he does. As a result, a person basically finds his identity in the experience of community.

Timasheff seeks to explain what constitutes a community, and he emphasizes first the bonds which unite people into social groups, the element of birth for the child in a family, and common attitudes and values for a group of friends, whether young boys in a gang or adults in a neighborhood group. The sharing of some great joy or sorrow may also serve as the bond of membership of a group which develops into a community. Central to the community, however, are common attitudes and values in which people are aware of their unity, and in the fulfillment of which they feel themselves as one, on the most basic levels of existence. Time, the span of years, generations, or centuries in which a group has existed and which now constitute its history or tradition, is a second important dimension. A third dimension is place, since every community must have a local reference. People feel they are somebody because they belong somewhere. They have land, fields, a shore, the city street, a nation. Goldenweiser says that "the basic character of locality as a social classifier has never been transcended."[2] The community can also be defined in terms of the nature of the interaction which takes place in it. It is generally face-to-face—the interaction of person to person, characterized by close acquaintanceship and direct communication. This interaction makes the individual aware of his oneness with the group. MacIver and Page emphasize the wholeness in the character of community experience. It does not deal with some segment or specific aspect of human life, but touches it in its totality: "The mark of community is that one's life *may* be lived wholly within it."[3] Some forms of community have a specific function (for example, the family's function is the reproduction and education of children). But for the most part, the function of community is psychosocial, providing for the individual the satisfaction of belonging to a group of fellow men, of being recognized and appreciated for what he is; of having a group supporting and perpetuating one's own values, and exercising a spontaneous, informal social control over its members.

It is in this kind of social group, in a community, that one has a deep sense of identity, and that the group is aware of its existence as a group. In this sense, community is closely related to the question of identity. Where community is strong, identity will be strong; where community is weak, identity is weak. If one wishes to strengthen the sense of identity, it is important first to strengthen the community.

[2]A. A. Goldenweiser, *Early Civilization* (New York: Alfred A. Knopf, 1929), Chap. XII.

[3]Robert MacIver and Charles Page, *Society* (New York: Rinehart, 1949), p. 9.

Community and the Process
of Assimilation

It is clear that community plays a central role in the experience of migration, uprooting, and assimilation into a new culture. The strength of the older community is weakened, perhaps lost, while the migrants face the task of reconstructing their community, strengthening it if it continues to exist, or adjusting to life in a new community.

The History of Assimilation

The relation of newcomers to the American nation and the process of assimilating them into its life have been marked by a great deal of ambiguity and controversy. The new immigrants were always needed by the nation. Without them, the nation could never have developed, for it would not have had the labor supply and the population it needed to expand and fill the land. Yet established citizens regularly received the newcomers with hostility. Intergroup conflict has been common on the American scene. Much of this was the understandable reaction of people whose way of life was upset and whose interests were threatened, and who therefore responded aggressively.

More serious were theories about assimilation which tended to glorify the way of life of the people of the United States and to disdain the way of life of the newcomers. Many nineteenth century writings glorified the white Anglo-Saxon and considered other races and ethnic groups as inferior. These writings attributed the achievement of democracy in the United States to the Anglo-Saxon, and explained the phenomenal developments of trade and industry as resulting from the initiative, vigor, and discipline of the Anglo-Saxon character.[4] This created an unfavorable

4Cf. E. N. Saveth, *American Historians and European Immigrants* (New York: Columbia University Press, 1948), for numerous examples of this theory. Other examples can be found in Edith Abbott, *Historical Aspects of the Immigration Problem* (Chicago: University of Chicago Press, 1926). Some of this was related to more theoretical principles of racial superiority, such as those of Arthur De Gobineau, *Essay on the Inequalities of Human Races* (New York: G. P. Putnam's Sons, 1932), and Houston Chamberlain, *Foundations of the Nineteenth Century,* tr. J. Lees (New York: John Lane Company, 1912). But a certain amount was the result of great enthusiasm about the obvious achievements of the United States, and a pride in the people who seemed responsible for it. The racial theories in their worst form cropped up again to influence United States immigration legislation; e.g., Madison Grant, and Charles Stewart Davison, eds., *The Alien in Our Midst* (New York: The Galton Publishing Co., Inc., 1930); *The Passing of the Great Race* (New York: Charles Scribner's Sons, 1916); Madison Grant and Charles S. Davison, *The Founders of the Republic on Immigration, Naturalization and Aliens* (New York: Charles Scribner's Sons, 1928). Even sociologist E. A. Ross, *The Old World and The New* (New York: Century, 1914), campaigned strongly

attitude toward the immigrant as one who would threaten the great achievements of the Anglo-Saxon, and therefore should be kept out of the United States, or compelled, when he came here, to adopt the ways of the traditional Americans (that is, the Anglo-Saxons) as soon as possible.

During and after World War I, this orientation shifted its emphasis. There appeared a willingness to accept the immigrant, accompanied by a determined effort to divest him of his traditional culture and get him to accept the American culture and way of life as quickly as possible. This has become known in sociology as the "Americanization" movement, and is commonly recognized as having been a mistake.[5]

While these theories were current, the concept of culture was being developed by anthropologists and sociologists. It began to appear noticeably in the immigrant literature in the study of Robert Park and Herbert Miller[6] and in the highly esteemed classic of W. I. Thomas and F. Znaniecki.[7]

CULTURAL PLURALISM

The new understanding of the nature of culture shed light on the experience of immigrants coming from a different culture and facing pressures to adjust to the American way of life. It became clear that the attitudes and customs of the newcomers were not trivial, something that could be adopted or discarded like a winter coat. They were rooted in the deepest values of life, and had a meaning for the immigrant that was related to his answer to the questions "Why am I alive?" and "Where am I going?" Thus traits such as the Irishman's apparent lack of thrift in spending for his family, the refusal of most immigrants to compete strongly against their fellow immigrants, and the unconcern of so many

---

against the admission of "inferior" races, attributing to this the decline of America. The racial theories were raised again at the time of the revision of the U.S. Immigration Law in 1952. Their influence was finally and fortunately ended with the Immigration Act of 1965 which did away with the use of immigrant quotas based on nationality origins.

[5]Read Lewis, "Americanization," in the *Encyclopedia of the Social Sciences,* Edwin R. A. Seligman, ed., Vol. II (New York: The Macmillan Company, 1930), pp. 33–35; Issac B. Berkson, *Theories of Americanization* (New York: Teachers College, Columbia University, 1920). Henry Pratt Fairchild, *The Melting Pot Mistake* (Boston: Little, Brown & Company, 1926), takes a somewhat modified position of "Americanization" which he modified still more in later works.

[6]Robert Park and Herbert A. Miller, *Old World Traits Transplanted* (New York: Harper & Brothers, 1921).

[7]W. I. Thomas and F. Znaniecki, *The Polish Peasant in Europe and America* (Boston: Richard G. Badger, 1918). This has been recently reissued by Dover Publications, New York, 1958.

immigrants with the making of money were not just the result of laziness or irresponsibility. Rather, when seen in the perspective of culture, they were often manifestations of a great sense of responsibility that expressed itself differently from that of the Anglo-Saxon. They came from a sense of obligation to give to one's relatives rather than save for oneself; from a love of children as a value in themselves above abundant earthly possessions; or from loyalty to "one's own kind" rather than a desire for self-advancement.

These cultural traits influenced behavior not only on its deepest levels, but also in many of its more superficial aspects, such as the kind of smile and when it was given; behavior at a wake or a wedding; the love of roughness at a celebration, and respect for physical strength; the way a friend was greeted, a meal served, or a type of clothing worn. These were all interwoven in an outlook on life that gave meaning to the work of a man's hands and the love of a man's heart; they gave life "the sense it made"; they were the source of a man's motivations and the support of his satisfaction. This was his culture.

Therefore, it was one thing to ask a man to become an American—millions of immigrants boasted that they wanted to be American. It was quite another thing to tell him that he had to discard the deepest values of his life, set aside all the traits that gave life its meaning, and adopt a pattern of ideas, attitudes, and customs which seemed to have no relationship to the lives of his fathers and grandfathers. In many cases the immigrants had become Americans precisely because they had conceived of America as the land where they would be free to live according to the values which they cherished.

In view of this, the concept of cultural pluralism was evolved. This viewpoint helped scholars to recognize the importance of the culture of the immigrant, and to acknowledge that his loyalties, values, and customs should exist in America together with the other culture that had come to be called American.

Practically all the current literature on immigration or migrant groups takes the concept of cultural pluralism for granted.[8] This is not to imply a naive belief that the immigrant culture is going to continue full-blown in an American environment. It is clearly recognized that it will eventually give way to a form of life which is predominantly Amer-

---

[8]See, e.g., Brewton Berry, *Race Relations* (Boston: Houghton Mifflin Company, 1951); Ruth Tuck, *Not With the Fist* (New York: Harcourt, Brace and Company, 1946), about the Mexicans of the Southwest; Pauline Kibbe, *Latin Americans in Texas* (Alberquerque: The University of New Mexico Press, 1946); C. Wright Mills, Clarence Senior, and Rose Goldsen, *Puerto Rican Journey* (New York: Harper & Row, Publishers, 1950); and the well-known college text, F. J. Brown and J. Roucek, *One America* (Englewood Cliffs, N.J.: Prentice-Hall, Inc., 1952).

ican. But this occurs most harmoniously when the culture of the immigrant is respected, and given every opportunity to survive in the midst of American society.[9]

This recognition of the importance of culture led to a new insight into the nature and function of the immigrant community. When the Irish began to cluster into their predominantly Irish neighborhoods, and the Little Germanys, Little Italys, and Jewish neighborhoods became so conspicious during the last century and the early part of this century, a great deal of concern was aroused among the older Americans. In many cases, the immigrants transplanted to the streets of New York almost the exact pattern of social relationships which had characterized their native habitats. The visitor to one of these sections could easily imagine that he was in a strange land.

The phenomenon was criticized because many people thought that these immigrant communities would prevent the members from becoming American. The immigrants continued to speak and to read newspapers in their native language; they went to churches where customs and religious practice reproduced the customs of the old country; they courted, married, raised their children, and died in an island of a culture different from that of the United States. As long as this continued, it was feared that they would not be exposed to American customs and ideas, and thus would never adopt those cultural traits which the Anglo-Saxon prized so highly, and to which he attributed the greatness of the United States. The immigrant community was seen as a threat to the great traditions of America. It became obvious as time went on that this was an unreasonable fear. Consistently, as the immigrant population went from second to third generation, the inevitable social process worked itself out; the third generation child, no longer a product of a foreign culture, was predominantly American.

Nevertheless, there seemed to be some regret that this should take

---

[9]Not all that has been said in the name of cultural pluralism has been said wisely. Every society, according to its values and the forms of behavior by which those values are expressed, places limits on variations which it will encourage or even tolerate. For example, Americans will not tolerate the practice of polygamy, regardless of how deeply rooted it may be in the culture of people who come here. Neither would Americans tolerate the selection of a marriage partner that gave no choice to either of the parties being married. Note the very strong opposition on the mainland to consensual unions among Puerto Ricans, which has been a fairly widespread practice in their culture despite the constant teaching of Catholicism to the contrary. Not infrequently, sociologists will describe as a tolerable cultural trait something that persons of other religious beliefs would condemn as immoral and inhuman. Cf. the difference between Ruth Benedict's consideration of culture traits in *Patterns of Culture* (Boston: Houghton Mifflin Company, 1961) and that of Father Andre Dupeyrat in *Savage Papua* (New York: E. P. Dutton & Co., Inc., 1954).

so long to accomplish. There was a widespread conviction that, if the immigrants could mingle more closely with Americans and be taught the language sooner, the process of adopting American cultural ways would advance more quickly. In some cases this was simply the rationalization of people who did not want the immigrants in the first place, but claimed that they would accept them "if they would only do things our way." In other cases, it evinced a sincere desire to hasten the process by which the immigrant would become "American." It was generally recognized that the factor which seemed to impede more rapid adoption of American ways was the immigrant community. Consequently, it was argued that if the bonds of the immigrant community could be weakened, and immigrants more directly exposed to American influence, they would become part of the American way of life much more quickly.

This last proposition has been strongly challenged in recent years, mainly because of growing appreciation of the role of culture in everyone's life. First, it has become clear that culture is the stabilizing factor in man's social life, giving it order and harmony. Any disintegration of a culture is attended by instability, insecurity, unrest, and even hostility. When the common values which govern people's actions, the common meanings that bind them together into a satisfying social unity, and the patterns of behavior that everyone takes for granted are shaken or shattered, man's social life becomes disorganized, perhaps chaotic. This was a particular problem for people moving from a "folk" culture, or from a traditional form of social life which was not consciously represented in their minds, but simply accepted from childhood as the "way things are done."[10]

The effect of this breaking down of cultures has been abundantly documented in studies of the second generation problem in America. The second generation are the people caught between two cultures. Born in the United States of foreign parents and raised at home in foreign ways, yet continually instructed outside of the home in a different culture, the members of this generation can easily slip into a cultural limbo.[11] If this distress is so marked among the second generation, imagine how much

[10]Oscar Handlin, *The Uprooted* (Boston: Little, Brown and Company, 1951), is an excellent description of the many aspects of the uprooting which points up the sadness mingled with the hope of the movement of people to a new culture.

[11]See Irvin Child, *Italian or American* (New Haven: Yale University Press, 1943), for an examination of the problem among second generation Italians. See W. F. Whyte, *Street Corner Society* (Chicago: University of Chicago Press, 1943); Hannibal G. Duncan, *Immigration and Assimilation* (Boston: D. C. Heath and Company, 1933), for an excellent treatment of first and second generation immigrants; see also Lawrence G. Brown, *Immigration; Culture Conflicts and Social Adjustments* (New York: Arno Press, 1969). Reprint of 1933 edition.

greater it would be among the first generation if they were deprived of the cultural surroundings of their traditional home, and the security that comes from the satisfaction of living among one's own.

It has become clear that the immigrant community played an important role in creating a stable and orderly situation in which the transition from one culture to another could take place. Instead of allowing him to fall into a completely disorganized life, which would have created serious problems for the immigrant as well as for the Americans, the immigrant community gave the immigrant security as he faced a bewildering new world. It offered protection and support in the face of a challenge to his traditional values, and exercised a strong social control that gave order and stability to his social relations. As a result, and despite the stress inherent in the transition, the immigrant moved toward a gradual acceptance of the ways of a new culture. Maurice Davie summarized the process:

> The essential functions of the immigrant community are to bridge the gap between the old country and the new, to prevent personal and social disorganization such as would result from too rapid change, and to interpret the American culture to the immigrant and prepare him to participate in it. . . . The newly arrived immigrant finds there a cultural haven without which he would be demoralized during the trying period of readjustment, and also assistance from the earlier arrivals in accommodating himself to the American scene.[12]

The result of these insights and discussions has been respect for the immigrant community as a form of transitional society which has enabled millions of immigrants to move gradually into acceptance of predominantly American attitudes and patterns of behavior.

In summary, the theory of cultural pluralism relating to the adjustment of people to a new culture would seem to suggest the following: No strong effort should be made to disorganize the community which immigrants or migrants may form as they move into the area of a new culture. They should be permitted to form communities of their own in which they will have security, stability, and order as they gradually learn American ways. Efforts should be made to help the immigrant preserve a genuine respect for his own culture as he acquires a knowledge of and respect for the new culture. Opportunities for association with older residents must not be blocked. The job and the school will be the first places to offer such associations. The neighborhood will become another place as the immigrant community begins to weaken and its members disperse.

[12]Maurice R. Davie, "Our Vanishing Minorities," in *One America* (3rd ed.), eds. F. J. Brown and J. Roucek (Englewood Cliffs, N.J.: Prentice-Hall, Inc., 1962), p. 547.

In this situation, the immigrant community will not shut its members off from gradual integration with their new culture; neither will it be blocked off in a ghetto-like segregation by the resistance of older residents. This is an ideal pattern which will never be wholly carried out in practice, but it has been the policy predominating in the last generation.

CONTEMPORARY THEORY

Community is a vital factor in immigrant assimilation because it is so contributory to the sense of identity of migrating peoples. To take apart the foundations of a person's identity before he has had the time and opportunity to develop a new identity in a new culture can be a serious threat to his whole personality. Consequently, the recent literature on immigration and assimilation centers its attention directly on the problem of identity in the experience of immigrants. The most significant contributions have been made by Will Herberg,[13] S. N. Eisenstadt,[14] Oscar Handlin in his classic on the subject, *The Uprooted*,[15] and in his more specific examination of the experience of Blacks and Puerto Ricans in New York, *The Newcomers*,[16] N. Glazer and D. Moynihan,[17] and Milton Gordon.[18] Three important developments, related to the problem of identity, are evident in these writings: (1) reemphasis on the importance of the immigrant community as the basis for a sense of identity in the process of transition from one culture to another; (2) recognition of the central role played by religion as the basis of social identification; and (3) clarification of the process of assimilation in the recognition that, in reality, there are two processes, not one. There is a process of cultural assimilation by which newcomers establish a practical working relationship with their new way of life, and a process of social assimilation in which the problem of identity and community is the crucial issue. An examination of the main points in this literature will provide the conceptual framework with which we can analyze the experience of the Puerto Ricans in New York.

[13]Will Herberg, *Protestant, Catholic, Jew* (Garden City, N.Y.: Doubleday & Company, Inc., 1955).

[14]S. N. Eisenstadt, *The Absorption of Immigrants* (New York: The Free Press, 1955).

[15]Handlin, *The Uprooted, op. cit.*

[16]Oscar Handlin, *The Newcomers* (Cambridge, Mass.: Harvard University Press, 1959).

[17]Nathan Glazer and Daniel P. Moynihan, *Beyond the Melting Pot* (2nd ed.) (Cambridge, Mass.: Harvard-M.I.T. Press, 1970).

[18]Milton M. Gordon, *Assimilation in American Life* (New York: Oxford University Press, 1964).

Will Herberg

Herberg's study is not formally a study of migration, but of religion. He was struck by the phenomenon of an increasing interest in and emphasis on religion in the United States concurrent with a noticeable increase in secularism. Herberg set out to explain the religiousness of a secularist people and the secularism of a religious people. However, in seeking light on these questions, he became involved in an extensive treatise on migration and assimilation, and his book is now a standard work on the subject of the assimilation of immigrants in the United States. The discussion of both religion and assimilation is focused on the problem of identification. There is one problem which Herberg considers to be central for all immigrants. As strangers in a strange world, how do they answer the questions: "Where are we?" and "What are we?" Briefly, Herberg concludes that religion has become the basis of social identification for third generation Americans.

The first generation become aware of themselves as strangers, and identify themselves by referring to the world from which they came. As Herberg says, they are conscious of their ethnic identity, thinking of themselves as Irish, French, Scotch, Polish, or Italian in a way in which they had never thought in their country of origin. The second generation, in an effort to identify themselves as Americans, tend to deemphasize their ethnic origins. They break away from the way of life of their parents, and from language, religion, and behavior patterns associated with the culture from which their parents came. The third generation, confident now of their identity as Americans, look for some symbol which would give them a specific identity. The one feature of the old world culture which they can revive, and which can be legitimately manifested in American life, is the religious identity of their forebears. Thus they revive their interest in the religion of their grandparents, return to practice of it with a decidedly American style, and use their religious affiliation and the pursuit of religious interests as the basis for their specific identity as Protestant, Catholic, or Jewish Americans.

Herberg's thesis has a number of significant implications for the theory of assimilation. Like most contemporary theories, it takes for granted the three generation hypothesis: by the third generation, the immigrant group has by and large adopted a common American way of life. Second, he recognizes the question of identity as the central problem of newcomers. Finally, he finds that a strong sense of community based on religious identification plays a crucial role in the process of assimilation.

Herberg published his book in 1955. In the intervening years the role of religion in American life has changed significantly. The radical changes in religious life, and in the social and cultural life of the nation, would require substantial modifications of Herberg's theory. Nevertheless, identity as the central problem remains the major issue in the immigrant experience.

Nathan Glazer and Daniel P. Moynihan

In their study of the ethnic and racial groups of New York City, Nathan Glazer and Daniel P. Moynihan present a theory which provides a new insight into the question of identity. The authors acknowledge, as do most contemporary scholars, that the need for identification results in the effort by immigrants to retain their ethnic identity. Their concern is to discover what happens to ethnic identity in the process of assimilation. Most previous studies of assimilation indicated that the immigrants had become an integral part of American society by the time of the third generation. The symbol of the "melting pot" has been used to describe that unity (admitting of some differences) which is the present state of those who constitute the third or later generation of migrating people. Glazer and Moynihan simply deny that the melting pot ever melted. As they describe it, the quest for identity takes a peculiar shift. In the process of assimilation, identity on the basis of national origin tends to weaken; it is no longer feasible for people to identify themselves by language, culture, or customs. Identification tends to rest more on common interests which become related to ethnic background rather than constituting an ethnic background themselves. "The ethnic groups of New York are also interest groups."[19]

Glazer and Moynihan find that "the specific pattern of ethnic differentiation . . . in every generation is created by specific events."[20] They believe that four specific events have provoked the crystallizing of ethnic loyalties: Nazi persecution and the establishment of Israel have been a focus of identification for Jews; the reemergence of the Catholic school controversy has done the same for Catholics; race is the focus of identification of the Negro; the experience of migration serves this purpose for Puerto Ricans. Around these four issues or experiences, a pattern of loyalties has developed which has resulted in a differentiation of New York into these four main groups. These groups, forming around particular interests, are the persistent ethnic groups of the present generation.

The question that emerges from the analysis of Glazer and Moynihan is: "What of the future?" If common interests replace nationality background as the basis for ethnic identity, how is this likely to affect

[19]Glazer and Moynihan, *Beyond the Melting Pot, op. cit.,* p. 17.
[20]*Ibid.,* p. 291.

the city or the nation? In other words, according to Glazer and Moynihan, it appears that the problem of cultural assimilation has been successfully met—people of diverse cultural backgrounds have been sufficiently integrated into a common American culture. Now a different type of problem presents itself, that of accommodating conflicting interests in one reasonably harmonious society. Conflicting interests have always been troublesome in the United States, and political institutions have been formed in order to give suitable representation to conflicting interest groups without endangering the common welfare. However, the interest groups which Glazer and Moynihan define as contemporary have a particular quality. Their interests crystallize around the basic and elemental loyalties which are characteristic of such fundamental human communities as an ethnic group. This gives the interest group a highly charged quality and an intense emotional tone. It is the division of interest groups on this level with which Glazer and Moynihan are concerned as a possible source of difficulty in the future:

> Religion and race seem to define the major groups into which American society is evolving as the specifically national aspect of ethnicity declines. In our large American cities, four major groups emerge: Catholics, Jews, white Protestants, and Negroes. . . .
> Religion and race define the next stage in the evolution of the American peoples. But the American nationality is still forming: its processes are mysterious, and the final form, if there is ever to be a final form, is as yet unknown.[21]

What happened, as Glazer and Moynihan explain it, is that the variety of interests which ordinarily mark a nation's life have become related in the American experience to the problem of identity. They agree with Herberg's view that as Americans come closer to sharing a common culture, they seek a specific identity, and the basis of this identity tends to be religious. But they add another factor, indicated by the four specific events cited earlier. Interests then tend to converge around this basic identity. This is the new phenomenon in the contemporary United States, and coping with it successfully will hopefully be one of the creative achievements of the future.

Glazer and Moynihan would expect the Puerto Ricans to follow the path of previous immigrant groups, identify with the interests of Catholics, and thus take their place in the mainstream of the nation's life. But they recognize that there are many obstacles to this development. The class differences between Puerto Ricans and other Catholics are making it difficult for the Puerto Ricans to establish themselves solidly with other Catholic groups. Furthermore, there are so many uncertainties

[21]*Ibid.*, pp. 314, 315.

about the relationship of the Catholic Church to the Puerto Ricans (this will be explored in Chapter Eight) that religion may fail to serve as a basis of identity. In addition, the Puerto Ricans are caught in the same depressed economic condition as the Blacks, and economic advancement is particularly difficult and unpredictable. Finally, many of them have to cope with the problem of color. In a revised edition published in 1970, seven years after the original edition of their book, Glazer and Moynihan find the Puerto Ricans at the lowest social and economic levels of the city's population, still struggling against great odds to establish the footholds which will enable them to move strongly into the city's life.

Milton Gordon

The latest extensive study of cultural assimilation (by Milton Gordon) is also the most complete and competent analysis now available of the nature of assimilation. The book consists of a statement of the nature of assimilation, a review of various theories of assimilation in American life, and a presentation of Gordon's own analysis of assimilation, with indications of its implication for practical policy and action in American society.

One of the major foci of Gordon's discussion is the problem of identity, the process whereby a person defines for himself who he is by becoming increasingly aware of his relationship to others in primary, face-to-face interaction. Beyond the range of the family, the basis for identity is the ethnic group, which is based on a number of common bonds such as values, religion, historical experiences, and race, and which gives to a large number of individuals the deep sense of being one, of being what Gordon calls "a people" distinct from those with other traditions, historical experiences, or values. Gordon specifies two other functions for the ethnic group: ". . . it provides a patterned network of groups and institutions which allows an individual to confine his primary relationships to his own ethnic groups throughout all the stages of the life cycle. Its third functional characteristic is that it refracts the national cultural patterns of behavior and values through the prism of its own cultural heritage."[22] The ethnic group is the carrier of the way of life, or culture, of its members. Consequently, whenever the ethnic group weakens or changes, there will be a problem of identity. When members of an ethnic group move into a society dominated by another ethnic group, and the contact raises a challenge as to whether the newcomers will continue to live according to their traditional culture or be absorbed into the new culture, the problem of identity becomes acute.

[22]Gordon, *Assimilation in American Life, op. cit.,* p. 38.

One of Gordon's significant contributions is his analysis of the relationships of the ethnic group to social class. The ethnic group does not always exhaust a person's social experience. In many cases, societal structures develop based on power, wealth or prestige in which "superiority and inferiority are reciprocally ascribed."[23] Particularly in the United States, which is the clearest example of an open class society, this kind of a class structure has developed distinct from the ethnic identities of many different groups; the same ethnic group may have members of many different classes. Therefore, a new kind of identity has developed, on the basis of social class. The ethnic identity is based on historical traditions, background, and a person's relationship to earlier history, thus giving him historical identity. His identity in terms of class tends to depend on his educational and occupational level, on day-to-day contacts in business, political activity, and active social life. This gives a person what Gordon calls his identity of social participation. The socal class develops its own values, patterns of relationships, and institutions. In other words, it takes on the characteristics of a culture of its own. In a society like that of the United States, the problem of identity is complicated by this relationship between ethnic identity and class identity. Gordon seeks to state this relationship in a number of hypotheses:

> (1) . . . With regard to cultural behavior, differences of social class are more important and decisive than differences of ethnic group. . . . (2) With regard to social participation in primary groups and primary relationships, people tend to confine these within their own social class segment of their own ethnic group. . . . (3) The question of group identification must be dealt with by distinguishing two types of such identification from one another—one the sense of peoplehood . . . the other a sense of being truly congenial with only a social class segment of that "people."[24]

The process of assimilation and the process of establishing identity must be examined in relation to these two factors of ethnic group and social class. The term that Gordon uses to identify this is "ethclass." As Gordon explains it, a middle class Puerto Rican probably feels a closer identity with a middle class Italian or Englishman than he feels with a lower class Puerto Rican; and a poor Italian or Black or Jewish person would probably feel closer to a poor Puerto Rican than to a middle class Italian or Black or Jewish person. Barring the factor of language, Gordon thinks that middle class people of various cultures share similar values and attitudes which are distinct from the ones they share with poor people of their own ethnic group. Therefore, in the analysis of Puerto Rican experience, it will be important to indicate the class levels and class rela-

23*Ibid.*, p. 40.
24*Ibid.*, p. 52.

TABLE 3–1

THE ASSIMILATION VARIABLES

Subprocess or Condition	Type or Stage of Assimilation	Special Term
Change of cultural patterns to those of host society	Cultural or behavioral assimilation	Acculturation
Large-scale entrance into cliques, clubs, and institutions of host society, on primary group level	Structural assimilation	None
Large-scale intermarriage	Marital assimilation	Amalgamation
Development of sense of peoplehood based exclusively on host society	Identificational assimilation	None
Absence of prejudice	Attitude receptional assimilation	None
Absence of discrimination	Behavior receptional assimilation	None
Absence of value and power conflict	Civic assimilation	None

source: Milton M. Gordon, *Assimilation in American Life* (New York: Oxford University Press, 1964), p. 71.

tionships of the Puerto Ricans in New York City, as well as their ethnic background. In other words, the ethclass of the Puerto Ricans is a necessary consideration in the analysis of their assimilation.

Gordon actually distinguishes the process of assimilation into seven processes related to seven stages. The first of these is a process of cultural assimilation in which the newcomers accommodate themselves to the basic values and behavior patterns of their new society, at least to a point which permits them to function reasonably well in it. The second is a process of structural assimilation by which the newcomers accommodate and are accepted into the primary groups of the new society, interact on a face-to-face basis, and feel themselves identified with members of the new society. In other words, newcomers can live in a society with a distinct culture and function effectively in it while their day-to-day lives remain quite isolated from primary relationships with members of the host society. Gordon presents all seven stages in the process of assimilation in a paradigm which is reproduced in Table 3–1.

In view of this analysis, Gordon states a few simple principles to summarize his theory:

1. Cultural assimilation is usually the first type to occur.
2. It is possible that cultural assimilation could occur without any of the other types occurring. In fact, the situation of "cultural assimilation only" may continue indefinitely.
3. Once structural assimilation has occurred, all other types naturally follow.

With the use of his scheme, Gordon analyzes the experience of the various ethnic groups in the United States. He concludes that the resulting situation is not really one of cultural pluralism, since all the ethnic groups have adapted themselves to an increasing degree to the dominant cultural themes of the American way of life, strongly influenced by the Protestant, Anglo-Saxon tradition. The pluralism that has emerged is a structural pluralism, the formation of primary, face-to-face interacting groups, ranging over all social classes, in which the fundamental basis for identity is religion (Protestant, Catholic, Jew) or race.

Gordon arrives at conclusions similar to those of Herberg and Glazer and Moynihan, although his theory is much more developed and his analysis much more refined. It is possible to use his analytical model to determine what level of assimilation a particular group has reached, and how the process of assimilation is taking place at a given place or time.

Summary of Contemporary Theory

The problem of identity emerges from all these studies as the central problem of a social group migrating to a new culture area. The initial cultural assimilation can take place to some degree without the newcomers losing their sense of identity based on history, traditions, and language. They may become extensively adapted to the new culture and develop a way of life of their own in the new culture. Structurally, they may retain an identity even though they have lost their traditional way of life, or they may seek a new identity by being absorbed into the primary groups of the new culture. This admits of degrees, and reaches its culmination in the acceptance of courtship and marriage between members of what had been culturally disparate groups. In approaching an analysis of the experience of Puerto Ricans, a conceptual framework can be developed out of the studies which have just been analyzed.

Cultural assimilation is the first and essential adjustment of newcomers. Therefore, it will be evident in the experience of the Puerto Ricans. Their progress may be compared with other groups in the speed and extent to which cultural assimilation has taken place. This would involve knowledge of the English language in areas where it is essential to their life in New York; ability to seek work and perform it satisfactorily; participation in political life; ability to find a suitable place to live, and to live in such a way that they may remain there; acceptance of the fundamental requirements of life in New York City; maintenance of the essential requirements of public health; compulsory education of children up to the sixteenth year; reasonable observance of law and reasonable respect for others.

These are obviously generalities, but they mean what Mills, Senior, and Goldsen[25] meant by their definition of assimilation: the ability to live in a society as inconspicuously as its ordinary citizens. It means that Puerto Ricans would not be permitted to live as squatters in Central Park; would have their young children in school instead of at work all day; would support themselves by some ordinarily accepted way of making a living; would live in reasonable peace with their neighbors. This is evidently the simplest aspect of assimilation to analyze.

SOCIAL OR
STRUCTURAL ASSIMILATION

The significant point of analysis at this level is the Puerto Rican community. To what extent does a Puerto Rican community exist in which the Puerto Ricans have a sense of belonging, where consciousness of common values and traditions is a bond of unity, in which face-to-face interaction is common, and in which the Puerto Ricans have psychosocial satisfaction from their identity as Puerto Ricans? To the extent to which the Puerto Rican community exists, social or structural assimilation has not taken place.

The presence of a strong Puerto Rican community among first generation Puerto Ricans is not an indication that assimilation will not take place in later generations. A strong community has been the condition from which assimilation has effectively proceeded among earlier immigrants. Therefore, one could argue on the basis of earlier experience that a strong Puerto Rican community would be evidence that social assimilation is likely to occur. Weakness of the Puerto Rican community at this point would be an unfavorable condition both for their own social life and for eventual assimilation. This is the point at which lack of strong identity may be a major difficulty.

The other levels of social assimilation could be described according to Gordon's paradigm. Gordon himself finds little or no assimilation of Puerto Ricans on any level.[26] He admits very little cultural assimilation,

25Mills, Senior, and Goldsen, *Puerto Rican Journey, op. cit.,* Chap. 8.
26Gordon, *Assimilation in American Life, op. cit.,* p. 76.

and partial civic assimilation. As will appear in later chapters, there was considerable evidence for both kinds of assimilation even in 1964, when Gordon's book was published, and developments since that time have been rapid and extensive. The analysis of the final chapter of this book will indicate that the drive for identity is taking some unexpected and interesting turns at present. It is taking the form of a strong assertion of the significance of Puerto Rican culture, including language, and also of a definition of Puerto Rican interests around militant types of political and community action. The consequences of this new orientation are still unforeseen. But as it is described in the chapters to follow, it will enable us to study the Puerto Ricans in the midst of a process in which they face the traditional problem of identity, but seek to settle it in some new and imaginative way.

THE ISLAND[1]

Puerto Rico is an island at the eastern end of the Caribbean Sea, 1,000 miles southeast of Florida. It is a small island, shaped like a rectangle, 100 miles from east to west and 35 miles from north to south. It was discovered by Columbus during his second voyage, on November 19, 1493. In 1508 Ponce de Leon began establishment of the Spanish colony on the Island. He called it the Island of San Juan Bautista, and gave the name Puerto Rico to the excellent harbor on the northern coast. By a strange transfer, the names became reversed, the Island becoming known as Puerto Rico, and the harbor city as San Juan. The island was strategically located at the eastern end of the Spanish colonial empire, and was heavily fortified as a military outpost. For nearly 400 years, until 1898, it was to remain a Spanish colony.

Prelude to Uncertainty: The Island Background

The Island became a possession of the United States as a result of the Spanish-American War. It was formally ceded by the Treaty of Paris, December 10, 1898. After two years of military occupation, the Foraker Act established the first civil government in Puerto Rico under United States' sovereignty in 1900. Under this Act, the effective government of the Island was vested in the President of the United States, who appointed a governor and an executive council which acted as an upper house. Provision was made for the popular election of a lower house. This was a disappointment to the Puerto Rican people, who had expected a larger measure of autonomy from the nation which had boasted that it had

[1]Unfortunately, no really good history of Puerto Rico is available in English. Knoulton Mixer, *Puerto Rico: History and Contribution—Social, Economic, Political* (New York: The Macmillan Company, 1926), is one of the few histories in existence, but it is inadequate. Probably the best source in English is the volume *Status of Puerto Rico: Selected Background Studies Prepared for the United States–Puerto Rican Commission on the Status of Puerto Rico* (Washington, D.C.: Office of the Resident Commissioner of Puerto Rico, 1966). It is regrettable that this volume, one of the really valuable sources of background information on political status, education, sociocultural development, and migration, had such limited circulation. Rafael Pico, *The Geographic Regions of Puerto Rico* (Rio Piedras: University of Puerto Rico Press, 1955), is an excellent description of the geographical features of the Island. Henry K. Carroll,

come to bring the blessings of liberal institutions to a former Spanish colony.

In 1917, the political status of the Island was modified by the Jones Act, which granted United States citizenship to the Puerto Ricans, and provided for the popular election of both houses of the legislature. The Act also provided for the popular election of a Resident Commissioner who would represent the Puerto Rican people (without voting rights) in Congress. Appointment of the governor, however, as well as appointment of the commissioner of education, the attorney-general, and members of the Supreme Court of the Island, was kept in the hands of the President of the United States. Congress also kept a veto power over all acts of the Island's legislature, a power which it never chose to exercise.

In 1947 the Congress of the United States amended the Act of 1917, granted the Puerto Ricans the right to elect their own governor, and provided that the governor appoint all officials except the auditor and the members of the Supreme Court. The first governor elected by popular vote was Luis Muñoz Marin, who took office in January 1949.

Under the leadership of Muñoz Marin, a new political status, called the Free Associated State of Puerto Rico, was instituted. This provided for widespread autonomy of the Island, and established a relationship of Puerto Rico and the United States similar to the status of a commonwealth. The constitution of the Free Associated State was approved by Congress and enacted into law on July 25, 1952. The day is called Constitution Day, and is celebrated as the most important civil holiday of the year.

However, the problem of civil status is still one of the most troublesome questions in Puerto Rico. There has always been a small but very vocal group demanding complete independence; these are represented by the Independence Party. There is a slowly but steadily increasing group organized as the Party for Statehood; and there is the majority voice, the

---

Report on the Island of Puerto Rico (Washington, D.C.: U.S. Government Printing Office, 1900), was the report prepared after the American occupation of the Island, and served as the basis for the formation of American policy toward the new possession. Rexford G. Tugwell, the last mainland governor of Puerto Rico, wrote a pessimistic analysis in *The Stricken Land* (Garden City, N.Y.: Doubleday & Company, Inc., 1946). *The Annals* (publication of the American Academy of Political and Social Science), Vol. 285 (January, 1953), *Puerto Rico, A Study in Democratic Development,* is a study of political, economic, and social developments of the early 1950's, but has some chapters which provide a sketchy coverage of the period 1900–1940. Earl Parker Hanson, *Transformation: The Story of Modern Puerto Rico* (New York: Simon and Schuster, Inc., 1955), and *Puerto Rico: Land of Wonders* (New York: Alfred A. Knopf, Inc., 1962), are about the only popular histories of the period of the 1930's and 1940's. Unfortunately, they are often enthusiastic testimonials by a devoted friend of Puerto Rico and Muñoz Marin, rather than serious histories. Gordon K. Lewis, *Freedom and Power in the Caribbean* (New York: Monthly Review Press, 1964), is a very good, although partisan, analysis of Puerto Rico's ambiguous political and economic status.

members of the Popular Party, demanding continuation of the present status of the Island as a Free Associated State. A commission on status was appointed by the Congress of the United States in 1963, held hearings for three years, and submitted its report in the summer of 1966.[2] It stated the advantages and disadvantages of each position as determined by the hearings, and recommended a plebiscite to be taken during 1967 in which the Puerto Ricans could express freely their choice from among the three alternatives.

The problem of status is not a simple matter of government, but rather a deeply rooted problem of identity. The proponents of *independence* insist that the Puerto Ricans will not really know who or what they are, will not be able to retain and strengthen a sense of national and cultural identity, unless they are completely independent. They insist that, if Puerto Rico becomes a state, it will lose its culture and the great vehicle and sign of its culture, the Spanish language. They insist that, even under the Free Associated State, they are neither first class citizens of the Republic nor a genuinely independent people. The proponents of *statehood* insist that only through first-class citizenship in the United States as a state of the Union will they have the genuine identity which they seek. They also insist that provision for retention of the Spanish language and Spanish cultural traditions will be possible even when they are a state. They are convinced that only through statehood can Puerto Rico have economic and political security and stability together with freedom. Proponents of the *Free Associated State* look upon their present constitution as a creative achievement providing the best of both other alternatives. It enables Puerto Rico to maintain a specific identity as a people with its own language, culture, and traditions, and enables them to have all the benefits of a close identity with the United States.

The Puerto Ricans voted in July 1967. The results of the plebiscite showed a preference for the Free Associated State; second preference was for statehood, while independence ran a poor third. However, most proponents of independence boycotted the plebiscite, since they claimed it was not a genuine plebiscite, but merely an expression of opinion. Meanwhile, the intensity of the controversy reflects the anxiety and uncertainty of a people in danger of losing themselves, and seeking to discover the political and social institutions which will enable them to preserve a genuine sense of identity in the presence of rapid changes with which they seek to cope. Thus, before any question of large scale migration arose, the Puerto Ricans had been facing a crisis of national and cultural identity.

[2]*Status of Puerto Rico. Report of the United States–Puerto Rico Commission on the Status of Puerto Rico* (Washington, D.C.: U.S. Government Printing Office, 1966).

In the elections of 1968, the Popular Party (Partido Popular), which was associated with Muñoz Marin and the Free Associated State, split into two. As a result, Luis Ferre, candidate of the New Party, an offshoot of the Statehood Party, won the election for Governor. Ferre is committed to eventual statehood for Puerto Rico. This appears to be creating a realignment of political loyalties on the Island. Some political observers believe it will polarize the population more sharply into two groups—those who seek statehood and those who seek independence.

ECONOMIC DEVELOPMENT[3]

Puerto Rico's economy has, until recent years, been primarily agricultural. Ginger, coffee, sugar, molasses, and hides were the early products. During the nineteenth century, sugar began to take predominance and, under United States rule, developed quickly into almost a monoculture. Coffee played a significant role in the Puerto Rican economy until the destruction of coffee trees in a 1928 hurricane. In the last decade of Spanish rule, 57,000 tons of sugar a year were produced. The rate had increased to 200,000 tons per year five years after American rule, and by 1930 it had risen to 900,000 tons per year.[4] It remained at this figure, or about one million tons, until the 1950's. The preeminence of sugar had two important consequences. First, it was a cash crop, and the cash income was used to purchase the staple foods which residents of the Island had to import. Puerto Rico still does not have a subsistence economy, which has left the Island dependent on economic fluctuations in international markets. Second, a sugar economy requires large amounts of labor for five or six months of the year, leaving the labor force with little or no employment for the other six months.

The economy of Puerto Rico has only recently begun to diminish the chronic poverty and destitution of its people. In 1929 the per capita income of the Island was $122 (at 1949 prices), one-fifth of what it was in the United States. It rose to $218 by 1939 (at 1954 prices) and to $706 in 1963–1964 (at 1954 prices).[5]

Beginning in 1948, under the leadership of Luis Muñoz Marin, Puerto Rico inaugurated a program of economic development called

[3]Victor S. Clark *et al.*, *Puerto Rico and its Problems* (Washington, D.C.: The Brookings Institution, 1930), is the best economic survey of the pre-1930 period. Harvey Perloff, *Puerto Rico's Economic Future* (Chicago: University of Chicago Press, 1950), updates the Clark report.

[4]Perloff, *op. cit.*, p. 28.

[5]*Facts and Figures, 1964–65* (New York: Office of the Commonwealth of Puerto Rico, 322 W. 45th Street, New York, 10036), p. 10.

"Operation Bootstrap."[6] The objective of the program was to introduce industry to the Island, locate it where there were pockets of unemployment, and thus help to raise the economic level of the people. Methods used to attract industry were: (1) building plants which the industries could occupy, (2) providing tax relief for ten years, and (3) training the labor force. The success of Operation Bootstrap has been unusual. Puerto Rico has become the most impressive example of the rapid development of an economically underdeveloped area. Over 1,066 new factories have opened since 1947, directly creating 68,410 new jobs, plus indirectly creating another 60,000 to 70,000 in service or trade. Family income has increased from $660 in 1940 to $3,818 in 1966.[7]

This industrial development has not occurred without profound social and cultural consequences. The Island has lost its predominantly agricultural character, with the traditional Spanish plaza and colonial style of life. Education is eliminating illiteracy; the automobile has given a surprisingly modern character to Island life (automobiles increased from 26,847 in 1939–1940 to 285,516 in 1963–1964), and the service station, shopping center, supermarket, housing project, superhighway, and expanding suburbs are marks of modern society. Television, motion pictures, advertising, installment buying, and all the institutions of a modern economy have become a major part of the life of the Puerto Rican people. As a result, the traditional culture and values of the Puerto Ricans have been deeply shaken. Such qualities as competitiveness for economic success, advancement measured in terms of economic achievement, the impersonality of a money economy, and a tendency to evaluate men in terms of income and gain rather than personal qualities have begun to shake the older emphasis of a traditional society on family loyalties, personal relationships, individual dignity, and respect.

This has given many Puerto Ricans second thoughts about the economic development. They recognize that a humanistic traditional culture is rapidly being replaced by a culture that appears to them as materialistic, competitive, and commercial. As a result, a deep reaction has become evident against the impact of the economic development. When he was Governor, Muñoz Marin saw the need to counterbalance the rise of modern commercial values with a reassertion of traditional values. He called

[6]No good comprehensive history of the Economic Development Program has yet been written. Reports of the Puerto Rico Industrial Development Company, used together with specialized studies, are the best sources of information about it. A. J. Jaffee, *People, Jobs and Economic Development* (New York: The Free Press, 1959), is a technical analysis of the economic development up to 1959. Stanley L. Friedlander, *Labor Migration and Economic Growth* (Cambridge, Mass.: M.I.T. Press, 1965), is a more recent study.

[7]*Facts and Figures, op. cit.*, p. 9.

for *Operación Serenidád,* Operation Serenity, as a reemphasis on the traditional culture, values, and qualities of Puerto Rican life, a balancing of commercialism with a sense of human dignity, an effort to create a blend of the best of the past with the best of the present and future.

THE RISE OF
THE MIDDLE CLASS

The most significant consequence of the economic development of the Island has been the rapid rise of the middle class. This is reflected statistically in a comparison of 1950 and 1960 census data on income, education, and occupation, the three standard indexes of class position in the United States.

However, the significant factor about the rise of the middle class is the shift in life style, cultural values, and personal experience. The rapidly expanding suburban areas around every large city in Puerto Rico indicate that the shift to suburban living is as much a characteristic of Puerto Rican life as it is of the cities of the mainland United States. This sudden shift has important cultural and personal consequences. It introduces a series of uncertainties and anxieties which are the common experiences of new middle class people in areas of rapid social transition. The advance to middle class status involves serious economic pressures. People find themselves in heavy debt paying for a home, an automobile, education of their children in private schools, and the external symbols of middle class status. They are in an economically precarious position. Furthermore, they have come from a cultural background in which social status was fixed. In such a traditional two class system, a person in the lower class has no anxieties about social position; he knows exactly what is expected of him. He may suffer great poverty, but he has no illusions about the things which gave a man prestige, respect, and personal dignity. But the person newly arrived in the middle class has none of these certainties. One of the major problems of a middle class person anywhere is determining the norms by which he can be confident that he belongs. These are always obscure and ambiguous, with the result that personal anxiety is a dominant experience of these people.

One aspect on which this uncertainty focuses is the factor of color, which will be analyzed at length in a later chapter. It is sufficient here to note that, in the uncertainty about symbols which indicate middle class status, the visible symbol of color often becomes important, and there is evidence that it has done so in Puerto Rico.

The uncertainty of the new middle class does not directly affect the migrating Puerto Ricans, who are mostly from the poorer levels of society. It does, however, add one more element of uncertainty to the general cultural features of the Island, and contributes to the problem of identity which complicates the adjustment of Puerto Ricans to New York.

THE ROLE OF RELIGION

In a period of distressing transition such as Puerto Rico is experiencing, the religious values of a people become deeply involved. As indicated in Chapter Three, religion has been a basic factor in the sense of identity of immigrants coming to the United States. The Catholic Church might have been a stabilizing factor in the period of unsettling transition in Puerto Rico, but a number of developments left the Church in such a position that, instead of modifying the increasing uncertainty, it sometimes contributed to it. Thus, added to other uncertainties, ambiguity in their Catholic background has left the Puerto Ricans both in Puerto Rico and on the mainland without the kind of consistency in strong religious identification which served earlier immigrants as the basis for community solidarity.

Puerto Rico has been traditionally Catholic in the style of Catholicism which was characteristic of the Spanish colonies[8] (the features of this Catholicism will be described in more detail in Chapter Eight). But in terms of religious experience on the Island, practically all Puerto Ricans were baptized. Identity as a Catholic was conceived mainly as identity with a community, a *pueblo* which was Catholic, rather than in terms of personal responsibility as a member of the Church or parish. Religious practice took the form of such community expressions of faith as processions, celebration of Saints' days, and observance of such days as Good Friday. The personal dimension of religion was generally practiced by wearing medals, maintaining shrines to saints in the home, and praying to particular saints in the church. Religion was thus deeply embedded in the culture as a set of folk beliefs and practices. Nevertheless it played a significant role in symbolizing the central values of the society; it provided a deep sense of solidarity among all classes in the possession of common values and a common meaning of life, and it has been the source of reassurance and consolation to the people in general and at critical

[8]Probably the best book for an understanding of the religious dimensions of the Spanish conquest is Robert Ricard, *The Spiritual Conquest of Mexico*, trans. L. B. Simpson (Berkeley: University of California Press, 1966). Although Ricard deals with the experience of Mexico, the insights he gives into the evangelization of the Spanish colonies are helpful in relation to Puerto Rico. There is nothing of particular value in English on the religious history of Puerto Rico.

moments in their lives. This deep religious sense is still present and still plays a significant role in the transition to life on the mainland.

However, the consistent strength which the Catholic Church might ideally have given became confused by a number of developments. When the Island became an American possession in 1898, American priests and religious personnel began to go there to provide the religious and spiritual care which had previously been given by a relatively few native priests and a large number of priests from Spain. This effort from the United States has continued, and has involved an impressive financial support and personnel for the development of the Church on the Island. However, the Church was under the leadership of American bishops until 1961. American religious personnel and the introduction of Catholic schools gave a particularly American character to much of the Church's work. Many of the Americans spoke Spanish poorly, if they spoke it at all, and complaints were repeatedly raised about the neglect of the language and cultural traditions of the Island. Finally, in the election for Governor in 1960, the Church placed itself into direct opposition to the Popular Party by supporting the Christian Action Party, a party formed to pursue "Catholic" interests by political action. Strangely enough, many of the people who had complained about the "Americanized" Church were active in this Christian Action Party, under the leadership of their "American" bishops. In taking this political stand, the Church gave the impression of opposing the efforts of the Popular Party for improvement of the social and economic situation of the Island. These developments introduced an ambiguity into the role of the Church in the lives of the Puerto Rican people, despite evidence of improvement in religious practice under the influence of American priests. The traditional sense of religious identity was weakened in the confusion between fidelity to the Catholic Church and to one's political role as a Puerto Rican.

After 1898, Protestant evangelists came to the Island with American sponsorship. Despite the steady increase in native Puerto Rican personnel in the Protestant effort, Protestantism is generally perceived as more American than Catholicism. It is difficult to ascertain what percentage of the Island population is Protestant; reasonable estimates indicate between 10 and 20 per cent.

These developments in Puerto Rico itself—the ambiguous political status, rapid social and economic development, the anxieties of a rapidly rising middle class, and the uncertainties provoked by developments in the Catholic Church—have all contributed to a problem of identity among Puerto Ricans on the Island before they begin the migration to the United States. This experience can be seen as a fortunate preparation for the uncertainties of life in the United States. But from the viewpoint of the central problem of all immigrants, the problem of identity, it leaves obscure that point of reference against which all things will be measured and tested in their experience on the mainland, namely, the cultural background from which they come.

With these points in mind, the analysis of their experience on the mainland can begin with a study of the general features of the Puerto Rican community on the mainland. Since the great majority of Puerto Ricans are clustered in New York City, it seems reasonable to examine that community first, and then compare it with other Puerto Rican communities.

NEW YORK CITY

Trying to define the Puerto Rican community in New York City is much more difficult than defining it in Puerto Rico. The Puerto Ricans who were to give the character to the later migration—the poor in search of work—began to settle in New York City during World War I.[1] The first settlement was in the area of the Brooklyn Navy Yard, probably responding to the demand for workers during the war years. About the same time, Puerto Ricans began to settle in Harlem, just as the newly arriving Blacks were settling there. The 1920 census reported 7,364 persons of Puerto Rican birth residing in New York City. Brooklyn Navy Yard and Harlem continued to be areas of settlement during the 1920's. A New York City Health Department Study[2] reported 44,908 persons of Puerto Rican birth living in New York City in 1930, an increase of 35,544 during the 1920–1930 decade. By this time, the great majority of Puerto Ricans were settling in Harlem, with 80 per cent of the Puerto Rican population of New York residing there. The Brooklyn Navy Yard section continued to be second, containing 16 per cent of the Puerto Rican population. Figure 5–1 indicates the place of residence of Puerto Ricans in Harlem in 1935; Figure 5–2 indicates the place of residence of Puerto Ricans in Brooklyn in 1935.

The Puerto Rican Community in New York City

Migration slowed during the depression years of 1930–1940. The 1940 census reported 61,463 persons of Puerto Rican birth residing in New York, an increase of 16,555 during the decade. Migration practically stopped during World War II, but after 1945 the rate began to increase rapidly. The population continued to settle in the Harlem and Brooklyn Navy Yard areas, but it flowed over from Harlem to East Harlem, and across the Harlem River into the South

[1]For the details of the early settlement of Puerto Ricans in New York, see Lawrence R. Chenault, *The Puerto Rican Migrant in New York City* (New York: Columbia University Press, 1938), Chaps. 4, 6.

[2]John L. Rice, "Health Problems among Puerto Ricans in New York City," unpublished Report of the Health Department of New York City, 1934. Quoted by Chenault, *ibid.*, p. 58.

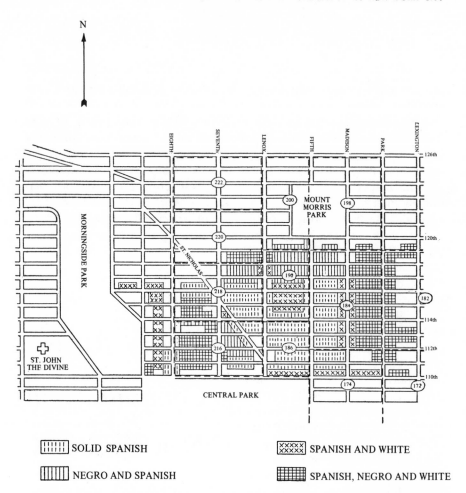

Fig. 5–1. Settlement of Spanish-Speaking Racial Groups in the Lower Harlem Area, New York City, 1935. Classifications of racial groups other than Spanish-speaking are omitted. Census tracts are indicated by broken lines. In the map, language takes precedence over color. Reproduced from Lawrence R. Chenault, *The Puerto Rican Migrant in New York City* (New York: Columbia University Press, 1938), Fig. 2, p. 95 [adapted from a map study prepared by the New York Urban League which appeared in the *Sun*, March 22, 1935, in *The New York Times*, March 24, 1935, and in James Ford, Katherine Morrow, and G. Thompson, *Slums and Housing* (Cambridge, Mass.: Harvard University Press, 1936), I, 323], by permission of Columbia University Press.

Bronx. From the Brooklyn Navy Yard the population pushed northeast into Williamsburg. Figure 5–3 traces the spread of the Puerto Rican population according to elementary school enrollment from 1958 to 1966. The densest concentration of Puerto Ricans since 1950 has been in the

Fig. 5–2   Area of Puerto Rican Settlement in Brooklyn by Census Tracts, 1935. Reproduced from Lawrence R. Chenault, *The Puerto Rican Migrant in New York City* (New York: Columbia University Press, 1938), Fig. 3, p. 105, by permission of Columbia University Press.

South Bronx, but the East Harlem community continues to be the area most completely associated with the Puerto Rican community. Called "The Barrio" (The Puerto Rican Neighborhood), it is identified with Puerto Ricans in a way that no other area of the city has been.

The significant thing about the population has been its rapid spread. By 1966, according to the school maps, in every school district in Manhattan, in all but one in the Bronx, and in all but three in Brooklyn, Puerto Ricans constituted 12.5 per cent or more of the public school population. In 1958, only one district in the City, the South Bronx, had a school population more than 50 per cent Puerto Rican; in 1966, four districts had gone beyond 50 per cent Puerto Rican. They were South Bronx, South Central Bronx, Manhattan's Lower East Side, and the Williamsburg section of Brooklyn. Statistics do not tell the entire story, however. Puerto Ricans have been a very mobile population within the

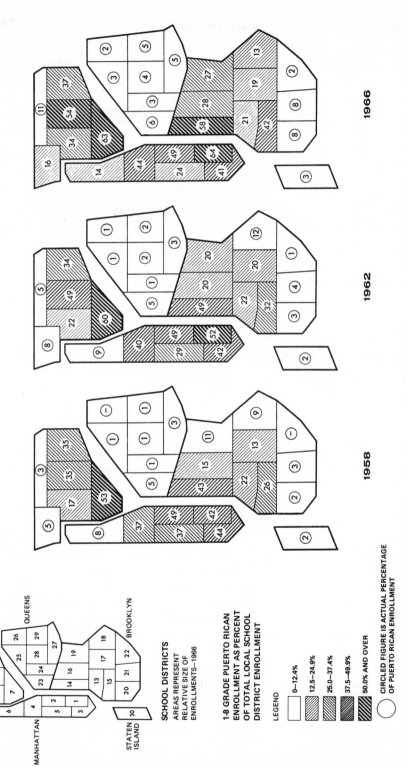

Fig. 5–3 Puerto Rican Student Enrollment in New York City, by Boroughs, 1958–1966. Reproduced from New York City Board of Education Special School Census, October 31, 1958, 1962, and 1966.

City because of large scale urban renewal projects, relocation due to housing developments, and a propensity to move quickly while looking for a little better place to live. In an unpublished study of a small section of the Lower East Side, Manhattan, carried out in 1958 by students of the Sociology Department of Fordham University, 28 Puerto Rican families were identified on one block in March 1958; there were still 28 Puerto Rican families on the block in November of the same year, but 21 of them were different families.

Although Puerto Ricans are scattered widely throughout the City, and are concentrated in some areas, it is doubtful whether they have established those geographical concentrations which were so important to the strong communities of earlier immigrant groups. One key to the strength of the earlier immigrants was the pattern of housing. At the point of second settlement, the earlier immigrants began to establish their tightly knit, strong communities. They could move into housing which was new, but within the rental range of poor working class families. This was private housing, and immigrants moved into the same house or block where brothers, cousins, aunts, relatives, or friends had moved before them. These dense concentrations gave rise to large areas which became the Little Dublins, or the Little Italies, the Little Germanies, the large concentrations of Jewish people, or others. They became stable, settled communities where a particular style of life was established and maintained. However, the only housing within reasonable range of the income of the Puerto Ricans is the public housing projects. Selection for these is on a nondiscriminatory basis according to policy norms of the New York City Housing Authority. Therefore, Puerto Ricans cannot easily move in where brothers, cousins, relatives, or friends are living, and find themselves within a conglomerate group. It is obviously much more difficult to maintain the cohesiveness of a stable Puerto Rican community similar to that of early immigrant groups.

Political Representation

One effect of this scattering of the Puerto Rican population is a weakening of its potential political strength. There are relatively few districts in which the Puerto Ricans alone could carry an election. Where they have a large percentage of the population, their voting power is affected by two other factors: a large percentage of the Puerto Rican population is still below voting age, and many of those who have reached voting age have not registered. Until 1964, Puerto Ricans in New York State were required to take a literacy test in English before they were permitted to register. This requirement was ruled out by the Civil Rights Act of 1965 and Puerto Ricans not literate in English may now register simply by showing evidence of having completed 6 years of schooling in Puerto Rico. The registration of Puerto Ricans which followed this change of the law was probably the reason for the election of Herman Badillo, a Puerto Rican, as Bronx Borough President in 1965. He won the election by a slim margin of about 2,000 votes, and probably would have lost without the support of newly registered Puerto Ricans. However, even with the new provisions for registration, Puerto Ricans have not been registering in large numbers. In the summer of 1969, a special drive was held to register Black and Puerto Rican voters. It fell far short of expectations. The Citizens Voter Registration Campaign estimated that 131,000 Puerto Ricans were registered in the City of New York out of a potential voting body of 435,000.[3]

When Puerto Ricans do register and vote, they vote predominantly Democratic. Hubert Humphrey received about 93 per cent of the Puerto Rican vote in the 1968 election. The tendency to vote Democratic, even against Puerto Rican candidates, was further evidenced in the 1968 elections. The vote in predominantly Puerto Rican East Harlem was 88 per cent for Hulan Jack, a Black candidate for the State Assembly on the Democratic ticket, against 14 per cent for a Puerto Rican on the Republican ticket. In the 1968 election for State Senator from the East Harlem–South Bronx District, three Puerto Ricans were running against each other. Roberto Garcia, the Democratic candidate, won 85 per cent of the votes.

The low percentages of Puerto Ricans in many districts, and their low percentage of registered voters, has left the Puerto Ricans with no elected representatives in the New York City Government as of 1970, and with only four elected representatives in the New York State Government, one State Senator, Roberto Garcia, and three Assemblymen, Armando Montano, Luis Nine, and Manuel Ramos. All three are from the South Bronx.[4] This weak position does not speak well for the political strength of the Puerto Rican community at the present moment. Strong political action both proceeds from community strength and contributes to an increase of community strength.

The most important political figure to appear in the Puerto Rican community thus far has been Herman Badillo Rivera. Born in 1929 in Caguas, a Puerto Rican city near San Juan, he came to the mainland after the death of his parents when he was 12 years old. He always calls attention to the fact that he put himself through school by working at three types of jobs, pin boy, elevator operator, and dishwasher, all of which

[3] *The New York Times*, August 26, 1969, p. 33.
[4] *The New York Times*, October 15, 1970, p. 30.

have since been eliminated by machines. He won his A.B. degree at City College and his law degree at Brooklyn Law School. He was one of a small group of bright, young Puerto Rican men and women who inaugurated a number of grass-roots movements in the 1950's to improve the life of Puerto Rican youth in the City of New York. He entered politics in 1961 and received his first important political appointment in 1962, when he was named Commissioner of the newly created Office of Relocation. When criticized for his handling of the relocation of many Puerto Rican families, he frequently told his audiences or his friends "I have been relocated so often in my life that I probably have a better understanding of relocation than most persons." He was elected Borough President of the Bronx in 1965; he resigned in the Spring of 1969 to run in the primary election for Democratic candidate for Mayor but was defeated. He ran in the 1970 election as the Democratic and Liberal Party candidate for the House of Representatives from the Hunts Point Section of the Bronx and was elected. He is the first elected Puerto Rican Congressman, and has also been named a Distinguished Professor of Urban Education by the Graduate School of Education of Fordham University in New York for the year 1970–1971. This is a record of success which matches the impressive rise to power of many of the best known political leaders of earlier immigrant groups. He is the outstanding political figure in the community. Antonio "Tony" Mendez has long been a figure in Democratic politics in East Harlem, and Mrs. Amalia Betanzos is active on the West Side. Mrs. Encarnacion Armas has been active in the Liberal Party but, despite her efforts, the Liberal Party has never been able to build a constituency among the Puerto Ricans of the City. Thus it is the younger people such as Badillo and Roberto Garcia who are giving the political character to the population at the present time.

Education and Occupational Levels

Occupationally and educationally, the Puerto Ricans are the poorest segment of the New York City population. In comparison with Blacks and the non-Puerto Rican population, they are heavily concentrated in the low occupational levels, and their median family income is considerably lower than that of the Blacks. The *Profile of the Bronx Economy*,[5] completed in 1967, indicated that median family income of Puerto Rican families in the Bronx was $400 lower than that of the Blacks. Table 5–1 presents the data on family income for the City of New York based on 1960 census reports. At that time, 53.7 per cent of the Puerto Rican fami-

[5] *A Profile of the Bronx Economy*, Institute for Urban Studies, Fordham University, Bronx, New York, 1967, mimeo'd.

TABLE 5–1

FAMILY INCOME BY ETHNIC GROUP,
NEW YORK CITY, 1960

	Percentages of Families with Income[a]		
Income	Puerto Rican	Nonwhite	Other White
Under $3,000	33.8	27.1	11.8
Under $4,000	53.7	43.6	19.2
$4,000 and over	46.3	56.4	80.8

SOURCE: U.S. Bureau of the Census. *U.S. Census of Population and Housing, 1960.* Census Tracts. Final Report PHC (1)-104. Part 1 (Washington, D.C.: U.S. Government Printing Office, 1962). Tables P-1, P-4, P-5.

[a]Nonadditive. Families with less than $4,000 income includes those with less than $3,000 income.

lies had family incomes below the $4,000 mark, whereas only 43.6 per cent of the nonwhite families were below that level. The *Profile of the Bronx Economy* also indicated that high rates of unemployment were found in the same areas where levels of education were low. Most of the Puerto Ricans covered by the study in the *Profile* had been born on the Island and migrated to the mainland. Of Puerto Ricans coming to the mainland between 1957 and 1961, 45 per cent were between 15–24 years of age; 53 per cent of all migrants had had no previous work experience.

Table 5–2 presents the occupational levels of the Puerto Rican population in New York City according to the 1960 census. In both 1950 and 1960 Puerto Ricans were concentrated in the operative and nonhousehold service categories. These are predominantly unskilled and semiskilled occupations. It is important, however, to note the difference between the first generation and the second, because an impressive improvement is indicated in the occupational levels of second generation Puerto Ricans. The only difficulty with this evidence for 1950 and 1960 is the fact that relatively few second generation Puerto Ricans were in the labor force in those years. At the time of the 1970 census, many more second generation Puerto Ricans had entered the labor force, so the results of that census will be significant in indicating whether the impressive progress of 1950 and 1960 continued during the following decade.

Statistics fail to reflect the impact of Puerto Ricans on the New York City job market. They dominate the hotel and restaurant trades to such an extent that these businesses would now be helpless without them. Puerto Rican women particularly constitute a significant part of the labor

TABLE 5–2

OCCUPATIONAL STATUS OF PERSONS BORN IN PUERTO RICO
AND OF PUERTO RICAN PARENTAGE, BY SEX,
NEW YORK CITY, 1950 AND 1960

	Born in Puerto Rico		Puerto Rican Parents	
Occupation	1950	1960	1950	1960
Males employed and occupation reported	46,275	118,288	3,585	9,096
Per cent	100.0	100.0	100.0	100.0
Professional technicians and kindred workers	2.4	1.8	5.4	7.4
Office managers and proprietors	5.5	3.7	4.4	4.0
Clerical, sales, and kindred workers	9.2	11.4	20.5	23.8
Craftsmen, foremen, and kindred workers	11.0	10.8	11.9	16.3
Operatives and kindred workers	37.4	45.2	35.4	29.8
Nonhousehold service workers	29.3	21.1	16.3	12.5
Household service	0.1	0.1	0.0	0.2
Laborers except farm and mine	5.0	5.7	6.0	6.0
Farm laborers and foremen	0.1	0.3	0.0	0.0
Females employed and occupation reported	31,730	61,225	2,955	5,893
Per cent	100.0	100.0	100.0	100.0
Professional technicians and kindred workers	1.7	2.6	5.6	6.3
Office managers and proprietors	1.0	1.1	1.2	1.7
Clerical, sales, and kindred workers	6.4	12.1	39.4	56.0
Craftsmen, foremen, and kindred workers	1.7	1.9	2.0	1.7
Operatives and kindred workers	80.8	74.0	40.9	24.4
Nonhousehold service workers	5.7	6.7	8.6	8.7
Household service	1.6	0.8	1.7	0.5
Laborers except farm and mine	1.0	0.8	0.5	0.6
Farm laborers and foremen	0.0	0.0	0.0	0.0

SOURCE: U.S. Bureau of the Census, *U.S. Census of Population, 1960. Subject Reports. Puerto Ricans in the United States.* Final Report. PC(2)-1D. (Washington, D.C.: U.S. Government Printing Office, 1963), Table 11.

force in the garment industry, which has always been the colorful and often turbulent source of employment for newcomers to the City. Irish and German tailors dominated the garment industry in the midnineteenth century. They were followed by the Jews and Italians, and now Blacks and Puerto Ricans constitute a large part of this labor force. The International Ladies Garment Workers Union, which has always been synonymous with immigrant efforts toward economic security, boasts that it is now the organization of the Black and Puerto Rican workers. However, Puerto Ricans have frequently complained that top union positions are still in the hands of an establishment from previous generations and of immigrant groups who prevent the advance of the Puerto Ricans to positions of union leadership and power. Unskilled and semiskilled factory work accounts for the employment of large numbers of Puerto Rican men and women, as reflected in the operative category of the census reports. The occupational advance from first to second generation is generally a move into the ranks of craftsmen and skilled workers for the men, and into the ranks of white collar clerical and sales employees for both men and women. At the same time, the increase in the percentage of second generation Puerto Rican men in professional and technical work is impressive.

Organizations of the
Puerto Rican Community

It is difficult to present a clear picture of the way the Puerto Rican community is structured, how it operates, and what gives it its community character. It is a highly dispersed community with a very large percentage of poor people, and it has not yet reached the level of sophistication in organizational activity which is evident in older, more established groups. Furthermore, the Puerto Rican community has been troubled by internal divisions and controversies.

In order to form some general outline of the way the Puerto Rican community functions, it seems best to give a brief description of a number of organizations which have played a significant role in its history in New York, and to indicate the particular significance of each of these organizations.

Two of the oldest Puerto Rican organizations in the city are the Puerto Rican Merchants Association and the Puerto Rican Civil Service Employees Association. The history of small business among Puerto Ricans is a colorful reflection of migrant experience in New York City. The small *Bodegas* or *Colmados* (grocery stores) dot every Puerto Rican neighborhood, as do the small cafes, bars, restaurants, and *botanicas*, which sell medicinal herbs, materials for spiritist activities, charms, religious goods, and a host of related objects. Travel agencies are numerous, with their attractive advertisements for travel back and forth to the Island: *Vuele ahora y paga despues* ("Fly now; pay later") brings a Puerto Rican to the Island for a few dollars down and small payments per month. The Puerto Rican Merchants Association has been an important economic network for the Puerto Rican community, although it has not been as politically or socially dynamic as the community organizations which will be mentioned later. Nevertheless, it has been a significant factor in assisting Puerto Ricans to advance into small private business.

The history of one of the founders of the Puerto Rican Merchants Association, Julio Hernandez, reflects the experience of upwardly mobile Puerto Ricans. Julio came from a family of eight children. His father had been well educated in Puerto Rico—eight years of schooling—had had a "good job" in Puerto Rico, and had been very interested in politics. In the late 1920's the family relocated to New York, where Julio was born shortly after. Caught in the depression, the family suffered from poverty in the early 1930's, but each of the children was educated at least to the end of high school. Julio Hernandez went on to Maritime Training School and served as an officer in the Merchant Marine for ten years. After his marriage he settled in Brooklyn, opened a grocery store, and then a restaurant. Out of these activities he moved toward the establishment of the Puerto Rican Merchants Association, and served as its Executive Secretary for several years. He became increasingly active in the Puerto Rican community, and during the 1960's became the director of several government programs to promote small business among Puerto Ricans in the city. He now serves on a wide range of boards of community centers, health associations, and civic and charitable organizations. He represents the Puerto Rican entrepreneur, as well as the merchant who seeks to relate himself to the service of a struggling community of newcomers to the City of New York.

Office of the Commonwealth of Puerto Rico. In 1948, when the post-World War II migration from Puerto Rico was beginning to increase, Governor Muñoz Marin established an office in New York, supported by the Government of Puerto Rico, to assist the increasing numbers of Puerto Ricans coming to the city. The office was created to fulfill a number of functions: (1) to supervise the program of contract farm workers who were brought to the mainland to work on farms, and were expected to return to Puerto Rico at the end of the three, four, six month, or other contract period; (2) to provide an employment service to assist Puerto Ricans in getting jobs; (3) to identify Puerto Ricans as Puerto Ricans;[6] (4) to provide a social service referral program to direct Puerto Ricans to a variety of social service resources which could help them; (5) to provide a function of educational counseling, involving location of financial assistance for promising Puerto Rican students, and provision of educational guidance for them; (6) to provide a variety of services

---

[6]Apparently many Spanish-speaking persons who are not citizens of the United States present themselves as Puerto Ricans in order to enjoy the privileges of citizenship. They are often challenged when they do so. In the process, however, many Puerto Ricans are also challenged, and they must establish their identity as Puerto Ricans. The Office of the Commonwealth undertook this function.

to the Puerto Rican community which can be defined as aspects of a community organization function, in other words, to assist the local Puerto Rican communities throughout the city to identify and exploit their resources for their own advancement and development. The Office was to fulfill another related function. As a public relations instrument, it has provided information about Puerto Rico and Puerto Ricans to New Yorkers, and information about New York to Puerto Ricans.

In many ways the Office of the Commonwealth found itself representing the New York Puerto Ricans. Its officials and employees were regularly called upon by public and private agencies to present "the Puerto Rican point of view." It provided testimony at public hearings in which Puerto Rico or Puerto Ricans had an interest. On many occasions it sought either formally or informally to coordinate the activities of other Puerto Rican organizations in the City. The Office has been a tangible point to which people turn when they wish to contact the Puerto Rican community. It has given visibility in an organized way to the Puerto Ricans of New York.

It has not been without its controversial aspects, however. Not only is it a government office, it is an office of the Government in Puerto Rico. This has involved a number of unfavorable consequences. New York Puerto Ricans who wish to manage their own lives and have confidence in their ability to do their own thing resent its presence in New York. They have been critical of a situation in which they, as New Yorkers, seemed to be represented by an arm of the Government of Puerto Rico. This has become more acute as the number of New York born Puerto Ricans has increased. Furthermore, as a government office, the Office of the Commonwealth has never been able to transcend political identification. During the regime of the Popular Party in Puerto Rico, the Office was staffed by people who shared their political position; with the election of Luis Ferre by the New Party, a director has been appointed who endorses his political ideas and goals. As a result, there has always been some ambiguity about the response of the Office to the political realities of Puerto Ricans in New York. During the 1960's, the Office of the Commonwealth was directed by Joseph Monserrat. He was born in Puerto Rico, came to New York as a small child and was raised there, so he identifies himself more a second generation than a first generation Puerto Rican. As Director of the Office he became a significant but continually controversial influence in the Puerto Rican community. He has been an articulate and intelligent spokesman for the community on many occasions, but his role was always complicated by the political character of the position he held. When he resigned from the Office in 1969, he was appointed to the interim Board of Education by then Bronx Borough President

Badillo; he was elected President of the Interim Board by its membership and distinguished himself at a moment of critical tension and transition for the educational system of New York City. Mr. Manuel Cassiano, appointed director in 1969, was born in the South Bronx and raised himself from poverty to become a skillful and wealthy business man. He represents that small segment of second generation Puerto Ricans who have advanced dramatically during the past 20 years. He now shifts into the area of community service, and brings to the task the expertise of the successful business executive. In late 1970, Cassiano was named Director of the Puerto Rico Industrial Development Company, a public corporation with responsibility for promoting the industrial development on the Island. Its activities are popularly known as "Operation Bootstrap." This is an interesting reversal, the appointment of a New Yorker to a position in San Juan. No one has yet been named successor to Cassiano as Director of the Office of the Commonwealth.

At the time of this writing, in the Fall of 1970, the Office was in a state of transition. Other grass-roots New York Puerto Rican organizations have emerged which deal with problems of education, social service, employment, and community organization, thus raising the question as to whether the Office of the Commonwealth should continue these services. The present thrust of the Office is in the direction of job development and training.

In view of the continuing migration of poor Puerto Ricans to New York, the Office may still have an important function to fulfill in helping them in their adjustment to the city. It is doubtful whether it will have much influence among young New York born Puerto Ricans who are moving into adulthood. Some militant young Puerto Ricans recently picketed the Office, protesting the role of the Office in the contract farm workers program. The young people claimed that Puerto Rican farm workers who were working under contract on farms of the mainland were being exploited and treated unjustly. They demanded that the Office terminate the program. The future of the Office therefore cannot be clearly seen at the present moment. It may continue to fulfill some important services but it is doubtful that it will be as significant an organization in the future of the New York Puerto Rican community as it has been in the past.

The Puerto Rican Forum. In the mid-1950's, a group of young, intelligent Puerto Ricans saw the need of a communitywide organization to promote the interests of Puerto Ricans in New York City, and so they established the Puerto Rican Forum. These young, vigorous, interested people of the early 1950's have since come to distinguish themselves for their service to the Puerto Rican Community.

They were primarily concerned with the development of Puerto Rican youth, and their efforts were in the direction of educational achievement. However, they were aware of the need for a range of other programs for the strengthening of the Puerto Rican community in New York City. Two major developments resulted from their efforts: the founding of Aspira, an organization to promote education among Puerto Ricans, and the Puerto Rican Community Development Project, a city-wide agency to promote programs of many kinds in local Puerto Rican communities.

The Forum remains a central and significant organization of Puerto Ricans. It probably comes closest to being a representative organization of Puerto Ricans in New York. It promotes programs which it carries out itself; it promotes programs and funding for programs which are carried out by local Puerto Rican organizations; it is generally represented at meetings or on committees where a Puerto Rican voice is expected to be heard. It is a highly respected and influential voice for the Puerto Rican community.

Aspira. One of the early organizations founded by the Puerto Rican Forum was an agency to promote higher education for Puerto Ricans. It was given the Spanish name of *Aspira*, which means *strive* or *aspire*. Founded in 1961 to provide inspiration and guidance to Puerto Rican youths to continue their education into the professions, technical fields, and the arts, Aspira has sought to identify promising Puerto Rican youths, to motivate them to continue their education, to provide educational guidance and leadership, and to promote scholarships and financial aid to assist them in financing their education. Aspira has also been devoted to the development of a sense of self-confidence and identity among Puerto Rican youth by familiarizing them with their own cultural background and the cultural achievements of the Island.

Of all the grass-roots organizations of the Puerto Rican community, Aspira has probably been the most effective. It has become nationally known, and its service to Puerto Rican youth has been remarkable. Many of the young people now coming out of colleges and professional schools received their early encouragement and guidance from Aspira. The Aspira staff has spoken for the Puerto Rican community on educational issues, and has had considerable influence in the development of programs promoting Puerto Rican education. They have established Aspira clubs in many of the high schools throughout the city, and have conducted workshops and conferences for both educators and youth. The Conference on Puerto Rican Education which Aspira conducted in 1968 received nationwide attention.

The inspiration and guiding spirit of Aspira was Antonia Pantoja, a Puerto Rican woman born on the Island, raised and educated in New York, and with a professional degree as a social worker. She was active with Puerto Rican youth groups in the early 1950's, and was one of the founders of the Puerto Rican Forum. She spent a number of years on the Mayor's Committee on Human Rights, and later began to devote almost all of her time to Aspira. In 1968 she returned to Puerto Rico, where she developed Aspira Clubs and acted as a consultant on private and public projects. In 1971 she returned to Washington, D.C. as a consultant. She has been one of the significant persons in the Puerto Rican community during the past decade.

Aspira represents an orientation toward education, professional training, and competence as the means of advancing in American society. It has not been without its critics. Another segment of the Puerto Rican community moved toward more direct forms of community and political action, leading to the founding of the Puerto Rican Community Development Project. There has been tension between the representatives of these two different orientations, the one intellectual and stressing the need for professional achievement, the other urging direct community action.

Criticism has also developed from among the militant student groups in the city. They tend to identify Aspira with the Establishment and reject an association with it in favor of action aimed at more radical educational reforms. But in terms of solid and tangible achievement, probably no other Puerto Rican organization can show as much evidence of accomplishment as Aspira.

Puerto Rican Community Development Project. Shortly after the founding of Aspira, members of the Forum saw the need for a more comprehensive development program for the Puerto Rican community. The leading figure in this movement was also Antonia Pantoja. The interested Puerto Ricans pursued a program which would promote a sense of identity among Puerto Ricans in New York, and would help them develop community strength. This was based on the sociological position (indicated in Chapter Three) that newcomers integrate from a position of strength, and that it was the strong, stable immigrant communities which enabled earlier immigrants to move steadily and confidently into the mainstream of American society.

This theory was elaborated in an excellent position paper prepared by Professor Frank Bonilla, then of the faculty of M.I.T., and a project was proposed which would provide a range of services to the Puerto Rican community aimed at promoting identity, community stability, and political strength. The Bonilla paper is a significant document in the literature on cultural assimilation, and the final proposal for the Puerto Rican Community Development Project[7] remains an impressive description of the Puerto Rican community in New York City as of 1964.

Two unfortunate things happened in the development of the proposal. First, the Puerto Ricans promoting the project split into two factions over the promotion of the proposal and the anticipated control of the project. The separation reflected the two orientations indicated above. One group represented the views of those Puerto Ricans who thought in terms of long range educational and professional advancement, and the development of high level competence among young Puerto Ricans. The other orientation looked to more immediate community action, and sought to mobilize community pressure for prompt improvement of conditions among Puerto Ricans. Second, the City of New York refused to fund the project while it was under the control of those with the long range orientation. City officials argued that: (1) they could not fund a project identified with one ethnic group (even though the Puerto Ricans agreed to provide services on a nondiscriminatory basis to all ethnic and racial groups of the city); (2) the project, which was intended as citywide, would duplicate services already provided by community corporations; and (3) the philosophy of the project, aimed at identity and strength for the Puerto Rican community, was much too vague. The city wanted to fund projects more on the "nuts and bolts" level of jobs and immediate income. The refusal to fund the project aggravated the split among the Forum members. The community action proponents were able to take over the proposal, and eventually succeeded in getting it funded. They have been the significant figures in it ever since.

The Puerto Rican Community Development Project was first funded in 1965 by the Office of Economic Opportunity. It is citywide, and, in turn, funds a large number of projects throughout the city. It has become involved in job training programs, tutoring programs, neighborhood youth corps, addiction prevention programs, and a block program of community organization. Even more important than these programs, however, has been the Project's role as a visible representative of Puerto Ricans in New York. The Project has been troubled by internal struggles for control, but it has succeeded in giving politically militant voice to the Puerto Rican community when Puerto Rican interests have been at stake. It has mounted demonstrations before City Hall and before numerous city agencies to protest mistreatment of Puerto Ricans or to demand

---

[7]Puerto Rican Forum, Inc., *The Puerto Rican Community Development Project: A Proposal for a Self-help Project to Develop the Community by Strengthening the Family, Opening Opportunities for Youth, and Making Full Use of Education.* Unpublished proposal, New York, 1963.

Puerto Rican rights. It is regrettable that much of this activity has been directed at Black citizens, with the charge that Blacks have gained strategic control over the poverty program. This controversy became intense in the Autumn of 1970 when an effort was made by the Community Development Agency of the Human Resources Administration of New York City to terminate the funding provided by the antipoverty program to citywide agencies.[8] Three of the most important citywide agencies are Puerto Rican: Aspira, The Puerto Rican Family Institute, and the Puerto Rican Community Development Project. The Director of the Community Development Agency happened to be Black, and the animosity of the Puerto Rican community was directed toward him in what appeared to be a Black vs. Puerto Rican conflict of interests over the control of antipoverty funds.[9]

If the funds from the antipoverty program are withdrawn, the Puerto Rican Community Development Project hopes to continue to operate with funds from a variety of other sources. It is one of the few citywide projects which serve Puerto Ricans and represent them in a militant style when the occasion arises.

The Puerto Rican Family Institute. The Puerto Rican Family Institute represents the grass-roots Puerto Rican effort in the area of professional social service. It was established as a voluntary agency in 1963 by a small group of Puerto Rican social workers led by Augustino Gonzales, assisted by a team of volunteers who were affectionately called, in Puerto Rican style, "Godparents." The objective of the agency was to create for newly arrived Puerto Rican families the support of an extended ritual kinship system which is a major feature of the culture of the Island. They sought to identify Puerto Rican families which had established themselves on the mainland, and, with their help, to enable newly arrived families to cope with the problems of establishing themselves firmly in New York City. The Family Institute was given support by the Council against Poverty as a citywide agency in 1965; with the help of antipoverty funds, it has been serving the Puerto Rican community ever since. It has extended its staff and, together with its program of attempting to match integrated families with those newly arrived, provides a range of direct

[8]The Community Development Agency claimed, among other things, that the antipoverty funds should be disbursed through the local community corporations in the poverty areas, and that the citywide agencies were not properly related to these local corporations. Community corporations are the local agencies established in sections of the city which are defined as "poverty areas," and administer the funds assigned to that area for local antipoverty programs. The governing boards of community corporations are elected by the people of the area.

[9]*The New York Times*, September 4, 1970, p. 24; September 7, 1970, p. 22; September 11, 1970, p. 83. See also notes 15 and 16 in Chapter Seven.

services to prevent family disruption through family case work, psychiatric and social work counseling.

The Puerto Rican Family Institute is the only grass-roots Puerto Rican family agency in New York City. Staffed by Puerto Ricans and conducted in a thoroughly Puerto Rican style, it provides a setting where Puerto Rican families feel at home and can seek assistance which is provided without the strangeness and unfamiliar complications of a professional New York agency. It has been criticized for its conventional, case work orientation. But, in terms of direct social service, it is a Puerto Rican oasis in a desert of bewildering agencies, and hundreds of Puerto Rican families seek it out as a refuge in a strange land.

These agencies, the Office of the Commonwealth, the Forum, Aspira, the Community Development Project, and the Family Institute represent, to a large extent, the organized face of the Puerto Rican community on a citywide basis.

There is a range of other organizations, including the clubs involving New York residents from practically every small town in Puerto Rico, which are centers of social activity, mutual help, and friendly support. There are active athletic leagues, and cultural organizations such as the Instituto de Puerto Rico and the Ateneo de Puerto Rico which are dedicated to cultivating literature, music, and the arts among New York Puerto Ricans. New theatre groups are beginning to appear, such as the eminently successful Puerto Rican Traveling Theatre, founded by Miriam Colon, which tours the streets in summertime presenting Puerto Rican dramas to the people of the neighborhoods. There are action groups, such as United Bronx Parents, which carries on a vigorous campaign for improvement of the schools in the poor sections of the Bronx. It was founded and continues under the militant guidance of a Puerto Rican woman, Evelina Antonetti. Although many of its participants are Puerto Rican, it provides a service to the entire neighborhood with regard to conditions in the schools.

What is the Puerto Rican community in New York? Is it an entity? How does it function? Does it have an identity, a visibility, the quality of a clearly recognizable segment of the city? Containing probably a million people in 1970, it constitutes the largest Puerto Rican city in the world, about one-third larger than the city of San Juan; its population is about 40 per cent of the size of the entire population of Puerto Rico. It is a population mainly of poor working people, the backbone of the labor force for hotels, restaurants, hospitals, the garment industry, small factories, and shops, without whom the economy of the city would collapse. It is youthful, now about one-fourth of the entire public school population of the city. Puerto Ricans constitute one-half of the membership of the entire New York Archdiocese, but there are only six Puerto Rican priests in the city. There is a small but steadily growing number of Puerto Rican policemen and firemen. There are five Puerto Rican school principals in the city, and a small percentage of Puerto Rican teachers. About 25 per cent of the eligible Puerto Rican voters are registered, and not a single Puerto Rican holds an elected office in New York City. There are three City Commissioners who are Puerto Rican (Marta Valle, Commissioner of the Youth Services Agency, Amalia Bentanzos, Commissioner of Relocation and Joseph Rodriquez Erazo, Commissioner of the Manpower and Career Development Agency), and some Deputy Commissioners in the Human Resources Administration and in the Housing Authority and Police Department. A large number of small businesses are represented in the Puerto Rican Merchants Association; a small number of professionals, social workers, doctors, and lawyers are beginning to take an active and militant role in support of their people. There are a few community corporations in which Puerto Ricans have an influential or dominant voice in East Harlem and the Lower East Side in Manhattan, Coney Island and Williamsburg in Brooklyn, and South Bronx, Hunts Point, and Tremont in the Bronx. There is one newspaper, *El Diario de Nueva York*, owned by a mainland American and staffed by Puerto Ricans, which is known as the Puerto Rican paper. Although they are only about 15 per cent of the city's population, Puerto Ricans constitute about 40 per cent of the recipients of public welfare in the form of Aid to Dependent Children; about 23 per cent of the registered heroin addicts are Puerto Rican.

All this adds up to a struggling, suffering, poor, but vital segment of the city. It is a community without a visible, powerful leader, and one which has not been able to make a unified impact on the city proportionate to its representation in the population. The community is continually losing experienced persons to the Island in return migration, and is replenishing its poorest ranks with newcomers from the Island. It stands at an uncertain moment in its struggle for stability, identity, and strength.

The second generation increases, but its future is still unknown. Available data reveal an impressive advance, socially and economically, of the second generation. A new style is appearing among the youth. The larger numbers entering college are militant and aggressive. They took a leading part in the demonstrations which shut down City College in the Spring of 1969, and in the militant action at Queens, Brooklyn, and Lehman Colleges which resulted in the establishment of Puerto Rican studies programs. Since 1968 the Young Lords have appeared as a demonstrative group of militant Puerto Ricans. They occupied a church in East Harlem in the Spring of 1970, engaged in militant action around Metropolitan and Gouverneur Hospitals, and were involved in aggressive demonstrations around Lincoln Hospital in the Bronx in the Autumn of

1970. As will be indicated later, although they constitute a controversial development within the Puerto Rican community, they are a clear sign that the second generation Puerto Ricans are likely to be different from the first.

All in all, it is a community in transition, facing all the strains of shock and adjustment, and affected by all the problems of New York of the 1960's. After a brief description of Puerto Rican communities elsewhere on the mainland, the following chapters will review the major segments of their life in detail, and an attempt at interpretation will be provided in the final chapter.

COMMUNITIES IN OTHER MAINLAND CITIES

Puerto Rican communities have been developing outside of New York for many years. As early as 1920 there were communities in Chicago, Boston, Miami, and New Orleans. The 1920 census reported Puerto Ricans in 15 states and the District of Columbia. The major concentrations at the present time are in Chicago and neighboring cities; in Northern New Jersey, particularly Newark, Jersey City, Hoboken, Passaic, and Paterson, and farther southwest in Trenton; in Philadelphia and its environs, with a large concentration across the river in the Camden, New Jersey area; in the Cleveland and Lorain, Ohio, areas, where Puerto Rican communities developed out of the demand for factory workers during World War II; in Milwaukee, where a Puerto Rican community also developed out of a demand for factory workers; and in Connecticut, which has large communities in Norwalk, Bridgeport, New Haven, and Hartford. There is a large Puerto Rican community in Miami, but it is completely overshadowed by the large numbers of Cubans who now live there.

Unfortunately few systematic studies have been made of these various Puerto Rican communities, and many of these studies are not up to date. Apart from newspaper reports, there has been no extensive study of the Puerto Ricans in Chicago. Small studies have been made of the communities in Lorain, Ohio,[10] Philadelphia,[11] Newark, New Jersey,[12] Milwaukee, Wisconsin,[13] and Bridgeport, Connecticut.[14]

[10]Robert W. O'Brien, *A Survey of the Puerto Ricans in Lorain, Ohio* (Lorain, Ohio: Neighborhood House Association, 1954).

[11]Commission on Human Relations, *Philadelphia's Puerto Rican Population* (Philadelphia: 1964).

[12]Mayor's Commission on Intergroup Relations, *Newark, A City in Transition* (Newark, N.J.: 1959).

[13]Rudolph Morris, *Some Aspects of Life of the Puerto Ricans in Milwaukee* (Milwaukee: Intercollegiate Council on Intergroup Relations, 1953).

[14]Ronald J. Pedone and T. P. Velli, *The Spanish-Speaking People of the Greater Bridgeport Area* (Bridgeport: Department of Sociology, University of Bridgeport, 1962).

In many ways, the characteristics of all these communities are similar. They have developed during and after World War II, and consist mainly of Puerto Ricans who were poor (but not the poorest) in Puerto Rico. In other words, this is not a middle class migration. They have more education than the average Puerto Rican on the Island, but it is very limited by mainland standards; they are found predominantly in factory jobs as operatives, and in service jobs in hotels, restaurants, and cafeterias. They suffer from poor housing; their children face educational problems which are complicated by language difficulties, since many of them do not speak English when they start school. They face the ambiguity of color, the difficulties of family and religious adjustment, and problems of public welfare and drug abuse, all of which will be discussed in detail in the chapters which follow. They are not powerful politically, but there are evidences of organization in a variety of forms, from the ever present Home Town Clubs through civic and political associations which hold the promise of future influence.

The general characteristics of these smaller communities of Puerto Ricans are similar to those of the Puerto Ricans in New York. The differences come from size, type of settlement, and level of social or community organization.

Some Puerto Rican communities are particularly citylike in character, and their problems are those of large cities. Chicago has always been the second largest Puerto Rican community on the mainland. It began to grow during and after World War II, but it has never compared in size with the Puerto Rican population in New York. It is now estimated to be somewhere between 50,000 and 75,000 persons. The Chicago population is even more dispersed than that of New York. The largest numbers are on the northwest side, about two or three miles from the Loop, but it is intermingled here with members of the former populations of Irish, Polish, Slovak, and others. Another smaller group is found on the south side, bordering the Black community, while a third group is mingled with large numbers of other Spanish-speaking people following the Lake shore. As in New York, they are not concentrated enough in any one area to make them a decisive political force. Unlike the situation in New York, they are overshadowed in Chicago by the much larger Mexican population and, more recently, increasing numbers of Cubans and other Spanish-speaking peoples.

Nevertheless, the Puerto Rican community in Chicago has been able to maintain some sense of solidarity in a much simpler way than the Puerto Ricans in New York. Very early in the life of the Chicago community an organization called the "Caballeros de San Juan" (the Knights of Saint John) was formed to develop leadership among Puerto Rican men, and to promote the interests of the Puerto Rican community in religious, cultural, and political affairs. The councils of the Caballeros were self-starting and self-sustaining and had a significant impact on the life of Puerto Ricans in the late 1950's and early 1960's. They have since come to resemble a Puerto Rican Knights of Columbus. The civic activity formerly carried out by the Caballeros has been taken up by organizations explicitly devoted to political participation; the religious activity has been taken up by groups of Puerto Rican laymen who devote themselves to the spiritural and religious formation of their people. These latter, called the *Hermanos* (Brothers), are modeled on the groups of lay religious teachers in Puerto Rico called the *Hermanos Cheos*. The Chicago Archdiocese has not attempted to establish national or language parishes[15] for the Puerto Ricans, but has sought to provide existing parishes with Spanish-speaking priests. In 1956, the Archdiocese established the "Bishop's Committee for the Spanish-Speaking in Chicago." Although the major responsibility of this Committee was the large Mexican population, it has always maintained contact with the Puerto Ricans as well.

The Commonwealth of Puerto Rico established a second mainland office in Chicago in the late 1950's, an indication that it considered Chicago second in importance only to New York in the matter of serving Puerto Rican migrants. The office has served the populations of Puerto Ricans in Milwaukee, East Chicago, Gary, Indiana, and other midwestern cities as well as the contract farm workers who came to the midwestern states.

The difficulties of the Puerto Rican community in Chicago came to a head in two days of rioting which erupted in June 1966[16] when a policeman shot a Puerto Rican youth who, the policeman alleged, was attacking him. Although the major issue in the riot focused on police brutality, the disturbance led to a general airing of grievances of Puerto Ricans in Chicago, including problems of housing, education and discrimination. The outbreak prompted the Mayor of Chicago to appoint a Puerto Rican to the Mayor's Committee on Human Relations.

Other large-city experiences can be found in Newark, Philadelphia, Cleveland, and Boston. The Puerto Rican population in Newark is part of the overflow of the New York population into northeastern New Jersey. Since Newark is more than 50 per cent Black, the Puerto Ricans form a small minority in both a white and a Black world. They have sought to exercise some political influence by forming a coalition with the Blacks, but their numbers are too few and their residential pattern too scattered to permit a concentrated political thrust. The Puerto Ricans celebrate

[15]These parishes will be explained at length in Chapter Eight.
[16]*The New York Times*, June 13, 1966, p. 1; June 14, 1966, p. 1; June 15, 1966, p. 1; June 16, 1966, p. 29; June 22, 1966, p. 22; June 23, 1966, p. 21.

an annual parade in Newark, an indication of a growing sense of unity and solidarity which may eventually become a significant force.

The situation in other New Jersey cities is more or less the same. The numbers are smaller than the Puerto Ricans in Newark, but the percentage of Puerto Ricans, as in Hoboken, may be much larger. Riots have marked the lives of Puerto Ricans in Jersey City,[17] Paterson,[18] Passaic,[19] Perth Amboy,[20] and Trenton.[21] These are generally set off by an incident such as a complaint of police brutality, but they reflect the accumulation of grievances around housing, education, welfare, employment, and discrimination.

The Puerto Ricans in New Jersey organized a statewide Puerto Rican conference in the Autumn of 1970. This may develop into a basis of political influence and power, since the Puerto Ricans living in the whole of New Jersey certainly number into the hundreds of thousands. Furthermore, the Young Lords have been organizing in some parts of New Jersey, and the militancy of the Lords and other Puerto Rican youths has begun to appear. In the first statewide conference of Puerto Ricans, there was a sharp confrontation between the militant young and the older Puerto Ricans who had organized the conference.

Another type of Puerto Rican experience can be found in such cities as Lorain, Ohio, Youngstown, Ohio, and Bridgeport, Connecticut. These represent concentrations of Puerto Ricans in highly industrialized smaller cities, where Puerto Ricans are likely to be employed in heavier industrial work, such as factories, machine shops, and steel mills. They live in one or two family dwellings, and are often in the process of buying the home in which they live. Life in these smaller cities is much quieter and better organized, and the Puerto Rican community gives the impression of managing its life more effectively. When Puerto Ricans began to reside in each of these cities during and shortly after World War II, the community developed a close relationship with a Spanish-speaking parish or mission which has been a major factor in community identity and strength.

As in New York, the Puerto Ricans in these communities face the struggle to establish themselves, to marshal their strength, to move into the mainstream of mainland society. The problem of identity will be a

17 *The New York Times*, June 11, 1970, p. 41; June 12, 1970, p. 27; June 13, 1970, p. 40; June 14, 1970, p. 38.
18 *The New York Times*, July 4, 1968, p. 8; July 5, 1968, p. 28; July 6, 1968, p. 22; July 7, 1968, p. 63; July 8, 1968, p. 42; July 9, 1968, p. 23; October 30, 1968, p. 18; November 16, 1968, p. 22; December 20, 1968, p. 33.
19 *The New York Times*, August 4, 1969, p. 11; August 5, 1969, p. 55; August 6, 1969, p. 33; August 7, 1969, p. 25; August 8, 1969, p. 42; August 17, 1969, p. 49.
20 *The New York Times*, August 1, 1966, p. 15; August 2, 1966, p. 13; August 3, 1966, p. 1; August 4, 1966, p. 41; August 7, 1966, p. 41.
21 *The New York Times*, June 14, 1969, p. 68.

factor in the process, not to the extent to which it exists in a large and complicated city like New York, but in simpler and perhaps more subtle ways. The New York experience will be the Puerto Rican experience writ large. An understanding of it will not provide an understanding of the unique political, social, economic, or religious features of a particular Puerto Rican community anywhere else in the nation, but, hopefully, it will provide an insight into the universal issues which Puerto Ricans must face as they lose familiar contact with their own culture, and seek to establish themselves in a new and strange way of life.

The heart of every culture is the family. As the major influence in the process of socialization, it is the institution which gives a person his basic sense of identity. It is the main strength and support of people in the process of migration, and the institution which is most directly challenged in the process of assimilation.

BACKGROUND OF THE
PUERTO RICAN FAMILY[1]

Four major influences have contributed to the structure of family life, kinship patterns, and the patterns of family living of the Puerto Ricans:

The

Puerto

Rican

Family

1. The culture of the Borinquen Indians, now generally referred to as the Tainos, the natives on the Island when it was discovered.
2. The influence of Spanish colonial culture.
3. Slavery.
4. The influence of the United States and of economic development.

Very little is known about the culture of the Borinquen Indians. Unlike those in other areas of the Spanish Empire, the indigenous people in Puerto Rico seem to have disappeared as an identifiable group early in the history of the colony. Some speculations are available about their culture and family life, but little of it is reliable. New studies are now in progress.

[1]The literature on the Puerto Rican family is extensive and uneven. Julian Steward, *People of Puerto Rico* (Champaign-Urbana: University of Illinois Press, 1957), is one of the best presentations of varied types of Puerto Rican families. Sidney Mintz, *Worker in the Cane* (New Haven: Yale University Press, 1960), is a life history which is really a study of family life in a small barrio on the southern coast of Puerto Rico in an area where rates of consensual union have been high. It is probably the finest single book on this kind of Puerto Rican family. David Landy, *Tropical Childhood* (Chapel Hill: University of North Carolina Press, 1959), is a study of socialization and life cycle among poor families in a town in the northeast section of the Island. It is an excellent study of family life and socialization. Lydia Roberts and Rose Stefani, *Patterns of Living in Puerto Rican Families* (Rio Piedras: University of Puerto Rico Press, 1940), is out of date, but it has detailed descriptions of many family habits and practices which are still common among the poor and rural families of the Island. J. Mayone Stycos, *Family and Fertility in Puerto Rico* (New York: Columbia University

Spanish Colonial Culture

The great influence in the past and present on all levels of Puerto Rican family life was the Spanish colonial culture, the important features of which will now be discussed.

Preeminence of the family. As in most cultures of the world, the individual in Latin America has a deep consciousness of his membership in a family. He thinks of his importance in terms of his family membership. This is not a matter of prestige (as in belonging to the Ford or Rockefeller family), but a much more elemental thing, and it is as strong among the families of the very poor as it is among those of the very wealthy. The world to a Latin consists of a pattern of intimate personal relationships, and the basic relationships are those of his family. His confidence, his sense of security and identity are perceived in his relationship to others who are his family.

This is evident in the use of *names*, the *technonomy* of Puerto Rican and Latin families. The man generally uses two family names together with his given name, e.g., José Garcia Rivera. Garcia is the name of José's father's father; Rivera is the family name of José's mother's father. Thus the name indicates that José comes from the family of Garcia in his father's line, and from the family of Rivera in his mother's father's line. In Spanish speaking areas, if the man is to be addressed by only one family name, the first name is used, not the second. José would be called Mr. Garcia, not Mr. Rivera. The mixing of these names by Americans is a source of constant embarrassment to Spanish speaking people. The

---

Press, 1955), was part of a study of attitudes toward birth control, but actually presents extensive information about the Puerto Rican family, particularly in attitudes toward marriage, children, and sex. Lloyd H. Rogler and A. B. Hollingshead, *Trapped: Families and Schizophrenia* (New York: John Wiley & Sons, Inc., 1965), is a study of the causes of schizophrenia in Puerto Rico, but it provides an excellent and detailed analysis of family experience, especially among poor Puerto Ricans. Oscar Lewis, *La Vida: A Puerto Rican Family in the Culture of Poverty—San Juan and New York* (New York: Random House, Inc., 1965), is a vivid and detailed picture of the day-to-day experiences of a family with a history of prostitution in a slum area of San Juan. The Introduction, which presents a lengthy analysis of what Lewis calls the "culture of poverty," is important as a setting for the rest of the book. R. Fernandez-Marina, "The Puerto Rican Syndrome: Its Dynamics and Cultural Determinants," *Psychiatry*, 25 (1961), 79–82, is an analysis of a form of hysteria common among Puerto Ricans, but the analysis involves a study of Puerto Rican family patterns; R. Fernandez-Marina, E. D. Maldonado Sierra, and R. D. Trent, "Three Basic Themes in Mexican and Puerto Rican Family Values," *J. of Soc. Psychol.*, 48 (1958), 167–181, is a study of the changes in the values of Puerto Rican families under the influence of the mainland. Reuben Hill, "Courtship in Puerto Rico: An Institution in Transition," *Marriage and Family Living*, 17 (1955), 26–34, and Howard Stanton, "Puerto Rico's Changing Families," in *Transactions of the Third World Congress of Sociology* (London: International Sociological Association, 1956), IV, 101–107, are also studies of family change.

former Governor of Puerto Rico, Luis Muñoz Marin, was regularly referred to in American publications as Governor Marin. It should have been Governor Muñoz. Referring to Muñoz Marin as Governor Marin would be similar to referring to John Fitzgerald Kennedy as President Fitzgerald.

On some formal occasions, Puerto Ricans, like other Spanish speaking people, will use the names of all four families from which they come. If José were announcing his wedding, or an important official appointment, he might write his name: José Garcia Diaz y Rivera Colon. By this he is telling the world that he comes from the families of Garcia and Diaz on his father's side, and Rivera and Colon on his mother's side. The Puerto Ricans are not as familiar and informal with their public figures as Americans are. They may refer to a person as Don[2] Luis, Señor Muñoz, Señor Muñoz Marin, or as Muñoz, but they would not refer to him with the equivalent of "Looie" the way Americans refer to Ike and Dick and Jack or Harry. Americans are more sensitive to the importance of the individual—it is Harry who is important, or Ike, or Dick—but Puerto Ricans emphasize the importance of presenting themselves in the framework of the family of which they are a part.

The wife of José writes her name Maria Gonzalez de Garcia. She retains the family name of her father's father, Gonzalez, and she adopts, usually with the "de," the first name of her husband, Garcia. She may use both his names and present herself as Maria Gonzalez de Garcia Rivera. On formal occasions she may retain both her family names, and would then present herself as Maria Gonzalez Medina de Garcia Rivera. The children of José and Maria would have the first family name of both mother and father. The son would be Juan Garcia Gonzalez, the daughter Carmen Garcia Gonzalez; in formal situations, they would be Juan or Carmen Garcia Rivera y Gonzalez Medina.

The family is much more involved in the process of courtship than would be the case with an American family. In the United States, boys and girls mingle freely, date each other, fall in love, and by various means ask each other to marry. If they agree to marry, they will advise their parents. If the parents agree, the marriage proceeds happily; if parents disagree, the couple may go ahead and get married regardless. In Puerto Rico, intermingling and dating is much more restricted. A young man interested in a young woman is expected to speak to the parents of the

[2]Don is a title of respect used generally in direct speech toward a man (Doña for a woman). It has no class implication. Very poor and humble people use it of their own family members or friends as a sign of respect. It is generally used with the first name (Don Luis or Doña Maria), never without it (Don Luis Muñoz, perhaps, but never Don Muñoz).

girl, particularly the father, to declare his intentions. A serious courtship may never get started if the families disapprove. As one Puerto Rican sociologist expressed it: in the United States, courtship is a drama with only two actors; in Puerto Rico, it is a drama of two actors, but the families are continually prompting from the wings. Marriage is still considered much more a union of two families than it would be in the United States.

Finally, Puerto Ricans have a deep sense of family obligation. One's primary responsibilities are to family and friends. If a person advances in public office or succeeds in business enterprises, he has a strong sense of obligation to use his gains for the benefit of his family. People of the United States also have a sense of family loyalty, but, to a much larger degree, they expect to make it on their own. Success does not make them feel obliged to appoint family members to positions, share their wealth with relatives, or use their position for the benefit of the family. They expect selection in business and government to be on the basis of ability and effort, not personal or family relationships. This is an oversimplification, since family influence operates in the United States and people in Puerto Rico are increasingly chosen on the basis of ability and effort. But, in Puerto Rico, the sense of family is much deeper. As economic development proceeds on the Island, or as its citizens adjust to American life, the need increases to sacrifice family loyalty and obligation to efficiency. The Puerto Rican finds this a very difficult thing to do.

Superior Authority of the Man. A second feature of the Puerto Rican family is the role of superior authority exercised by the man. This is not peculiar to Latin cultures; it is the common situation in most cultures of the world. The man expects to exercise the authority in the family; he feels free to make decisions without consulting his wife; he expects to be obeyed when he gives commands. As a larger middle class emerges in Puerto Rico, the role of the woman is in the process of being redefined. But, in contrast to the characteristics of cooperation and companionship of American families, the woman in Puerto Rico has a subordinate role.

This must not be interpreted as meaning that women do not have subtle ways of influencing men. The influence of mother over son is particularly strong in the culture of the Puerto Ricans. Furthermore, women have played an unusually important role in public and academic life. In 1962, of the 76 municipios in Puerto Rico, 10 had women as mayors, the most famous being Doña Felisa Rincon de Gautier, who was Mayoress of the capital city of San Juan for 20 years. Women are Department Chairmen of many of the departments of the University of Puerto Rico. Oscar Lewis found the Puerto Rican women among the families he studied to be much more aggressive, outspoken, and even violent than the women in the Mexican families he had studied.[3] Nevertheless, the role is culturally defined and ordinarily maintained as subordinate to the authority of the husband. Until recently, and still to a surprising extent, women will not make such decisions as consultation of a doctor, or sending children for medical treatment, without seeking permission of the husband.

The superior position of the man is also reflected in what Americans call a *double standard of morality* in reference to sexual behavior.[4] In Latin cultures, as in most cultures of the world, a very clear distinction is made between the "good" woman, who will be protected as a virgin until marriage, and then be protected as a wife and mother, and the "bad" woman, who is available for a man's enjoyment. Puerto Ricans are concerned about their girls, and fathers and brothers feel a strong obligation to protect them. On the other hand, a great deal of freedom is granted to the boys. It is rather expected, sometimes encouraged, that a boy have sexual experiences with women before marriage. After marriage he may feel free to engage in what Puerto Ricans sometimes jokingly refer to as "extracurricular activities." These patterns of protection of the woman and freedom for the man are changing, but they are still quite different from patterns of sexual behavior on the mainland. It is also true that patterns of sexual behavior are going through a revolution on the mainland, but the revolution to greater sexual freedom in the United States involves boys and girls equally, and thus draws us even further away from the style of life in Puerto Rico.

Compadrazgo. Another consequence of the influence of Spain on the Puerto Rican family has been *compadrazgo*,[5] or the institution of *compadres*. These are people who are companion parents, as it were, with the natural parents of the child; the man is the *compadre*, the woman is the *comadre*. Sponsors at Baptism, for example, become the godparents (padrinos) of the child, and the compadres of the child's parents; this is also true of sponsors at Confirmation. Witnesses at a marriage become compadres of the married couple. Sometimes common interests or the intensification of friendship may lead men or women to consider themselves compadres or comadres. The compadres are sometimes relatives, but often they are not. They constitute a network of ritual kinship, as

---

[3]Lewis, *La Vida, op. cit.*, p. xxvii.

[4]See references to machismo in Stycos, *Family and Fertility, op. cit.*, pp. 34–35, 42–44, 175–180.

[5]There is some evidence that compadrazgo may have existed among the indigenous people. Some traces of it have been found among the Mayans. But it definitely was a significant Spanish institution which the colonizers either implanted or reinforced when they arrived.

serious and important as that of natural kinship, around a person or a group. Compadres frequently become more formal in their relationships, shifting from the familiar "Tu" to the formal "Usted" in speech. They have a deep sense of obligation to each other for economic assistance, support, encouragement, and even personal correction. A compadre may feel much freer to give advice or correction in regard to family problems than a brother or sister would. A compadre is expected to be responsive to all the needs of his compadre, and, ideally, he supplies assistance without question. When Sidney Mintz was doing his anthropological study of a barrio of Santa Isabel, Puerto Rico, his principal informant was a remarkable man, Taso Zayas, a farm worker who cut sugar cane. Mintz reached a degree of close friendship with Taso, and later decided to do his life history. Mintz describes the relationship which had developed between himself and Taso. Taso had reached a point where he felt free to ask Mintz for money. "In his own words he would not 'dare ask' if he were not sure I would respond; and failure to do so, if it were a matter of free choice, would end our friendship."[6] In other words, Mintz and Taso had become compadres.

Slavery

Another influence on family life in Puerto Rico was that of slavery. As will be described elsewhere,[7] slavery was a milder institution in Puerto Rico than in the United States. But slavery in the Western World has had a devastating effect on family life. Little effort is made to provide for the stability and permanence of the slave family; men and women, relatives, children, are bought, sold, exchanged, and shifted with little or no regard for permanent family union. Slave women are defenseless before the advances of free men.

The usual consequences of slavery in the broken family life of Negroes have been as evident in Puerto Rico as elsewhere. A number of features of Spanish culture modified the effects to some extent. Consorting with a woman who was not one's wife was a practice of upper class men in the Spanish colonial tradition, and was not confined to Negro women. Therefore, the extramarital relationships of white men and Negro women tended to follow a pattern similar to that of white men with white women. Cultural patterns formed around these relationships which provided some advantages to the women and children involved in them. However, the mother-based family—the family with children of a number

[6]Mintz, *Worker in the Cane, op. cit.*, p. 6.
[7]See Chapter Seven for references to slavery.

of fathers and no permanent male consort—has been a common phenomenon in Puerto Rican history.

The United States and Economic Development

Within recent years, two other major influences have become important: (1) the influence of the United States has affected the Island through the educational system which, for many years after annexation, was in the hands of Americans and conducted on the American model; (2) religious influence from the mainland. Most of the Catholic priests, brothers, and nuns working among Puerto Ricans during the past 50 years have come from the United States. Protestant denominations have been established on the Island since the turn of the century, and Pentecostal sects have preached a strong and effective gospel among the poor. Finally, and most important, Puerto Ricans returning from the mainland either to visit or to stay bring with them a strong and direct influence of mainland culture in relation to the family. The consequences, particularly of this last influence, will be indicated later.

STRUCTURE OF THE PUERTO RICAN FAMILY

As a consequence of the above influences, a fourfold structural typology can be identified among Puerto Rican families.

1. *Extended family systems.* These are families in which there are strong bonds and frequent interaction among a wide range of natural or ritual kin. Grandparents, parents, and children may live in the same household, or they may have separate households but visit frequently. The extended family is evident, regardless of the type of marriage (regularized or consensual), and it is a source of strength and support.

2. *The nuclear family.* With the rise of the middle class, the conjugal unit of father, mother, and children, not living close to relatives and with weak bonds to the extended family, is becoming more common. It is difficult to get reliable evidence on the number of these families, but observant Puerto Ricans are noticing that, with migration and upward mobility, their number is rapidly increasing. This is an expected response to social and economic development.

3. *Father, mother, their children, and children of another union or unions of husband or wife.* This is not an uncommon phenomenon among Puerto Rican families. New Yorkers have complained about the difficulty

of understanding the differing names of children in some Puerto Rican households. In places on the Island where this phenomenon is common, children will identify themselves accordingly. If a visitor asks a boy if the girl with him is his sister, he may respond: "Yes, on my father's side," or "Yes, on my mother's side."

4. *The mother-based family, with children of one or more men, but with no permanent male consort in the home.* These four types of family structure are evident among Puerto Ricans on the mainland.

Consensual Unions

Important in relation to family structure is the phenomenon of consensual unions,[8] which in former years have been common on the Island but have been rapidly declining. A consensual union is a relatively stable union of a man and a woman who have never gone through a religious or civil marriage ceremony. They begin living together and raising their family, and may live this way throughout their lives. At some later date, they may regularize the union in a civil or religious ceremony.

This is not the "common law" marriage which is an institution in English Common Law. The Roman Law tradition which has prevailed in Puerto Rico never recognized a union as a marriage unless it was regularized, but Roman Law always acknowledged the situation in which two people would live together without getting married. This state was defined as *concubinatus* or *concubinage*. Concubinage has unfavorable connotations in the English language, but it never had these in the Roman Law tradition. Puerto Ricans who live consensually, or in concubinage, refer to themselves as *amancebados*, living together without marriage. The United States census reports consensual unions as a recognized "civil status" and consequently asks people if they are living consensually. According to the decennial census, of all couples "living together" on the Island, the following percentages were reported as "living consensually":

1899	34.7%	of all unions
1920	26.3	of all unions
1950	24.9	of all unions
1960	13.5	of all unions

[8]The phenomenon of consensual union is widely discussed in the literature. The best insight into this cultural practice is found in Mintz, *Worker in the Cane, op. cit.,* pp. 253–277. A broader but less detailed description is found in Mintz' chapter, "Canamelar," in Steward, *People of Puerto Rico, op. cit.,* pp. 375–391. A more detailed study of different rates of consensual unions in different parts of Puerto Rico is found in Dorothy M. Dohen, *The Background of Consensual Union in Puerto Rico,* in *Two Puerto Rican Studies* (Cuernavaca, Mexico: Center of Intercultural Documentation, 1967). Some lengthy descriptions are also found in Lewis, *La Vida, op. cit., passim,* and Rogler and Hollingshead, *Trapped, op. cit., passim.*

It is a status, therefore, which has always been culturally and officially acknowledged, and Puerto Ricans, unless they are speaking with strangers who they think may not understand, are very open about admitting that they are living consensually. They do not look upon this as an immoral state, as it would be considered in many parts of the Christian world. The partners generally are not well instructed in any religious faith, and consequently have no guilt feelings about living without religious marriage.[9] In addition, they are usually poor people with no property, and civil marriage makes sense only as a legal protection for property rights related to marriage. These simple people recognize that a man needs a woman and a woman needs a man, and they begin to live together and bring up the children resulting from their union, or from other unions which either one might have had. They judge the moral quality of the union in terms of their relationship to each other. He is a good man if he works to support the woman and children, treats them respectfully, and does not abandon them. She is a good woman if she keeps his house, cooks his meals, keeps his clothes, and raises his children properly. In fact, people in consensual unions are sometimes more concerned about the basic moral relationships than are people preoccupied with the regularization of the union. More important than the percentage of consensual unions for the whole Island is the uneven distribution of consensual unions. For example, if one selected a number of representative municipios for low, medium, and high percentages of consensual union, it would break down as shown in Table 6–1. The table indicates that family patterns differ sharply from one section of the Island to another. All of the low percentage municipios are in a small corner of the northwest tip, all of the medium percentage municipios are in the central mountains, while all the high percentage municipios are on the southeast corner.

The percentage of existing consensual unions has been declining sharply. It dropped from 25 per cent in 1950 to 13.5 per cent in 1960. The report of the 1970 Census, when it is available, will probably indicate a further decline. A number of factors help to explain the decline. First, the increase in religious and spiritual care has created a wider concern for religious marriage. Second, important economic benefits have come to be associated with regularized unions; e.g., widow's pensions, family benefits, social security, and admittance, particularly in New York, to public housing projects. Finally, the rapid emergence of a middle class has been important. Consensual union has always been a phenomenon of the poor population. As persons from the poorer classes advance to

[9]This does not mean they do not respect religious marriage. Many of them do not enter religious marriage because they understand its binding character, and do not wish to commit themselves this way until they are sure they mean it.

TABLE 6–1

PERCENTAGE OF ALL EXISTING UNIONS
WHICH WERE CONSENSUAL, 1930, 1950, 1960,
FOR SELECTED MUNICIPIOS OF PUERTO RICO

	1930	1950	1960
Low rates:			
Aguada	6.8	8.2	6.2
Aguadilla	11.3	14.3	6.0
Camuy	11.4	10.8	7.0
Isabela	9.6	9.4	9.0
Moca	6.3	6.9	4.0
Quebradilla	8.9	9.0	5.0
Rincon	8.5	8.6	5.0
Medium rates:			
Barceloneta	22.3	19.8	13.0
Barranquitas	15.3	15.4	7.0
Ciales	20.3	17.6	16.0
Jayuya	21.4	14.5	12.0
Orocovis	23.7	18.8	9.0
High rates:			
Arroyo	41.	35.6	14.
Cayey	42.2	34.9	20.
Coamo	41	29.4	20.
Guayama	46.6	32.7	20.
Juana Diaz	40.5	44.5	28.
Maunabo	41.6	29.5	19.
Salinas	55.9	51.7	33.
Santa Isabel	51.6	43.8	19.

SOURCE: For 1930: U.S. Bureau of the Census, *U.S. Census of Population, 1930* (Washington, D.C.: U.S. Government Printing Office, 1933), Vol. VI, Puerto Rico, Families, Table 18; for 1950: U.S. Bureau of the Census, *U.S. Census of Population, 1950* (Washington, D.C.: U.S. Government Printing Office, 1953), Vol. II, Parts 51–54, Territories and Possessions, Table 39; for 1960: U.S. Bureau of the Census, *U.S. Census of Population, 1960* (Washington, D.C.: U.S. Government Printing Office, 1963), Vol. I, Characteristics of the Population, Part 53, Puerto Rico, Table 29.

middle class status, they become aware of regularized marriage as a middle class value, and so they get married. Increase in education, and the gainful occupation and changing status of women have also contributed to the decline. In other words, the social conditions in which it was functional have disappeared.

Illegitimacy

Related to consensual unions is illegitimacy, about which at least brief mention must be made. International reports of population use the term "illegitimate" to designate the children of parents who are not married. Children of consensual unions are included in this. This is a misleading designation. In Puerto Rico, as in the Roman Law tradition generally, the term "illegitimate" was never used.[10] A child of a marriage which was legalized, and whose rights before the law were thus protected, was called "legitimate," he was a "legal" child. "Natural" was the term used for all other children. Thus no pejorative connotation was related to the term for a child of unmarried parents. A third term has come into use in Puerto Rico, the *hijo reconocido*, the recognized child.[11] In Puerto Rico, if the father of a child is known, whether he is living consensually with the mother or whether the child resulted from a casual union, he is required by law to recognize the child. This gives the child a number of rights before the law, including the right to use the father's name, the right to support, and some rights of inheritance. Therefore, in examining statistics on legitimacy from areas like Puerto Rico it is important to note that many of the children reported as illegitimate may actually be the children of stable consensual unions.

MARRIAGE AND FAMILY
IN PUERTO RICO:
THE DEMOGRAPHIC PICTURE

The tendency to marry is lower in Puerto Rico than that proclivity in the United States. According to the 1960 census, 62.6 per cent of the men over 14 years of age were ever married, as were 71.4 per cent of the women. In the United States the percentages were higher. Differences which appear may be a reflection of the age at marriage, which is lower in the United States than in Puerto Rico. Median age at marriage for men in Puerto Rico was 23.01 in 1960; in the United States it was 22.8;

---

[10] In contrast to English Common Law, which was concerned with illegitimacy, Roman Law always acknowledged that some people would live together without getting married, in a state of concubinage. English Common Law, however, had the principle of common law marriage: if a couple lived together long enough, it recognized the union as legal.

[11] In the late 1960's the vital statistics reports do not use the category "recognized child" as they once did. As a result, it is difficult to determine how many there are.

for women in Puerto Rico in 1960 it was 21.75; for women in the United States it was 20.3. However, age at marriage has been declining steadily in Puerto Rico. In 1950, of all men entering marriage, only 6.4 per cent were under 20 years of age; in 1960, 10.3 per cent were under 20; of the women in Puerto Rico entering marriage in 1950, 32.1 per cent were under 20; in 1960, 36.1 per cent were under 20.

Type of Ceremony

Apart from consensual unions, which are not registered, another distinction among marriages in Puerto Rico which is quite significant is difference in type of ceremony, whether civil, Protestant, or Catholic. The different percentages of these types of ceremonies are very marked throughout the Island (see Tables 6–2 and 6–3). When one realizes that Aguada

TABLE 6–2

TYPE OF CEREMONY FOR ALL MARRIAGES
IN PUERTO RICO, 1949, 1956, 1960, 1969

	Civil (%)	Catholic (%)	Protestant (%)
1949	24.3	61.4	14.3
1956	26.5	59.5	14.0
1960	36.2	45.8	17.6
1969	40.0	40.0	20.0

SOURCE: Registro Demografico, Departamento de Salud, San Juan, Puerto Rico.

TABLE 6–3

TYPE OF MARRIAGE CEREMONY FOR SELECTED
MUNICIPIOS OF PUERTO RICO, 1960

	No.	Civil (%)	Catholic (%)	Protestant (%)
Aguada	206	22.6	71.4	6.0
Aguadilla	400	12.7	34.3	53.0
Barranquitas	115	31.0	69.0	0.0
Guayanilla	125	27.0	55.0	18.0
Santa Isabel	111	71.0	23.0	17.6

SOURCE: Registro Demografico, Departamento de Salud, San Juan, Puerto Rico.

is the municipio contiguous to Aguadilla, the difference in type of marriage ceremony is striking. It is difficult to explain the absence of any Protestant marriages in Barranquitas and the high rate of civil marriage in Santa Isabel. What is clear is that type of marriage ceremony differs sharply from one area of the Island to another. There is no consistent pattern which can be called "Puerto Rican."

Fertility

Fertility has generally been high in Puerto Rico, although it appears to be dropping in recent years.[12] This may be due largely to the migration of large numbers of young people to the mainland during their most fertile years. In any event, the rate of population increase on the Island has been declining. Puerto Rico has been one of the classic examples of "population explosion," and efforts to control the population increase have been widespread, well known, and at times very controversial. The estimated natural increase of the population during the period 1887–1899 was 14.3 per 1,000 population; the crude birth rate during the same period was 45.7, and the crude death rate was 31.4. The introduction of better hygiene caused the death rate to decline consistently but the birth rate to remain high, so population increase has been rapid. The average annual increase during the period 1930–1935 was 18.9 per 1,000; during the period 1940–1945 it was 24.9; in 1950 it was 28.6; in 1965 it had declined to 23.4; the estimated rate for 1969 is 18. Crude rates such as these are not very helpful in explaining population changes, but they give a general picture of increases and decreases. Actually, the continuing migration of Puerto Ricans to the mainland has been the safety valve of population increase. Had all the migrants remained in Puerto Rico, the population would be doubling every 20 years, a rate of growth which would have caused major problems on the Island.

Family Values

Some aspects of the values of Puerto Rican family life have already been mentioned in relation to the influences which have helped to form it.

[12]The problem of population policy and birth control has been a troublesome issue between the Government and the Catholic Bishops on the Island. For an analysis of the problem up to 1950, see Harvey S. Perloff, *Puerto Rico's Economic Future* (Chicago: University of Chicago Press, 1950), Chaps. 12 and 13. For the more modern period, José L. Vasquez, *Fertility Trends in Puerto Rico* (Section on Biostatistics, Department of Preventive Medicine and Public Health, School of Medicine of Puerto Rico, San Juan, 1964), brings the data up to date. An intensive study of backgrounds of fertility was done during the 1950's in Puerto Rico. The first publication, Paul Hatt, *Background of Human Fertility in Puerto Rico* (Princeton, N.J.: Princeton University Press, 1952), was a survey of public attitudes toward large or small families. This was followed by Stycos, *Family and Fertility, op. cit.*, which sought to determine why people said they preferred small families but continued having large ones; the final study was Reuben Hill, J. Mayone Stycos, and Kurt W. Back, *The Family and Population Control: A Puerto Rican Experiment in Social Change* (Chapel Hill, N.C.: University of North Carolina Press, 1959), which reports the results of various methods to bring people to the practice of birth control.

In the following paragraphs, the range of values will be indicated which distinguish the Puerto Rican family from the predominant middle class family values of the mainland.[13]

Personalism. The basic value of Puerto Rican culture, as of Latin cultures in general, is a form of individualism which focuses on the inner importance of the person. In contrast to the individualism of the United States, which values the individual in terms of his ability to compete for higher social and economic status, the culture of Puerto Rico centers attention on those inner qualities which constitute the uniqueness of the person, and his goodness or worth in himself. In a two class society where little mobility was possible, a man was born into his social and economic position. Therefore, he defined his value in terms of the qualities and behavior that made a man good or respected in the social position where he found himself. A poor farm laborer was a good man when he did those things which made a man good on his social and economic level. He felt an inner dignity (*dignidad*) about which the Puerto Rican is very sensitive; he expected others to have respect (*respeto*) for that *dignidad*. All men have some sense of personal dignity and are sensitive about proper respect being shown them. But this marks the Puerto Rican culture in a particular way. Puerto Ricans are much more sensitive than Americans to anything that appears to be personal insult or disdain; they do not take to practical jokes which are likely to embarrass, or to party games in which people "make fools of themselves." They do not "horse around," as Americans would say in an offhand, informal manner; they are unusually responsive to manifestations of personal respect, and to styles of personal leadership by men who appeal to the person rather than a program or a platform. Although the old two class society in which these values developed has been disappearing, the values themselves are still very strong.

Personalism and Efficiency. It is this personalism which makes it difficult for the Puerto Rican to adjust easily to what Americans call efficiency. For a Puerto Rican, life is a network of personal relationships. He trusts persons; he relies on persons; he knows that, at every moment, he can fall back on a brother, a cousin, a compadre. He does not have that same trust for a system or an organization. The American, on the other hand, expects the system to work; he has confidence in the organization. When something goes wrong, his reaction is: "Somebody ought to do something about this"; "Get this system going." Thus, an American

13One of the best brief treatments of Latin values which are shared by Puerto Ricans can be found in John Gillin, "Some Signposts for Policy," in *Social Change in Latin America Today*, Richard N. Adams, *et al.*, eds. (New York: Vintage, 1960), pp. 28–47. Another good treatment is found in Henry Wells, *The Modernization of Puerto Rico* (Cambridge, Mass.: Harvard University Press, 1969), Chaps. 1 and 2.

becomes impatient and uneasy when systems do not work. He responds to efficiency. The Latin becomes uneasy and impatient if the system works too well, if he feels himself in a situation where he must rely on impersonal functions rather than personal relationships.

The Padrino. Related to personalism is the role of the *padrino.* The padrino is a person, strategically placed in a higher position of the social structure, who has a personal relationship with the poorer person in which he provides employment, assistance at time of need, and acts as an advocate if the poor person becomes involved in trouble. The padrino is really the intermediary between the poor person, who has neither sophistication nor influence, and the larger society of law, government, employment, and service. He is a strategic helper in times of need, but the possibilities of exploitation in this relationship are very great. The poor person can become completely bound to the padrino by debt or by obligations to personal service to such an extent that his life is little better than slavery. The role of the padrino has decreased in Puerto Rico, but the tendency to seek a personal relationship in one's business affairs is still strong.

Machismo. Another aspect of personalism is a combination of qualities associated with masculinity. This is generally referred to as *machismo,* literally, maleness. Machismo is a style of personal daring (the great quality of the bullfighter) by which one faces challenge, danger, and threat with calmness and self-possession; this sometimes takes the form of bravado. It is also a quality of personal magnetism which impresses and influences others and prompts them to follow one as a leader—the quality of the conquistador. It is associated with sexual prowess, influence, and power over women reflected in a vigorous romanticism and a jealous guarding of sweetheart or wife, or in premarital and extramarital relationships.

Sense of Family Obligation. Personalism is deeply rooted in the individualism which has just been described; it is also rooted in the family. As explained above, the Puerto Rican has a deep sense of that network of primary personal relationships which is his family. To express it another way, he senses the family as an extension of the person, and the network of obligations follows as described above.

Sense of the Primary of the Spiritual. The Latin generally refers to American culture as very materialistic, much to the amazement of Americans, who are conscious of human qualities, concerns, and generosity in American culture which are missing in the Latin. What the Latin means is that his fundamental concerns are not with this world or its tangible features. He has a sense of spirit and soul as much more important than the body, and as being intimately related to his value as a person; he tends to think in terms of transcendent qualities, such as justice, loyalty, or love, rather than in terms of practical arrangements which spell out justice or loyalty in the concrete. On an intellectual level, he strives to clarify relationships conceptually with a confidence that, if they can be made intellectually clear and precise, the reality which they express will have those relationships. He thinks of life very much in terms of ultimate values and ultimate spiritual goals, and expresses a willingness to sacrifice material satisfactions for these. In contrast, the American preoccupation with mastering the world and subjecting it, through technological programs, to man's domination, gives him the sense of reversing the system of values, of emphasizing the importance of mastering the physical universe rather than seeking the values of the spirit. It is striking to note how many important political figures are also literary men with a humanistic flair. Former Governor Muñoz Marin is a poet and is affectionately called *El Vate*, the Bard, in Puerto Rico; the former Resident Commissioner in Washington, Santiago Polanco Abreu, is a literary critic; some of the best known figures in public service in the Puerto Rican community in New York, such as Juan Aviles, Carmen Marrero, and Luis Quero Chiesa, are accomplished writers and artists.

Fatalism. Connected to these spiritual values is a deep sense of fatalism in Puerto Ricans. They have a sense of destiny, partly related to elemental fears of the sacred, partly related to a sense of Divine Providence governing the world. The popular song *Que será, será*, "Whatever will be, will be," is a simple expression of it, as is the common expression that intersperses so much of Puerto Rican speech: *Si Dios Quiere*, "If God wills it." The term "destiny" recurs frequently in Puerto Rican popular songs. This quality leads to the acceptance of many events as inevitable; it also softens the sense of personal guilt for failure. If, after a vigorous effort, an enterprise does not succeed, the Puerto Rican may shrug his shoulders and remark: "It was not meant to be."

Sense of Hierarchy. The Puerto Ricans, like other Latins, have had a concept of a hierarchical world during the whole of their history. This was partly the result of the two class system, in which members never conceived of a world in which they could move out of the position in which they were born. Thus they thought of a relationship of higher and lower classes which was fixed somewhat as the various parts of the body were fixed. This concept of hierarchy contributed to their concept of personal worth as distinct from a person's position in the social structure.

TRANSITION TO THE MAINLAND

The institution which faces the most direct shock in the migration to the mainland is the family, and the progress of Puerto Ricans can be measured to a large extent by a study of the family. First a statistical description of Puerto Rican families can be presented, followed by an analysis of the effect of migration on the family.

It has long been recognized that the migration of Puerto Ricans is a family migration, in the sense that they either come as families, or expect to stay and found their families here. This is reflected in the percentage of the population on the mainland which is married. According to the 1960 census, of all Puerto Rican males over 14 years of age, 70 per cent were married; of females, about 80 per cent.[14] Age at marriage shows a sharp decline from first generation to second generation, indicating an adaptation to mainland patterns.

Type of Ceremony

Another indication of change can be found in the type of religious ceremony of Puerto Rican marriages on the mainland. As indicated before, this varies considerably from one area of Puerto Rico to another. Comparison of type of religious ceremony for all marriages in Puerto Rico for 1960 with type of religious ceremony for Puerto Rican marriages in New York City for 1959 brings results as shown in Table 6–4.

TABLE 6–4

TYPE OF RELIGIOUS CEREMONY FOR ALL MARRIAGES
IN PUERTO RICO AND ALL PUERTO RICAN MARRIAGES
IN NEW YORK CITY FOR SELECTED YEARS

	Civil (%)	Catholic (%)	Protestant (%)
Puerto Rico, 1949	24.3	61.4	14.3
Puerto Rico, 1960	36.2	45.8	17.6
New York City, 1949 (n. 4514)[a]	20.0	27.0	50.0
New York City, 1959 (n. 9370)	18.0	41.0	38.0

SOURCE: J. P. Fitzpatrick, "Intermarriage of Puerto Ricans in New York City," *Amer. J. of Sociol.*, 71, 4 (1966), 403.

[a]A small number of other types of ceremonies are included in this total.

Two things are evident from Table 6–4. The pattern of marriage ceremony differs considerably between Puerto Rico and New York, and the pattern in New York, as in Puerto Rico, changed greatly between

[14]J. P. Fitzpatrick, "Intermarriage of Puerto Ricans in New York City," *Amer. J. of Sociol.*, 71, 4 (1966), 401, Tables 4 and 5.

1949 and 1959. The increase in Catholic ceremonies can be explained by the widespread efforts of the Catholic Archdioceses of New York and Brooklyn to develop special programs for the religious care of Puerto Rican people between 1949 and 1959. In addition, ceremonies in Pentecostal and Evangelical Churches declined from 1949 to 1959, particularly between first and second generation. If the Protestant marriages performed by ministers of Pentecostal and Evangelical sects are taken separately, the decline is very evident. In 1959, 38.4 per cent of first generation grooms were married by Pentecostal ministers, but only 33.3 per cent of second generation grooms; among brides, 37 per cent of first generation, but only 30.1 per cent of the second generation were married by Pentecostal ministers.[15] The implications of this for religious practice will be discussed in Chapter Eight. The consistent drop from first to second generation tends to confirm the theory that association with sects and storefront religious groups is a first generation phenomenon. When the second generation becomes more familiar with American life, they tend to withdraw from the sects.

Out-Group Marriage

The most significant evidence of adjustment to life on the mainland has been the increase of marriage of Puerto Ricans with non-Puerto Ricans. In his study of New York marriages, 1949 and 1959, Fitzpatrick established that there is a significant increase in the rate of out-group marriage among second generation Puerto Ricans over the first. The data are presented in Table 6–5.

The increase in the rate of out-group marriage among Puerto Ricans in both 1949 and 1959 between the first and second generation was as great as was the increase for all immigrants in New York City in the years 1908 to 1912.[16] It is legitimate to conclude from this that, if out-group marriage is accepted as an index of assimilation, the assimilation of Puerto Ricans in New York is moving as rapidly as the assimilation of all immigrant groups during the years 1908–1912.

Changes in Values

Much more important than the statistical description of the Puerto Rican families in the United States or in New York City is the study of the

---

[15]*Ibid.*, 404, Table 10.

[16]The data for marriages of immigrants, 1908–1912, which were used in the Fitzpatrick study were taken from Julian Drachsler, *Intermarriage in New York City* (New York: Columbia University Press, 1921).

TABLE 6–5

RATE OF OUT-GROUP MARRIAGE OF PUERTO RICANS
IN NEW YORK CITY, 1949 AND 1959, BY GENERATION;
AND OF ALL IMMIGRANTS IN NEW YORK CITY, 1908–1912

	First Generation		Second Generation		Increase in Second Generation
	%	No.	%	No.	%
Grooms:					
Puerto Rican, 1949	5.2	3,079	28.3	378	23.1
Puerto Rican, 1959	3.6	7,078	27.4	638	23.8
1908–1912	10.39	64,577	32.4	12,184	22.01
Brides:					
Puerto Rican, 1949	8.5	3,077	30.0	523	21.5
Puerto Rican, 1959	6.0	7,257	33.1	717	27.1
1908–1912	10.1	61,823	30.12	14,611	20.02

SOURCE: J. P. Fitzpatrick, "Intermarriage of Puerto Ricans in New York
City," *Amer. J. of Sociol.*, 71, 4 (1966), 398.

changes in values which they face. Probably the most serious is the shift
in roles of husband and wife. There is abundant evidence that this is a
common experience of immigrants. It is provoked by a number of things.
First, it is frequently easier for Puerto Rican women to get jobs in New
York rather than Puerto Rican men. This gives the wife an economic
independence which she may never have had before, and if the husband
is unemployed while the wife is working, the reversal of roles is severe.
Second, the impact of American culture begins to make itself felt more
directly in New York than on the Island. Puerto Rican women from the
poorer classes are much more involved in social, community, and political
activities than they are in Puerto Rico. This influences the Puerto Rican
wife gradually to adopt the patterns of the mainland.

Even more direct and difficult to cope with is the shift in role of
the Puerto Rican child. Puerto Rican families have frequently lamented
the patterns of behavior of even good boys in the United States. Puerto
Rican parents consider them to be disrespectful. American children are
taught to be self-reliant, aggressive, and competitive, to ask "why," and
to stand on their own two feet. A Puerto Rican child is generally much
more submissive. When the children begin to behave according to the
American pattern, the parents cannot understand it. A priest who had
worked for many years with migrating Puerto Ricans remarked to the
writer: "When these Puerto Rican families come to New York, I give the
boys about 48 hours on the streets of New York, and the difference be-

tween his behavior and what the family expects, will have begun to shake the family."

The distance which gradually separates child from family is indicated in much of the literature about Puerto Ricans in New York. In the autobiography of Piri Thomas, *Down These Mean Streets*,[17] it is clear that his family—and it was a good, strong family—had no way of controlling him once he began to associate with his peers on the streets. The sharp contrast of two life histories, *Two Blocks Apart*,[18] also demonstrates the difficulties of a Puerto Rican family in trying to continue to control the life of a boy growing up in New York. His peers become his significant reference group. A considerable number of scholars and social workers attribute much of the delinquency of Puerto Ricans to the excessive confinement which the Puerto Rican families impose in an effort to protect their children. Once the children can break loose in the early teens, they break completely. When Julio Gonzalez was killed in a gang fight on the lower East Side in reprisal for the murder of a Negro girl, Theresa Gee, in 1959, he was buried from Nativity Church. Julio's father, a poor man from a mountain town in Puerto Rico, was like a pillar of strength during the wake. He was a man of extraordinary dignity and self-possession. After the funeral Mass, he went to the sacristy of the Church, embraced each of the priests who had participated, and thanked them. Here was a man who sought to pass on to his son the qualities of loyalty, dignity, and strength. But when the son reached the streets, different definitions of loyalty and dignity took over. As Julio was dying, after the priest had given him the last rites of the Catholic Church, he fell into unconsciousness, mumbling: "Tell the guys they can count on me; tell them I'll be there."[19]

Probably the most severe problem of control is the effort of families to give their unmarried girls the same kind of protection they would have given them in Puerto Rico. When the girls reach the early teens, they wish to do what American girls do—go to dances with boys without a chaperone, and associate freely with girls and boys of the neighborhood or school. For a good Puerto Rican father to permit his daughter to go out unprotected is a serious moral failure. In a Puerto Rican town, when a father has brought his daughters as virgins to marriage, he can hold up his head before his community; he enjoys the esteem and prestige of a

---

[17]Piri Thomas, *Down These Mean Streets* (New York: Alfred A. Knopf, 1967).
     [18]Charlotte Leon Mayerson, ed., *Two Blocks Apart* (New York: Holt, Rinehart and Winston, Inc., 1965).
     [19]For a lengthy discussion of this change of values and its relation to delinquency, see J. P. Fitzpatrick, "Crime and Our Puerto Ricans," in *Catholic Mind*, LVIII (1960), 39–50. This is reprinted in Gus Tyler, *Organized Crime in America* (Ann Arbor: University of Michigan Press, 1962), pp. 415–421.

good father. To ask the same father to allow his daughters to go free in New York is to ask him to do something which the men of his family have considered immoral. It is psychologically almost impossible for him to do this. This tension between parents and daughter(s) is one of the most difficult for Puerto Rican parents to manage. It is frequently complicated because Americans, including school teachers and counsellors, who are not aware of the significance of this in the Puerto Rican background, advise the parents to allow the girls to go out freely.[20]

Finally, the classic tension between the generations takes place. The parents are living in the Puerto Rican culture in their homes. The children are being brought up in an American school where American values are being presented. The parents will never really understand their children; the children will never really understand the parents.

Weakening of Extended Kinship

Apart from the conflict between generations, the experience of migration tends to weaken the family bonds that created a supporting network on which the family could always rely. To a growing extent, the family finds itself alone. This is partly the result of moving from place to place. It is also due to the fact that the way of life in mainland cities is not a convenient environment for the perpetuation of family virtues and values. The Department of Social Services provides assistance in time of need, but not with the familiar, informal sense of personal and family respect. Regulations in housing, consumer loans, schools, and courts create a requirement for professional help, and the family is less and less effective.

Replacement of Personalist Values

Closely related to all the above difficulties, and creating difficulties of its own, is the slow and steady substitution of impersonal norms, norms of the system rather than norms of personal relationships. The need to adjust to the dominant patterns of American society requires a preparation to seek employment and advancement on the basis of merit or ability. To people for whom the world is an extensive pattern of personal relationships, this is a difficult adjustment.

This process of uprooting has been described before in the extensive literature about immigrants. It leads to three kinds of adjustments. The first involves escape from the immigrant or migrant group and an effort

---

[20]Protection of the girls generates its own problems in Puerto Rico, a form of "cloister rebellion" which may lead to escape from the home or elopement. It is well described in Stycos, *Family and Fertility, op. cit.,* Chap. 5.

to become as much like the established community as possible in as short
a time as possible. These people seek to disassociate themselves from their
past. They sometimes change their name, they change their reference
groups, and seek to be accepted by the larger society. They are in great
danger of becoming marginal. Having abandoned the way of life of their
own people, in which they had a sense of "who they were," there is no
assurance that they will be accepted by the larger community. They may
find themselves in a no man's land of culture. In this stage, the danger
of personal frustration is acute.

A second reaction is withdrawal into the old culture, a resistance to
the new way of life. These people seek to retain the older identities by
locking themselves into their old way of life.

The third reaction is the effort to build a cultural bridge between
the culture of the migrants and that of the mainland. These are the
people who have confidence and security in their own way of life, but
who realize that it cannot continue. Therefore, they seek to establish
themselves in the new society, but continue to identify themselves with
the people from whom they come. These are the ones through whom
the process of assimilation moves forward.

PRESENT SITUATION OF
PUERTO RICAN FAMILIES

In view of the above discussion, it is important to discover at what
level of assimilation the Puerto Rican family now stands, and how it is
affected by the problem of identity. In terms of intermarriage, the data
indicate that the increase in the rate of out-group marriage between first
and second generation is as great as it was for all immigrants to New
York, 1908–1912. Replication of the study for 1969 which is now in progress at Fordham University, New York, will involve many more first and
second generation marriages, and will give a much more reliable indication of the trend. In this regard, Puerto Ricans are simply repeating the
consistent pattern of immigrants who preceded them.

Second, in view of the character of the migration from Puerto Rico
(i.e., the return of many Puerto Ricans from the mainland and the continuing movement of large numbers of new migrants to the mainland),
there continue to be large numbers of Puerto Rican families in the early
and difficult stages of adjustment to New York, struggling for a satisfactory cultural adjustment as defined by Gordon and Eisenstadt.

The increase in the number of second generation Puerto Ricans
indicates that the classical problems of newcomers, the problems of the
second generation, are very likely at a serious level and will continue to

be so for a considerable length of time. In Chapters Nine to Twelve, some problem areas as they affect the Puerto Ricans will be reviewed—problems of education, mental illness, need for public assistance, and drug addiction. It is not clear just how family difficulties contribute to these larger problems, but it is certain that these problems contribute immeasurably to family difficulties. In the early 1960's, a group of Puerto Rican social workers founded the Puerto Rican Family Institute in an effort to assist Puerto Rican families in New York. The objective of the Institute was not simply to provide family casework, but rather to identify well established Puerto Rican families in New York and match them as *compadres* to newly arrived families which showed signs of suffering from the strains of adjustment to the city. This was an attempt to use the traditional forms of neighborhood and family help which were characteristic of Puerto Rico. Where families could be matched, the program has been very helpful. But recently the Institute has found that the percentage of families with serious and immediate problems has been increasing. This may reflect the fact that, as agencies around the city learn of a Puerto Rican Institute, they refer their Puerto Rican problem cases to it; it may also reflect the shock of uprooting upon the newly arriving families, or the disruption which occurs as the numbers in the second generation increase. The growth of militancy among the young will be another factor which will increase tension. However, in the demonstrations at City College of New York in the Spring of 1969, in which militant Puerto Rican students played a major part, observers commented that the parents of the Puerto Rican students were very much on hand supporting their sons and daughters, bringing them food, clothing, and supplies.   *145/22*

In the period during which the Puerto Ricans struggle for greater solidarity and identity as a community, the family remains the major psychosocial support for its members. In many cases it is a broken family; in others it is hampered by poverty, unemployment, illness; but it remains the source of strength for most Puerto Ricans in the process of transition. In the turbulent action of the musical *West Side Story*, when Bernardo, leader of the Puerto Rican gang, sees Tony, a youth of another ethnic group, approaching his sister Maria, Bernardo pulls Maria away from Tony to take her home; he then turns to Tony in anger and shouts: "You keep away from my sister. Don't you know we are a family people!"

During 1966 the first presentation in New York of *The Ox Cart* took place. This is a play by a Puerto Rican playwright, René Marqués, which presents a picture of a simple farm family in the mountains of Puerto Rico, struggling to survive but reflecting the deep virtues of family loyalty and strength. Under the influence of the oldest son, the family moves to a slum section of San Juan in order to improve itself. But deterioration sets in as the slum environment begins to attack the solidarity and loyalty of the family members. The family then moves to New York, where the strain of the uprooting becomes worse, the gap between mother and children more painful, and the virtues of the old mountain family seem even more distant. After the violent death of the son, the play ends with the valiant mother setting out to go back to the mountains of Puerto Rico, where she hopes to regain the traditional values of Puerto Rican family life which were destroyed in San Juan and New York.

This is an ancient theme, and it may be as true for Puerto Ricans as it was for earlier newcomers. But if the Puerto Ricans make it on the mainland, it will be through the same source of strength which supported the immigrants of earlier times—the solidarity of the family.

CHAPTER SEVEN

Nothing is so complicating to the Puerto Ricans in their effort to adjust to American life as the problem of color.[1] They represent the first group ever to come to the United States in large numbers with a tradition of widespread intermingling and intermarriage of people of different color. Both in the population on the Island and the mainland, racial character- istics of the Puerto Ricans range from completely Caucasoid to completely Negroid. Apart from small groups of the upper or middle class, any ordi- nary gathering of Puerto Ricans represents a striking example of the com- plete acceptance of social intermingling of people of different color and racial characteristics. Therefore, despite the problem of color which will be explained below, the sense of identity of Puerto Ricans on the Island never rested on the basis of a person's color. Yet they come to a mainland society in which a person's color plays a crucial role in identifying who a man is and where he belongs.

The Problem of Color

DESIGNATION OF COLOR IN PUERTO RICO

Designation of a Puerto Rican according to color is a very compli- cated matter. The United States Cen- sus of 1950 designated 80 per cent of the people in Puerto Rico as "white," and 20 per cent as "non-white." The 1960 census of the Island omitted the designation altogether. Actually, any designation of Puerto Ricans according to these categories is meaningless. Puerto Ricans use a number of terms when referring to color or racial

[1]The problem of the extent of discrimination on the basis of color has often been debated in Puerto Rico. For general background in the institution of slavery, the recent edition of Luis M. Diaz Soler, *Historia De La Exclavitud Negra en Puerto Rico* (Rio Piedras, Puerto Rico: Editorial Universitaria, Universidad de Puerto Rico, 1965), is very helpful. Frank Tannenbaum, *Slave and Citizen, The Negro in the Americas* (New York: Alfred A. Knopf, 1947), is an excellent treatment in English of slavery and social conditions of the Negroes. José Celso Barbosa, an outstanding Puerto Rican figure, was a Negro, founder of the Republican Party on the Island. In the compilation of his articles, *Problema de Razas* (San Juan: Imprenta Venezuela, 1937), he consistently contrasted the situation of the colored person in Puerto Rico with that of the United States. He insisted that racial discrimination did not exist on the Island. Tomas Blanco in *Prejuicio Racial en Puerto Rico* (San Juan: Biblioteca de Autores Puertorriqueños, 1942), also makes a strong case for the lack of racial discrimination in Puerto Rico in

characteristics: the term "Negro" is very rarely used. In fact, *negra* or *negrita* may be used as a form of endearment in reference to a person who is completely white. The term *de color* is the term most commonly used to designate a Negro. The really difficult problem arises in the identification of people who are in between white and colored. Marriage and baptismal records display a number of terms—*pardo, moreno, mulatto*—but the word most commonly used for the group in-between is *trigueño. Indio* is used for people with Indian features. *Grifo* is for people with kinky hair, frequently someone who is of light color but has the texture of hair characteristic of the Negro. *Pelo malo*, bad hair, is used in the same context. Characteristics of hair, much more than of color, seem to play a decisive role in identifying the racial background of the individual. To simplify matters, *trigueño* will be used in this chapter to designate people who are not obviously white or Negro, but in the range between. *Trigueño*, a Spanish word meaning the color of wheat, was originally applied to a person who had dark color but obviously *Caucasoid* features. It is the condition an American seeks when he strives for a deep tan.

---

contrast to its existence in the United States. In their book about Puerto Ricans in New York, C. W. Mills, Clarence Senior, and Rose K. Goldsen, *Puerto Rican Journey* (New York: Harper & Row, Publishers, 1950), p. 7, have presented as accurate and clear an analysis of the problem of race in Puerto Rico as the reader will find anywhere. It reveals why there is no discrimination in the American sense, although there is a racial problem.

An excellent discussion of the existence of racial discrimination in Puerto Rico is in Maxine Gordon, "Race Patterns and Prejudice in Puerto Rico," *Amer. Sociol. Rev.,* XIV (April 1949), 294, 301; and "Cultural Aspects of Puerto Rico's Race Problem," *Amer. Sociol. Rev.,* XIV (June 1950), 382–392. Jose Columban Rosario and Justina Carrion had presented a strong case for racial discrimination in *El Negro, Boletin de la Universidad de Puerto Rico,* Serie X, #2 (Rio Piedras: University of Puerto Rico, 1939). Charles Rogler has some helpful insights in "The Morality of Race Mixing in Puerto Rico," *Social Forces,* XXV (October 1946), 77–81; and in "Some Situational Aspects of Race Relations in Puerto Rico," *Social Forces,* XXVII (1948), 72–77. Renzo Sereno, "Cryptomelanism, a Study of Color Relations and Personal Insecurity in Puerto Rico," *Psychiatry,* X (August 1946), 261–269, finds a great deal of discrimination based on color in Puerto Rico, and, with the help of psychiatric concepts, attributes much of it to anxiety over legitimacy. Julian Steward (ed.), *People of Puerto Rico* (Champaign: University of Illinois Press, 1946), has a great deal of information about color. Note especially his index under "Racial Attitudes." See also Ivan Illich, "Puerto Ricans in New York," *Commonweal,* LXIV (June 22, 1956), 294–297; E. J. Dunne, "Puerto Ricans in New York," *Commonweal,* LXIV (August 3, 1956), 442; J. P. Fitzpatrick, "Puerto Ricans in New York," *Commonweal,* LXIV (September 14, 1956), 589–590, for an exchange of letters concerning the same problem. A brief treatment of the issue can also be found in J. P. Fitzpatrick, "Attitude of Puerto Ricans Toward Color," *American Catholic Sociological Review,* 20, 3 (1959), 219–233. E. Seda Bonilla, in "Social Structure and Race Relations," *Social Forces,* XL, 2 (December 1961), 141–148, reviews the question extensively, but finds a widespread consciousness of discrimination in Puerto Rico which becomes compounded in the experience of Puerto Ricans in New York.

Actually, Puerto Ricans will sometimes notice color differences in a white person by remarking: "The last time I saw you, you were much more *trigueño* than you are now." The *trigueño*, and especially the *trigueña*, the dark woman, were considered handsome and beautiful. As will become clear later, the identification of a person as *trigueño* or *trigueña* can become the focal point of anxieties over race and color among Puerto Ricans.

Relationships based on color or race are not the same in Puerto Rico as they are in the United States. No such thing as the segregation characteristic of either the American South or North ever existed on the Island, and there has been a common cultural pattern of social intermingling and intermarriage. This was particularly true of the people in the lower class, the poor class, in contrast to the upper class in Spanish times. The traditional upper class always prided itself on being white, and has always been very sensitive to the matter of color or racial characteristics. They became important factors in any attempt to claim identity with a pure Spanish lineage. Anyone who had characteristics of color obviously proceeded from a union of Spanish with Negro or Indian somewhere in the past. Some of the poorer people also apparently seek distinction by identifying themselves as pure white. It is surprising to observe the preoccupation with color in some of the poor mountain sections. "Look, do you notice how white everyone is here!" is mentioned with a spontaneity and candor that is quite striking. These same people, however, will deny that there is racial prejudice or discrimination in Puerto Rico. They insist that the distinction is one of class, not of color. People are excluded from social participation not because they are colored, but because they are lower class. When these white people deny that this practice constitutes racial discrimination, they distinguish their own practice from that of the United States by saying: "In the United States, a man's color determines what class he belongs to; in Puerto Rico, a man's class determines what his color is." There is a great deal of subtle truth to this remark.

They mean that a white person of the upper class will behave toward a white person of the lower class in the same way he would behave toward a colored person of the lower class. The class relationship rather than the color defines how the person will be treated. In other words, color is simply one indication of a person's social status: living in a certain barrio is a sign that he is lower class; if he is illiterate, he is lower class; and if he is colored, this is also a sign that he is lower class. Consequently, what the upper class person relates to in his behavior toward the colored person is not the person's color, but the class position, of which color is one of a number of signs.

FACTORS WHICH TEMPERED
DISCRIMINATION IN
PUERTO RICO

A number of cultural and historical factors contributed to a softening of discrimination on the basis of color in Puerto Rico.

Spain had had long experience with dark people, especially the Moors from North Africa who dominated Spain for a long period and had frequently married white women. Consequently, there has never been the strange abhorrence of color which has characterized the Anglo-Saxons.

In the wars of the Christians against Moors and Saracens, slavery became an experience of white men as well as colored. Laws were developed for the protection of slaves somewhat similar to today's international agreements governing the treatment of prisoners of war. This tradition carried over to the treatment of Negroes, who were brought to the Spanish colonies as slaves. Although it is difficult to think of anything making the experience of slaves more human, the tradition of legal protection did serve to soften the harsh treatment of slaves in the Spanish colonies.

It was the practice of upper class men in the colonies to recognize the illegitimate children born to them by colored women. It is quite impressive to look through old baptismal records and see the frequency with which colored children were given their freedom at baptism. The records read: "Juan, son of Carmen, slave of Don and Doña Felipe _____, baptized into freedom on this _____ day of June, 1835." It is reasonable to presume that many of these children may have been the children of Carmen's master or the master's sons.

Another important factor has been the practice of the *compadrazgo*, in which outstanding white members of the community would frequently be the godparents of colored children at Baptism. Although becoming a godparent was sometimes a mere social formality, the godparent relationship is generally taken very seriously among the Latin peoples. The *padrino* or the *compadre* was a significant person in the life of the child. Perhaps nobody knew who the father of a slave child was, but everybody in the community knew who his godparents were. They were not just children, legitimate or illegitimate, of a colored woman. They were bound by ties of a serious and sacred relationship into the web of a living community. This was a relationship which Negro children did not enjoy in Anglo-Saxon areas.

Finally, the Puerto Rican town, the Pueblo, was definitely planned as a community, where a sense of identity of all, rich and poor, white and colored, was given expression in the plaza where residents gathered for the community celebration of fiestas, religious processions, and public events. As a consequence of all these factors, colored persons were conscious of a place which they shared with many white people in the town. This distinguished the experience of the colored in Puerto Rico from what it was in the United States. Furthermore, if the people from the poorer classes found some way to advance through education or achievement, they were able to move among the whites with an ease and familiarity which would not have been possible in the United States. José Celso Barbosa, founder of the Republican Party in Puerto Rico, enjoyed a position in the Puerto Rican community which would have been quite unheard of at that time for a Negro in the United States. His picture still holds the most prominent place in the City Hall in Ponce.

However, with the dynamic cultural changes since the annexation of the Island to the United States in 1898, and with the rapid development of education, industry, and government services, a new middle class has been growing rapidly, recruiting many members from the lower classes, and pressing for recognition and acceptance by the upper class as well. Therefore, upward social mobility related to upward economic mobility has become a noticeable phenomenon on the Island, and complicates the role that color plays in designating the class to which a person belongs. Admission to certain societies and clubs, social acceptance by some groups of middle and upper class people, and particularly marriage, are seriously hindered for a person who is identified as colored (and to a somewhat lesser degree for someone who is not identified definitely as white).

Regardless of the class in which it takes place, the heart of the color problem in Puerto Rico rests in this: identification of a person as white, *trigueño*, or colored depends very largely on the attitude of the person making the judgment. One phenomenon that puzzles the observer in Puerto Rico is that one person will identify an individual as white or *trigueño*, while a second person will identify the same individual as colored. Three examples will clarify this.

1. An American friend of the writer had arranged a luncheon date in Puerto Rico for the two of us and a number of Puerto Rican friends of ours. All these Puerto Ricans would be accepted as white anywhere in the United States. The luncheon was arranged for a place which did not admit colored people. The morning of the luncheon, one of the Puerto Ricans called my American friend, and suggested that he choose another place for lunch because "X, one of the Puerto Ricans in the party, was 'colored.' "

2. We were questioning some young ladies about their going to dances and dancing with young men whom we, as Americans, would

identify as colored. The young ladies insisted that these young men were not colored; they were *trigueño*. We pressed the point, trying to get them to explain how they identified these young men as *trigueño* when there were other young men, just as light, whom they identified as colored. Finally one of the young ladies phrased it briefly and well when she explained: "Father, if two young men are somewhat dark, and have similar features, if one of them is socially acceptable to me and my family, we will call him *trigueño*; if he is not socially acceptable, we will call him *de color*."

3. I had met a young Puerto Rican man in New York who would be taken as white even in Mississippi. I met him later in Puerto Rico after he had been back on the Island for some time. He mentioned one point of great distress. He had started going with one or two young ladies, but after a while they had both dropped him. This had happened, he mentioned, after they had run their fingers through his hair. The young man was in a state of anxiety because he was afraid they had the opinion he was partly colored. In the United States, when a person is a Negro, his identification is clear, no matter how light he may be. But in Puerto Rico, the many intermediate people may never know exactly what they are because their identification as white, *trigueño*, or colored will depend much more on the observer's judgment than on the characteristics of race or color which they themselves possess. In his study of the top 200 families in Puerto Rico, Julian Steward found that some of the members of these families had a Negro background, and some had Negro features. But, since they were accepted as upper class people, they were not considered to be *de color*, or colored. Steward's interesting comment is that "an individual is 'whiter' in proportion to his wealth."[2]

THE PROBLEM OF COLOR
IN NEW YORK

When Puerto Ricans migrate to New York, they meet an attitude toward color and a type of discrimination that they have never experienced on the Island. The 1950 Census reported nearly 250,000 Puerto Ricans in New York City, 92 per cent of them white, 8 per cent nonwhite. In 1960, the Census reported 612,000 Puerto Ricans in New York City, 96 per cent of them white, 4 per cent nonwhite. The category "nonwhite" is as meaningless in New York City as it is in Puerto Rico, because it is subject to all the same ambiguities of color designations.

It is interesting to note that, in self-identification of color, a higher

---

[2]Steward, *People of Puerto Rico, op. cit.,* p. 425.

percentage of Puerto Ricans identify themselves as black, brown, or colored than appears in the census reports. Couples seeking a marriage license are asked to identify themselves according to color (not race). A study of every marriage record of 1949 and 1959 involving a Puerto Rican indicates the self-identifications presented in Table 7–1. If one

TABLE 7–1

SELF-IDENTIFICATION OF COLOR BY PUERTO RICANS
IN NEW YORK CITY ON MARRIAGE LICENSE REQUESTS,
1949 AND 1959[3]

| | 1949 | | 1959 | |
	Men	Women	Men	Women
White	91.45%	92.78%	88.19%	89.77%
Black	2.5	2.48	3.82	3.16
Brown	4.05	2.92	7.02	6.41
Colored	1.53	1.62	0.39	0.46
Other	0.47	0.20	0.57	0.19
	100.00	100.00	100.00	100.00
	(4,128)	(4,188)	(8,263)	(8,411)

SOURCE: J. P. Fitzpatrick, unpublished data.

adds the black and colored together, the percentage of Puerto Ricans identifying themselves as nonwhite in 1959 is about the same as the percentage in the census reports. The category missed by the census is the in-between category of brown.

Identification as colored in New York involves handicaps for Puerto Ricans far greater than a similar identification in Puerto Rico. First, the intermediate category tends to disappear. People are considered simply as white or colored. Second, Puerto Ricans feel the resentment of the existing residents to their coming, and the pressure to win acceptance for themselves becomes extremely strong. It is not long before they realize that acceptance by the American community is much easier if one is white. Finally, the pressure for social and economic advancement that works so dynamically in every group of newcomers to New York works also with the Puerto Ricans, with the result that they quickly become sensitive to the social and economic advantages of being white.

All of this complicates a concern about color which was already

[3]These are unpublished data from a study of intermarriage among Puerto Ricans in New York City, 1949 and 1959. The published data from this study can be found in J. P. Fitzpatrick, "Intermarriage of Puerto Ricans in New York City," *Amer. J. Sociol.*, 71, 4 (1966), 395–406. See particularly n. 8.

present, but in a much different context, in Puerto Rico. The survey made in 1947 of the Puerto Ricans in New York[4] gave evidence of the problem this created for the Puerto Ricans. The survey indicated that intermediate Puerto Ricans gave least evidence of being assimilated to the New York community. Not accepted as white, reluctant to be classed as Negroes, they were clinging to everything that gave them identity as Puerto Ricans, thus slowing their assimilation. More recent studies of the Puerto Ricans in New York single out Negro-white relations as one of the most difficult points of adjustment.[5] A medical study of migration and health among 80 Puerto Rican families concluded that anxiety over race and color was definitely related to health problems. The study quoted the report of a skilled social worker that in a group of 20 young Puerto Rican drug addicts with whom she had come into contact, the addict, with one exception, was the darkest member of his family.[6]

Will Herberg expects the Puerto Ricans to split into two completely separate groups, with those who can pass for white becoming assimilated to the white community, and those who cannot pass gradually becoming assimilated to the Negro community.[7] One of the most powerful and poignant pieces of literature to come from the Puerto Rican community is the life history of a Puerto Rican youth who was born and brought up in East Harlem. Piri Thomas, in his autobiography *Down These Mean Streets*,[8] tells what it is like to grow up as a Puerto Rican who is constantly troubled by his uncertainty over whether he is Black or Puerto Rican. No one knows how many youths there are like Piri Thomas, but it can be assumed that the number is not small. In an impressive little book which compares the upbringing of a middle class Irish boy with a poor Puerto Rican boy who lives two blocks away, the same problem of color is evident. The book ends on a particularly pathetic note: "Me, I'm Puerto Rican, colored, and I'm not going to turn my back on that, but if you ask me, if I could say: 'Which would you rather be?' Well, I mean, you've got to face it. I mean anybody would. If you ask me, which I'd rather be, well, man, I'd rather be white."[9]

[4]Mills, Senior, and Goldsen, *Puerto Rican Journey, op. cit.*, p. 152.

[5]Elena Padilla, *Up From Puerto Rico* (New York: Columbia University Press, 1958), pp. 61–81.

[6]Beatrice R. Berle, *Eighty Puerto Rican Families in New York City* (New York: Columbia University Press, 1959), p. 49. See pp. 45–49 for the full discussion.

[7]Will Herberg, *Catholic, Protestant, Jew* (Garden City, N.Y.: Doubleday & Company, Inc., 1955), p. 56, n. 11.

[8]Piri Thomas, *Down These Mean Streets* (New York: Alfred A. Knopf, Inc., 1967).

[9]Charlotte Leon Mayerson (ed.), *Two Blocks Apart* (New York: Holt, Rinehart and Winston, Inc., 1965), p. 114.

It is obvious, therefore, that attitudes toward color are the focus of serious difficulties among Puerto Ricans in New York. It is likely that the Puerto Ricans of intermediate color, the *trigueños,* will have the greatest difficulty. All the people who have worked with the Puerto Rican and Black communities in New York City have recognized two things. First, the Puerto Ricans make a clear distinction between an American Negro and a Puerto Rican who is *de color.* The colored Puerto Rican is identified primarily as Puerto Rican, not as a Negro. Furthermore, relations between Puerto Ricans and American Negroes are often characterized by tension.

One of the complicating factors in this difficult relationship is the fact that the Puerto Ricans arrived in New York in large numbers at the very moment that the Civil Rights movement was at its height. The Puerto Ricans never quite succeeded in coping with the problem this created for them. The Puerto Ricans are already a racially integrated community. For example, a school roster which is 70 per cent Puerto Rican will include Puerto Ricans of every color, so integration focused on color has no meaning for the Puerto Ricans as a community. In their participation in Civil Rights activities related to education, what they demanded was better schools. However, the leaders of the Civil Rights movement, predominantly American Negroes, were defining the problem in terms of color, and discrimination on the basis of color and de facto segregation were seen as the situations to be corrected. Therefore, when Puerto Ricans became involved in Civil Rights action, they were fighting an issue which they did not recognize as their issue.[10] Furthermore, in associating themselves with the Civil Rights movement, they were afraid of appearing to identify Puerto Ricans with American Negroes, so they tended to withdraw from vigorous participation in general Civil Rights movements. For example, when Rev. Milton Galamison inaugurated the boycott of the Public Schools in January 1964, many New York Puerto Rican leaders supported him. But shortly thereafter they withdrew from the movements led by Galamison, established their own National Committee for Puerto Rican Civil Rights, and began to demonstrate on their own.[11] The development of the Black Power movement was to create another type of problem for the Puerto Ricans which will be discussed later.

[10]One of the clearest statements of the issue from the Puerto Rican point of view can be found in an address by Joseph Monserrat, former Director of the Office of the Commonwealth of Puerto Rico and more recently member of the interim Board of Education of New York City. Copies of the address are available from the Office of the Commonwealth of Puerto Rico, 322 W. 45 St., New York City.

[11]*The New York Times,* February 4, 1964, p. 1; March 2, 1964, p. 1; March 13, 1964, p. 20.

CONTINUANCE OF
RACIAL INTEGRATION

As indicated above, the main question in relation to the attitude of Puerto Ricans toward color is this: As they become assimilated to American life, will they continue widespread intermingling of people of different color, or will they split into two groups, one identifying with the white people, another identifying with the Negro people of the mainland? Reliable evidence of either trend is not yet available. It will depend on more detailed studies of the second and third generation. What evidence there is indicates that, up till now, the intermingling of people of different color carries over to the mainland.

Every gathering of Puerto Ricans which this writer has attended in recent years, with the exception of some meetings of some well-to-do charitable ladies, has been marked by a mingling of people of various colors such as would never be found anywhere in New York outside the Puerto Rican community. Furthermore, the social intermingling of these people has been spontaneous and wholehearted, and the participants seemed to take it for granted as the normal and natural thing to do. The gatherings reflected the wholesome attitude toward color which is typical of gatherings in Puerto Rico.

Interviews with Americans and Puerto Ricans who work with the Puerto Rican community consistently evoke the same opinion, namely, that the social intermingling of people of different color is typical of social gatherings of Puerto Ricans held for the general community, and not a specialized group. In certain areas where the majority of Puerto Ricans are more of the middle class, they are predominantly white, and the more established, more highly educated people who are active around the Church are generally white. In poorer sections, members of Church societies are quite mixed, reflecting the racial characteristics of the neighborhood. In one parish where the Puerto Rican community is described as having practically no "colored people," the pastor reported to the writer that a dance of Puerto Rican parishioners provoked some rather strong protests from the mainland Americans in the parish. They objected to what they called the dancing together of whites and Negroes. Another American priest with long experience in Puerto Rico expressed his opinion in this fashion: "I used to think the white Puerto Ricans discriminated against the colored Puerto Ricans, but my experience here in this New York parish has been forcing me to change my mind. They are careful about the matter of marriage, but in ordinary social gatherings and parish functions, there is no sign of discrimination of any kind." One of the leaders of the Puerto Rican community, herself completely white, described her Christmas party for poor Puerto Rican children as follows: "What a wonderful lesson it was for the American people who were with me. There were two things they admired most: the free and friendly intermingling of dark and light Puerto Ricans; and the great respect the children showed to their elders." Therefore, regardless of the anxieties over color which certainly exists, the predominant impression that Puerto Ricans give to the New York community is unquestioned acceptance of the social intermingling of people of different color and racial characteristics.[12]

The study of Puerto Rican marriage records indicates the self-identification of the color of bride and groom. Table 7–2 gives the color combinations of these marriages. According to these data, 3.49 per cent

TABLE 7–2

MARRIAGES OF PERSONS OF DIFFERENT COLOR AMONG
PUERTO RICANS IN NEW YORK, 1949 AND 1959

Groom	Bride	1949	1959
White	White	90.25%	84.83%
Black	Black	3.06	2.21
Brown	Brown	2.37	4.14
White	Black	.73	1.32
Black	White	.93	1.85
White	Brown	.35	1.99
Brown	White	1.37	—
Brown	Black	.11	2.64
Other		.82	1.02
		100.01	100.00
		(4,074)	(7,949)

SOURCE: J. P. Fitzpatrick, unpublished data.

of the marriages in 1949 were between people who identified themselves as of different color; in 1959, the figure was 7.8 per cent. Neither of these figures indicates a high rate of intermarriage, but it is worthy of note that the rate is far higher than the general rate of interracial marriages in the United States. However, in order to avoid the difficulties involved in self-identification of color, the writer did a study in 1957 of a sample of Puerto Rican marriages over a six-month period in six different localities in New York City. The identification of color was made by the priest (in every case an American) who performed the ceremony. He was simply

12E. Seda Bonilla, "Social Structure," op. cit. indicates the importance of distinguishing between different groups of Puerto Ricans in observing social intermingling. Among the upwardly mobile Puerto Ricans whom he interviewed, some sought to disassociate themselves from their identity as Puerto Ricans; others proudly identified themselves and worked closely with the poorer Puerto Ricans of the city.

asked to identify the color of the bride and groom as he thought they would be generally identified in the United States. Out of a total of 115 marriages, 26 (22.6 per cent) were judged to be of people of noticeably different color—19 between a white person and a *trigueño*, 3 between white and colored, and 4 between *trigueño* and colored. This was even higher than the rate indicated on marriage records where identification of color was made by the individuals themselves. In her study of *Eighty Puerto Rican Families*, Beatrice Berle gives a detailed description of the structure of each family; in the cases of families with husband and wife (or man and woman in a relatively permanent union), she was able to give the color of husband and wife in 66 instances. Of these, 16, or 25 per cent, were unions between people of noticeably different color.[13] This evidence is sufficient to indicate that a reasonably widespread practice of marriage between people of different color is continuing in New York. Continuation of this practice could represent the establishment, in cities where Puerto Ricans are numerous, of a pattern of intermingling of people of different color which could hasten the integration of white and colored in the mainland populations.

The situation differs from one area to another, and the impact of the Puerto Rican pattern is likely to be uneven. In a recent farewell celebration for an American who was well known to the Puerto Ricans and at which the writer was present, the Puerto Rican neighbors presented a little act in which six small Puerto Rican children participated. Two of them were noticeably *trigueño*. A number of middle class Puerto Ricans were obviously upset. They felt that all the Puerto Rican children should have been white in a performance before an audience of Americans. The writer was also present recently at a benefit to raise funds for a Community Center for Puerto Ricans, at which the guests were almost all upper middle class and upper class Americans. During the affair, a group of 20 Puerto Rican children was introduced to entertain with some dances. The children, typical of any ordinary gathering of Puerto Ricans in the city, ranged in color from very dark and Negroid to very white. They danced together, a white boy with a colored girl and vice versa, and the American guests were delighted with the performance. But some middle class Puerto Ricans who were also guests were quite indignant. They insisted that the directors of the benefit should have chosen all white Puerto Rican children lest the Americans get the impression that Puerto Ricans are colored.

It is doubtful that this kind of reaction would ever be found among Puerto Ricans of any social class level on the Island. It indicates that as

---

[13]Berle, *Eighty Puerto Rican Families, op. cit.*, Appendix.

Puerto Ricans advance to middle class status in New York City, they become sensitive to American definitions of race, and are uneasy about the danger of being identified as colored on the mainland. It is difficult at present to determine how widespread this attitude is among Puerto Ricans who are moving into middle class status, or whether it is widespread enough to suggest that a Puerto Rican influence on American racial attitudes may be lost. But the next generation will not come directly from Puerto Rico into neighborhoods where they feel they must struggle for middle class acceptance. They will have gone through the schools together, and their integration will have been achieved through years of spontaneous intermingling with all various racial and ethnic groups as children and teenagers. It is likely that this will result in the unquestioning acceptance of the variety of colors as the normal, natural thing.

The intermingling of Puerto Ricans with American Negroes is an ambiguous feature of the problem of color. Relations between the two communities have not been particularly friendly. Some of this tension is due to the fact that Puerto Ricans and Negroes find themselves in a struggle against each other for power and control in political, social, and economic issues. The conflict in the elections for Community Corporations in the Anti-Poverty program in the Bronx provoked the intervention of the Mayor.[14] The problem of Black control in districts where large numbers of Puerto Ricans live has also been an issue in the struggle over school decentralization. In November 1967, when the first plan for school decentralization was presented to the Mayor of New York, considerable apprehension was expressed by Herman Badillo, at that time Borough President of the Bronx:

> I can't think of anything that would be more conducive to civil strife. The election of local neighborhood boards would create strife because in many areas candidates would be running on ethnic lines. It makes no sense at all. It assumes a civil stability which does not exist. It's an incredible proposal. It shows a lack of understanding of New York City today. There are many groups that don't get along. In many parts of the City, busing would be abolished and extremists would be running for office.[15]

Speakers at the Kings County Puerto Rican Leadership Conference were more explicit. They informed the Mayor that the Puerto Rican community did not want the local boards to have complete control of education "because certain extremist groups push out minority groups like Puerto Ricans *and other whites* [ital. mine]."[16] On the other hand, Puerto Ricans

14*The New York Times*, January 26, 1968, p. 19.
15*The New York Times*, November 9, 1967, p. 1.
16*The New York Times*, March 18, 1968, p. 22.

were definitely involved in cooperation with Blacks in the bitter conflict over the Ocean Hill-Brownsville experimental school district in 1968–1969, and militant organizations like United Bronx Parents, which is predominantly Puerto Rican, are also cooperative with Blacks.

One further development is important. The young militant students have been organizing and becoming articulate within the past year or two. Puerto Ricans have been closely associated with Black youth in much of the militant activity, such as the disturbances at Queens College and City College of the City University of New York in the Spring of 1969. It is not possible at this moment to tell in what direction the militant youth movement will go. If it continues to make common cause with the Black students, the integration of Black and Puerto Rican may begin to develop from this direction. If this occurs, it could very well reinforce the tendencies of the Puerto Rican community to continue the pattern of intermingling of people of different colors which they have brought to the mainland from the Island.

Religion has played a central role in the experience of immigrants who have come to the United States. Some, like many of the Jews, were fleeing religious persecution, and sought religious freedom of the United States; others, like the Irish, had struggled for nearly two centuries in defense of their faith against the oppression of the English, and they brought with them that same deep loyalty to their Catholic religion. However, in all cases, religious identity became the basis for a deep and strong sense of social identity. In seeking to make clear to themselves or to others who they were, they regularly pointed to their faith as Jews, Catholics, Lutherans, or Methodists as a sign of their identity. Furthermore, the congregation or parish became a focus of social organization and social activity which gave the immigrant support, a sense of belonging, the satisfaction of being among his own. It was the basis of the immigrant com-munity described above. The proc-ess whereby identity became secured through religious identification has

Religion

been explained at length by Will Herberg, Glazer and Moynihan, and Milton Gordon, as indicated in Chapter Three.[1]

It is doubtful whether religion will play the same role for the Puerto Ricans. Religious experience is as important to them as to others, but the framework of religious life makes more difficult the formation of a strong community based on religious identification.

RELIGIOUS BACKGROUND
OF THE ISLAND

Like all areas of the Spanish empire, Puerto Rico became a "Roman Catholic" colony.[2] The faith was brought to the Island with conquest. The conquistadores were motivated strongly by "God, Gold, Glory." Emphasis on the conquest as a pursuit of gold and glory is sometimes exaggerated to a point that obscures the fact that the conquistadores also

[1]The literature on the relation of religion to immigrant experience in the United States is abundant. Much of it is reviewed in Will Herberg, *Protestant, Catholic, Jew* (Garden City, N.Y.: Doubleday & Company, Inc., 1955). A reexamination of the Herberg thesis and a review of the role of religion in immigrant life can be found in Dorothy M. Dohen, *Nationalism and American Catholicism* (New York: Sheed & Ward, 1967).

[2]Cf. Robert Ricard, *The Spiritual Conquest of Mexico*, trans. L. B. Simpson (Berkeley: University of California Press, 1966), for the background of Spanish colonial Catholicism.

had God very much in mind. To a Spaniard, whether conquistador or not, the Catholic faith was the one true faith, the most important thing for which a man should live or die, and the most important gift he could give to another. The conquistadores had strange ideas about how the faith should be given to others, but they were determined to pass it on to the indigenous peoples they met in the New World. As a consequence, they created communities in which the Catholic faith was communicated, together with the Spanish language, colonial organization, and economy. In this way it was brought to Puerto Rico.

In order to develop this Spanish colonial culture and transfer it to the natives, the Spanish formed the *pueblo*,[3] the town, and thus created a community. It was a positive principle of colonial policy that a man could not be a man unless he was a member of a community. Every community was formed in the same way. A plaza was designed which was to be the center of community life, the place where all members of the community could meet, celebrate fiestas, and participate in religious ceremonies. The main building on the plaza was the Church; no community could exist unless God were a member of it. Thus all the members of the pueblo were conscious of being members of a community, and the community of necessity was Catholic. When a Latin American said he was *catolico*, or, more commonly, *muy catolico*, very Catholic, he did not necessarily mean he had been at Mass or the sacraments; he simply meant that he was a member of a people, a *pueblo*, which was Catholic. Periodically the *pueblo*, the community, worshipped God in great public demonstrations. In the United States, the *pueblo* in this sense (the community) never worships God. It guarantees to the individual the right to worship God according to his conscience. But practice of the faith in the United States is not a community manifestation; it is a matter of personal choice or commitment. The Latin, on the other hand is "Catholic" because he belongs to a Catholic people. This sense of identity, based on religion, which came to penetrate the life of Latin Americans very deeply, was related to a style of Catholicism with which they were familiar—the Catholicism of the *pueblo*, the community of which they were a part.

Two observations are helpful about this style of Catholicism. First, in Latin America, being religious is not perceived, as it is in the United States, in terms of adherence to the organized Church. A person in the United States is Catholic because he is affiliated with the Church, belongs

---

[3]The term *pueblo* is used to mean both the town or city as a place, and the people or population in it.

to its associations, and identifies himself with its structures. In Latin America, religious practice is marked by the quality of *personalismo*, the pattern of close, intimate personal relationships which is characteristic of Spanish cultures everywhere. Thus the individual perceives his religious life as a network of personal relationships with the saints, the Blessed Virgin, or various manifestations of the Lord. He looks on these as his *compadres*, his close friends. He prays to them, lights candles to them, carries them in procession, builds shrines to them in his home, makes promises to them, and expects them to deliver the favors, help, or protection he needs. Just as in his human relationships he needs the *padrino*, the *patrón*, or the *compadre*, so the *santo* is the counterpart in the realm of religion. But this personal relationship with the saints takes place quite outside the organized structure of the Church. Indeed, if the organized Church should be shut down, the relationship would go on as usual. Latins could be very anticlerical toward the hierarchy of the Church without in any way thinking they were departing from the Catholicism which penetrates their lives. It has often been told that, during the Spanish Civil War, men would risk their lives to rescue their *santos* from the Catholic Churches which they had just set on fire.

Second, the effort to absorb all the natives into a Spanish colonial culture and a Catholic community was never entirely successful. Remnants of pre-Discovery religious rites have continued among many of the indigenous peoples, and African rites were brought by Negro slaves and intermingled with some of the folk practices of the Catholics. The result is a syncretism of cults and practices which is still very much alive in many parts of Latin America, e.g., the *costumbre* of Central America, the *macumba* or *candomblé* of Brazil. Although there is little evidence of this in Puerto Rico, there is widespread practice of spiritism which will be described later in this chapter. These practices are often called superstitions by the North Americans, and elements of superstition are no doubt intermingled with them. But actually they are a mixture, sometimes of pre-Columbian indigenous rites, a variety of Catholic devotions, and an elemental response to the sense of the presence of the sacred in everyday life.

Both of these features of Latin Catholicism—its traditional community character and its personalistic character in devotion to the saints —are very difficult for North Americans to grasp. Ordinarily, when North Americans face the task of working with Latin American Catholics, they want to bring them around to a North American style as soon as possible. In Puerto Rico, more than in any other Latin American area, the meeting of these two different types of Catholicism took place.

PUERTO RICO

Puerto Rico was not only a major administrative and military center for Spain in the Colonies, it was the first administrative center of the Catholic Church in the Western world.[4] The first diocese in the Western Hemisphere was established in San Juan in 1511, and the first Bishop was Bishop Alonso Manso. San Juan has remained a diocese, but with the development of the Church in other areas of the Western world, its jurisdiction has become limited to Puerto Rico and the Virgin Islands. There are now four dioceses for Puerto Rico itself, San Juan, Ponce, Arecibo, and Caguas, and a vicariate for the Virgin Islands.

The Church in Puerto Rico was compelled to operate under the conditions required for the colonies by the Spanish king, that is, under the system called the *patronato*. The Church was given grants of land or the right to land revenues, this source of income intended to support the ecclesiastical, educational, and charitable activities which the Church generally undertook. In return, the Spanish king had a major voice in naming the bishops to the dioceses of the colonies. This left the Church in a difficult position in regard to rebellions against oppression or for independence. When most of the nations of Latin America had succeeded in gaining independence from Spain, Puerto Rico remained a Spanish colony with a close relationship to the Spanish crown and Church. In the history of Puerto Rico until 1898, although the number of native Puerto Rican priests had been impressive, only one Puerto Rican had ever been named as a bishop in San Juan. This was Bishop Juan Alejo Arizmendi, 1803–1814.[5]

In 1898, when Puerto Rico became a possession of the United States, American priests and religious personnel began to go to the Island. This effort increased steadily, and has involved an unusually generous expenditure of personnel and funds for development of the Church on the Island.

This extraordinary effort has had significant results in the life of the Church in Puerto Rico. Religious instruction and practice have im-

[4]There is nothing in English of any value about the early period of the Catholic Church in Puerto Rico. Antonio S. Pedreira, *Bibliografía Puertorriqueña, 1493–1930* (Madrid: Imprenta de la Librería y Casa Editorial Hernando (S.A.), 1932), lists all the titles in Spanish and English. A suitable reference in Spanish would be the standard work on the early Colony, Salvador Brau, *La Colonización de Puerto Rico* (San Juan, Puerto Rico: Cantero, Fernández & Co., 1930).

[5]The problem of native bishops has been the source of longstanding controversy in Puerto Rico. For the documents around this issue, cf. Alejandro del Corro, S. J. (compilador), *Puerto Rico: Obisbos Nativos; Documentos y Reacciones de Prensa, 1962–65* (Cuernavaca, Mexico: Centro de Documentacion Intercultural, Dossier 15, 1967).

proved considerably; an increasing respect for the Church has become evident; men as well as women have been responsive to religious practice, and the number of young men entering the priesthood had been increasing until the last few years. However, the Puerto Rican Church has acquired a noticeably American character in the conduct of Catholic life, in emphasis on the sacraments, and particularly in the development of the parochial school and the Catholic High School on the American model. Many of the parishes have become well organized and adequately equipped with financial aid from the United States; the Catholic schools have also been supported principally from the mainland and staffed with mainland personnel. In terms of generosity of service, this has represented an important contribution to the life of the Church in Puerto Rico. But it has left the majority of Puerto Ricans untouched. Lack of effective contact with the Church and lack of formal instruction have remained a rather general condition of the people; the religion that characterizes the lives of many is still the folk religion described above.[6]

At the same time, the experience with those Puerto Ricans whose lives have been touched most directly by the religious and spiritual effort of American Catholics has not been without its problems. Most of the Catholic schools found it necessary to charge tuition, which restricted the student body largely to the more affluent classes. The schools were also very demanding in their selection of students, and limiting the student body to those who had the best preparation usually meant the children of more affluent families, who had been sent to better schools during the earlier grades. Scholarships have always been available for poor students, but the number of poor students on scholarship has never been sufficient to counterbalance the impression that the schools were for the more privileged people of the Island. In addition, the emphasis on English and the mainland American character of the schools resulted in American rather than the Spanish or Latin traditions of the Island being stressed. A large part of the religious enterprise represented a formation of Puerto Rican Catholicism on a mainland model. Many religious personnel never learned Spanish, or spoke it quite poorly. The schools and the American religious personnel have not distinguished themselves by achieving a creative relationship between the Spanish cultural tradition and the de-

[6]For a review of the religious situation on the Island, see William Ferree, John Illich, and Joseph Fitzpatrick, *Report on the First Conference on the Spiritual Care of Puerto Rican Migrants* (New York: Office of Coordinator of Spanish Catholic Action, 451 Madison Avenue, N.Y.C., 1956). See also Dorothy M. Dohen, *Two Studies of Puerto Rico: Religious Data and Background of Consensual Union* (Sondeos #3, Cuernavaca, Mexico: Center of Intercultural Documentation, 1966).

veloping American influence. They largely neglected the first and reinforced the American influence at a time when it was upsetting the traditions of the Island.[7]

From 1898 until 1961, the Bishops of Puerto Rico were mainland
Americans. In 1960, when there were two dioceses (San Juan and Ponce)
on the Island, both with mainland American Bishops, a third diocese
was created in Arecibo and a Puerto Rican who had been born and raised
in the United States was appointed its Bishop. In 1961, the first native
Puerto Rican to be made a Bishop in 150 years, Luis Aponte Martinez,
was consecrated in Ponce. He was later named Archbishop of San Juan.
Since that time, three other natives have been consecrated bishops, the
American Bishops have returned to the United States, and the hierarchy
of the Island is in the hands of four native Puerto Rican bishops and one
Puerto Rican from the United States. Development of a native hierarchy,
however, has not succeeded in forming a Church which would be strongly
Puerto Rican, or which could mediate effectively between Spanish Cath-
olic traditions and modern religious developments. The structure of the
Church is still very much based on the style brought to it by the American
clergy; some Puerto Ricans complain that the native Puerto Rican
Bishops are more American than were the native Americans.

Apart from the problem of developing according to an American
model, the Church further handicapped itself in the presence of rapid
social and political developments. At a time when the social and economic
aspects of the Island were beginning to move ahead remarkably, some
Church leaders took vigorous public objection to a number of the points
involved. They charged that the government was promoting birth control as part of the program of economic development, and that the government's impressive development of education was guided by a secularist
philosophy. This created the image of the Church as opposed to the
extraordinary efforts of the government toward social and economic development on an Island where poverty was widespread and there was a
crying need for social justice. Furthermore, at a time when rapid social
and economic development was beginning to create problems of anxiety
and uncertainty, the Church was incapable of mediating the change by
reaffirming traditional spiritual and religious values in the presence of
an intelligent understanding of the social and economic developments.
This led in 1960 to the unfortunate development of a Catholic political

[7]The Catholic schools became involved in a serious controversy over language
some years ago. This was part of a general concern about the neglect of the Spanish
language in the education of Puerto Ricans. For the documentation, cf. Tarsicio
Ocampo (compilador), *Puerto Rico: Idioma Escolar; Reacciones de la Prensa, 1962–65*
(Cuernavaca, Mexico: Centro de Documentacion Intercultural, Dossier 1, 1966).

party, the *Partido Acción Cristiana*,[8] which brought the Church and its full influence into the center of the political arena in opposition to the Partido Popular, the party which had created the impressive economic and social gains after 1948. The disastrous defeat of the Catholic party (it gained less than 8 per cent of the votes) left the Church discredited not only as a political participant but as a moral influence in public life. The Church thus contributed to anxiety and uncertainty by appeals to traditional morality in opposition to the Partido Popular, and left itself unable to provide any creative reassurance to the Puerto Rican people in their effort to relate their cultural traditions to rapid social and economic changes.

PROTESTANTISM

Protestants came to the Island when the United States took possession in 1898[9] It is roughly estimated that 20 per cent of the residents of the Island in 1970 may be Protestant. Most of these are probably members of Pentecostal sects, which have been the most vigorous group in their evangelizing. When the Protestant groups first came to the Island, they agreed among themselves to avoid competition in their evangelizing efforts. They divided the Island into territories, each one assigned to the responsibility of a particular Protestant denomination. As a result, almost every municipio in Puerto Rico has a Protestant Church, either Baptist, Methodist, Episcopal, and so on. The Pentecostal groups disregarded this agreement, and have carried on a vigorous campaign of evangelization wherever they chose. Consequently, small Pentecostal Churches appear everywhere, and many of them have very active congregations.

The attraction of Pentecostal Churches for the Puerto Ricans has been explored by Sidney Mintz in his life history of a poor cane worker in a small barrio of Santa Isabel.[10] Mintz attributes it to the sense of being "uprooted" from a traditional way of life as the economic system

[8]For the documentation on this development, cf. Tarcisio Ocampo (compilador), *Puerto Rico: Partido Acción Cristiana, 1960–62* (Cuernavaca, Mexico: Centro de Documentacion Intercultural, Dossier 11, 1967).

[9]For a brief history of Protestantism in English, see Donald T. Moore, *Puerto Rico para Cristo* (Cuernavaca, Mexico: Centro de Documentacion Intercultural, Sondeos, #43, 1969). This includes the history of the Pentecostal sects as well as the Protestant denominations. See also Jerry Fenton, *Understanding the Religious Background of The Puerto Rican* (Sondeos #52, Cuernavaca, Mexico: Center of Intercultural Documentation, 1969).

[10]Sidney Mintz, *Worker in the Cane* (New Haven: Yale University Press, 1960). See also the article by Joseph P. Fitzpatrick, "The Puerto Rican Story," *America* 103 (September 3, 1960), 593–597.

changes from one of "family" workers on a plantation to wage workers in an impersonal system that stresses advancement through economic activity, deferred gratification, and accumulation of consumer goods. Adaptation to a style of life related to industrial and commercial development, according to Mintz, leaves a social and psychological vacuum which many of the poor Puerto Ricans seek to fill through involvement in the Pentecostal congregations. They provide an ideology, a sense of community and purpose, which compensates for the loss of a traditional style of life.

SPIRITUALISM

One other aspect of religious life in Puerto Rico that must be mentioned is the widespread interest in spiritualism.[11] Spiritualism is a form of religious practice which is rooted in the belief that man can establish contact with the spirit world, and can use his power to influence the spirits, either restraining the unfavorable action of evil spirits or effecting the favorable action of good spirits. The practice of spiritualism proceeds on many levels, from the seances of sophisticated and learned people, to sessions in which sincere people evidently provide genuine help to the needy, to a level of manipulation of good and evil spirits which can be tormenting to its victims. The medium, the person who claims the power to contact the spirit world, is the center of most spiritualist activities; however, there are a large number of folk practices which devotees follow on their own.

The distinction between the spiritualist medium and the *curandero/a* is not always clear. The *curandero* is a man, or more frequently a woman (*curandera*), who has a wide knowledge of folk practices of medicine. He recommends herbs, potions, and practices of heating or cooling which are folk remedies for all kinds of human illnesses. Sometimes these techniques border on types of superstitious practices which differ little from some of the methods of spiritualists. Almost every Puerto Rican barrio has a *botanica*, a store that sells herbs, potions, prayers, ritual instructions, and devices such as little dolls to be pierced by pins at the spot where a person wishes to do harm to an enemy or to protect or cure a friend. The personal attention of the *curandero* is often an important factor in people's lives. He or she is the substitute for the doctor, and

[11]There is no good book or article about spiritualism among Puerto Ricans. One of the best descriptions of a spiritualist seance can be found in Dan Wakefield, *Island in the City* (Boston: Houghton Mifflin Company, 1957), Chap. 3. See also Joseph Bram, "Spirits, Mediums and Believers in Contemporary Puerto Rico," *Transactions of the New Academy of Medicine* (1957), pp. 340–347.

can take advantage of the confidence of people in that which is familiar, simple, uncomplicated, and traditional.

Probably the most valuable service of the spiritualist is the help he gives in times of mental illness. Rogler and Hollingshead[12] have described this role clearly. If a poor Puerto Rican who is mentally disturbed seeks the help of a psychiatrist or is committed to a mental hospital, the people define him as *loco* (crazy), and are inclined to reject him. If he seeks the help of a spiritualist, he is defined as suffering from evil spirits and the people are sympathetic to him. In this way the spiritualist, by helping the individual to manage the spirits which are troubling him, is often successful in keeping the disturbed person functional within his own community.

TRANSITION TO THE MAINLAND

Out of the above varied religious background, the Puerto Ricans come to the mainland and face the transition to a religious environment with which they are not familiar. As with earlier immigrant groups, it is important to examine the role of religion in the process of adjustment. According to Herberg, the parish or congregation became an important basis of identification for the first generation. Religious life and practice represented the transfer to the new land of an important segment of life in the old country. Furthermore, many values of a former way of life were supported by the religious life. In New York, for example, in 1902, among the Roman Catholics alone, there were 13 German churches, 2 French, 1 Bohemian, 4 Polish, 1 Maronite, 2 Slovak, 1 Hungarian, 1 Spanish, and 11 Italian, apart from the English speaking churches which were predominantly Irish.[13] These national parishes served three major functions: (1) they maintained effective contact between the immigrants and the Church so that religious faith and practice continued strong; (2) they provided the basis for a strong community life; they were a beachhead in the new country in which the customs, practices, and close relationships of the old country provided security and satisfaction during the period of transition; and (3) they gave the newcomers a sense of identity. The physical buildings of the parish, and their identity as parishion-

---

[12]Lloyd H. Rogler and August B. Hollingshead, "The Puerto Rican Spiritualist as a Psychiatrist," *Amer. J. of Sociol.*, LXVII, 1 (July 1961), 17–22.

[13]Cf. Joseph P. Fitzpatrick, "The Role of the Parish in the Spiritual Care of Puerto Ricans in the New York Archdiocese," *Studi Emigrazione*, III, 7 (October 1966), 1–27, for a more detailed examination of the problem of creating national or language parishes for the Puerto Ricans.

ers, gave them a sense of belonging, and were the symbols by which they were known to the larger community.

Furthermore, according to all contemporary theorists, a new kind of relationship develops around religious identification in the third generation. The interests of ethnic groups which crystallize around nationality in the first generation, tend to form around religious identification when the sense of nationality has diminished in the third generation. Thus a pluralism of nationalities leads to a pluralism of religious interest groups in America.

These functions have been much more difficult for the Puerto Ricans to fulfill. Since there were so few Puerto Rican priests on the Island, none were available to accompany the immigrants to the mainland. Puerto Ricans were geographically much more scattered in the mainland cities, and they moved into cities which were generally completely built up, and into areas where active Catholic parishes already existed. As a result, few Puerto Rican parishes were established. Those that were formed were often staffed by priests who were Spanish speaking but not Puerto Rican.

In most cases, Puerto Ricans have been received into what is known as the integrated parish. The existing parish into which they moved was staffed by one or more Spanish speaking priests who sought to help the Puerto Ricans to become part of the established Irish or Italian or Polish parish population. This generally meant that special Masses and services were provided for the Puerto Ricans in their own language, often in a basement chapel, a school hall, or a small chapel elsewhere in the parish.

The integrated parish was a practical answer to the pressing problem of large numbers of Puerto Ricans suddenly appearing in the area of an existing parish. However, it tends to perpetuate among the Puerto Ricans the feeling that they are newcomers who are inheriting something established rather than creating something of their own. They have not had the confidence of knowing that this parish, church, or school is "theirs" in the sense in which Italians, for example, knew the Italian parish was "theirs." As a result, the parish has not been able to serve as the basis of a strong, stable Puerto Rican community the way it had served for earlier immigrant groups.

The decision to follow a policy of integrated rather than national or language parishes was not easy for officials of the New York Archdiocese to make. In the late 1920's, the Archdiocese began to repeat the earlier tradition of language or national parishes. The first church founded for the Puerto Ricans was La Milagrosa, established in 1926 in a converted synagogue on 114th Street and Seventh Avenue. A second, Holy Agony, was established in 1930 on Third Avenue and 103rd Street. The decision to deviate from earlier practices and follow a policy of integrated parishes was made by Cardinal Spellman in 1939 shortly after he arrived in New York. He turned Saint Cecilia's in East Harlem over to American priests of the Congregation of the Most Holy Redeemer who had been working in Puerto Rico since 1900. The parish remained a geographical parish staffed by American priests who could continue to serve members who remained from the earlier Irish and German populations, but who spoke Spanish, were experienced in work with Puerto Ricans, and could make the adaptations in parish life needed for the newcomers.

A number of factors prompted Cardinal Spellman's decision. As indicated above, Puerto Ricans had no priests to bring with them. The Island had only a small number of native priests, and it was considered important that they should remain there. Furthermore, the history of the national or language parishes was beginning to reveal important disadvantages. When the third generation of Germans, Italians, or Polish had grown up, few of them still spoke the language of their forebears, and most had become assimilated to American ways and were moving away from the area of the language parish. As a result, clusters of old national churches, sometimes two and three in a few square blocks, continued to exist with a handful of members. It was clear that although the national parish was important in the first generation, it became a troublesome burden in the third generation. The integrated parish might involve problems of adjustment for the first generation, but it would be free of the problems of the third generation national parish that had lost its usefulness. Finally, as Puerto Ricans moved into poor areas from which older residents had departed, the existing geographical parish had valuable resources in the form of church buildings and parochial schools which could be used for the newcomers.

As the policy of the integrated parish was increasingly followed, it became clear that mainland American priests staffing these parishes would require training in the Spanish language and preparation in an understanding of the cultural background of the Puerto Rican people. A special office, The Coordinator of Spanish Catholic Action, was created in the New York Archdiocese in 1953. It has been the function of this office to study the needs of Puerto Ricans coming into the New York Archdiocese, and to coordinate the efforts of the parishes in providing special services. It has promoted special programs for the Puerto Ricans, most important of which has been an annual religious and civic festival called the Fiesta de San Juan. This festival is held on the Sunday in June closest to the feast of Saint John the Baptist, the Patron of Puerto Rico. It consists of a religious procession, devotions, and recreational and civic programs. It generally attracts large numbers of Puerto Ricans and has come to be a widely observed festival in the city. There are other citywide Puerto Rican civic celebrations, but the Fiesta de San Juan is the only widely observed religious fiesta of Puerto Ricans in New York. The Office of Coordinator also has sponsored other religious programs, such as the *Cursillo Movement*, a surprisingly effective spiritual exercise aimed at the renovation of one's life, and parish activities designed to help older residents to know and understand the Puerto Rican newcomers.

The major institution established to prepare priests, religious personnel, and lay people to work with Puerto Ricans on the mainland has been the Institute of Intercultural Communication, founded at the Catholic University, Ponce, Puerto Rico, in 1957 by Monsignor Ivan Illich, and sponsored by Francis Cardinal Spellman. The Institute is a three month summer course at which priests, religious personnel, and lay people from the mainland would study Spanish and receive instruction in Puerto Rican culture and the problems of migration and adjustment to mainland life. The course also gave the participants an opportunity to become familiar with life in Puerto Rico on all social and economic levels. Thus students at the Institute could return to the mainland better prepared to work with Puerto Rican newcomers. In the 14 years of its existence, the Institute has dealt with more than 2,000 people. It has been the largest single influence in training people from the mainland, and has also exerted a strong indirect influence on the policy of mainland Dioceses in their effort to provide spiritual care for Puerto Ricans. The guiding spirit of the Institute has been the conviction that a mainland pattern of religious practice must not be imposed on Puerto Ricans; rather, they must be given every opportunity to be "at home" in the practice of their faith in cities. They must have special services in their own language and according to their own style, and every effort must be made to enable them to preserve whatever richness exists in their own religious practices. Gradual adaptation to an American style of religious practice would come spontaneously as they became more adjusted to mainland life.

Various types of Puerto Rican religious or religio-civil organizations have appeared in other cities, such as the Caballeros de San Juan in Chicago, and the Centro Catolico Puertorriqueño in Jersey City, which have given considerable strength and support to these communities.

It is difficult to evaluate the numerous facets of the Catholic effort among Puerto Ricans on the mainland. The major effort has taken place in the parishes. The New York Archdiocese in 1970 had more than 200 American priests who speak Spanish. There are 75 other priests from Spain or other Spanish speaking areas. These priests are working in 136 parishes, where they provide for the Spanish speaking the whole range of religious services which are characteristic of a New York City parish.

It is through the parish that ordinary contact is established and main-tained with Puerto Ricans. Many of the Catholic hospitals are in poor sections of the city and have large numbers of Puerto Rican patients. Many of the staff workers and more than half the clients of Catholic Charities of the New York Archdiocese are Puerto Rican. In 1970 more than 20,000 children in the parochial schools of Manhattan and the Bronx were Puerto Ricans, representing 20 per cent of all children in the Catholic schools of these two boroughs. A very active program in religious instruction for children in the Public schools is also held. Yet, with all these efforts, the priests of the Archdiocese judge that they are in effective contact with only about 20 per cent of the Puerto Ricans in New York.

As indicated earlier, 27 per cent of all marriage ceremonies in 1949 involving a Puerto Rican were marriages with a Catholic ceremony; in 1959 this had increased to 41 per cent. Many more second generation than first generation Puerto Ricans marry in Catholic ceremonies: in 1949, 25 per cent of the ceremonies of first generation and 40 per cent of the second generation were Catholic. In 1959, 40 per cent of the first gen-eration and 48 per cent of the second generation were Catholic ceremonies. This does not mean that the Puerto Ricans do not consider themselves Catholics. They have their children baptized, and many of them follow the folk practices with which they were familiar in Puerto Rico. But in the absence of a Catholicism of the *pueblo*, only a small percentage of Puerto Ricans in New York follow those religious practices which identify one as a practicing Catholic on the mainland. The enormous effort made by the Archdiocese of New York is still far from adequate to meet the spiritual needs of the newcomers.

PROTESTANTISM ON
THE MAINLAND

It is as difficult to evaluate Protestant activity among Puerto Ricans in New York as it is to evaluate Catholic activity. The top ranking polit-ical leader of the Puerto Ricans in New York, Herman Badillo, comes from a well-known Protestant Puerto Rican family; Carlos Rios, a former City Councilman from East Harlem is a Protestant minister; Ruben Dario Colon, a community leader among the Puerto Ricans, is also a Protestant minister; Ralph Rosas, for many years Director of the New York Office of the Commonwealth of Puerto Rico is a Protestant. The presence of influential Protestants in the Puerto Rican community is impressive.

It is more difficult to get accurate information about the overall

Protestant population. A survey report published by the Protestant Council of the City of New York in 1954 estimated that 26,000 Puerto Ricans were then affiliated with Protestant work in New York City; the number in contact with Protestant work, whether formally affiliated or not, was probably 50,000. At that time, the Puerto Rican population of New York City was estimated at 425,000. If the 1954 estimates of the Protestant Council were accurate, it would indicate that about 12 per cent of the Puerto Ricans were in contact with Protestant work, and about 5 per cent were affiliated. A much more detailed report, published in 1960,[14] estimated a Spanish speaking membership of 31,126 in Protestant Churches, including the Pentecostal and Evangelical sects. This would have been about 6 per cent of the Puerto Rican community.

The best known Protestant work among Puerto Ricans has been the East Harlem Protestant Parish, a project in which clergymen and divinity students have lived in the midst of the area, and in which a wide range of social action programs have been promoted with the cooperation of the community, a drug addiction rehabilitation center operated, and a religious influence exerted in the predominantly Puerto Rican barrio. Similar types of religiously related social action programs are conducted in many other Protestant centers in the city.

If the Protestant estimate of 6 per cent of the Puerto Rican community being Protestant is at all reliable, and if the Catholic estimate that the Catholic Church is in effective contact with about 20 per cent of the Puerto Ricans is likewise at all reliable, the great majority of Puerto Ricans are, for all practical purposes, out of contact with any definite religious affiliation, and have no solid basis in religious activity for the building of a strong community.

This seems to be confirmed by an excellent study of the attraction of Pentecostal and Evangelical sects for Puerto Ricans. Renato Poblete and Thomas F. O'Dea,[15] found that Puerto Ricans were attracted to Pentecostal Churches in their search for the experience and satisfaction of community. These were largely self-starting and self-maintaining congregations, formed and directed by a minister who was a working man like the members themselves. They were small, informal, and intimate, with the religious style reflecting the style of life of poor, uprooted Puerto

[14]*A Report on the Protestant Spanish Community in New York City*, Protestant Council of the City of New York, Department of Church Planning and Research, 1960. See also E. C. Parker, "Spanish Speaking Churches," *Christian Century*, 78 (August 12, 1961), 466–468 and F. L. Whitman, "New York's Spanish Protestants," *Christian Century*, 79 (February 7, 1962), 162–164.

[15]Renato Poblete and Thomas F. O'Dea, "Anomie and the Quest for Community: The Formation of Sects among Puerto Ricans in New York," *Amer. Cath. Sociol. Rev.*, 21 (Spring 1960), 18–36.

Ricans. Members participated actively, expressing themselves emotionally in song, responses to prayer, invocations, and clapping of hands. They were concerned for each other, greeted each other warmly, and sought to help each other. Guilt was openly expressed and pardon prayed for; sympathy and support were provided by the brothers and sisters of the small congregation. Poblete and O'Dea concluded that the phenomenon of the Pentecostal or Evangelical storefront church represented a search for community, for the satisfaction of knowing that one belonged to, was respected by, and had a function to fulfill in the group. It is doubtful that their influence will be widespread enough to give character to the entire Puerto Rican community. Pentecostal congregations tend to be small and intimate, of about 60 to 100 members. As indicated in the study of Puerto Rican marriages, they appear to be a first generation phenomenon. Marriages of Puerto Ricans in Pentecostal ceremonies drop sharply from first generation to second. In view of the total New York population of Puerto Ricans, the Pentecostal basis for community appears to be limited and of short duration.

Folk religious practices continue; spiritualism is widespread. But neither of these can provide that basis for community which the immigrant parish or congregations supplied to the newcomers of last century or the early part of this century. In view of this, it is doubtful that religious identification will play the role in assimilation or cultural pluralism which it played at earlier periods.

No institution has played a more central role in the assimilation of immigrants to American life than the schools, particularly the public schools. They have been the main link between newcomers and established society; they have transmitted the predominant culture of the United States to children from a wide variety of cultural backgrounds; they have been a major factor in forming the newcomers in the ideas, motivations, and styles of American life.

In the process, however, the school has also contributed to the problem of insecurity as immigrant children passed from an old world culture into the new. It has always been the focus of the "second generation problem," the experience of the young who were born and raised in the home of parents of an old world culture, but who are being schooled into the new culture of the new land. Caroline Ware's book about second generation Italians in New York City,[1] and William F. Whyte's study of Italian boys in Boston[2] are part of the abundant literature which documents the problem. The same problem of the "second generation" can therefore be expected among the Puerto Ricans in New York, and its focus will be the experience in the school.

Puerto Ricans and the Schools of New York City

The role of the school, however, has been shifting in the past generation, and its relation to Puerto Rican children has become more complicated and ambiguous for both the schools and the Puerto Ricans. Recognition in recent years of the massive failure of the schools to educate the Puerto Ricans and other minority groups effectively, the growing insistence that the process of schooling be adapted to the cultural background of the Puerto Rican children, experiments in bilingual education, and the organization of community strength to cope with the problem have all affected the relationship of the Puerto

[1]Caroline Ware, *Greenwich Village, 1920–1930* (Boston: Houghton Mifflin Company, 1935).

[2]William F. Whyte, *Street Corner Society* (Chicago: University of Chicago Press, 1943).

This chapter was prepared with the assistance of Mary Lou Mayo and John Murphy, research assistants at Fordham University to whom I am greatly indebted. It is based on a paper originally prepared for the Center for Urban Education in New York City.

Ricans to the schools. From one point of view this suggests that the schools may not be the transmission belt into the new culture as they were for earlier immigrants; from another angle, community response to the problem may result in increasing community solidarity and strength.

For many years educators, public officials, and, especially, Puerto Rican citizens have recognized the low level of achievement of Puerto Rican children in the New York City schools. But the Puerto Rican community has now become restless and demanding about the problem. Militant Puerto Rican students have begun to engage in vigorous demonstrations and protests in the schools and colleges; the community has proposed new programs and directions with a sophisticated sense of political and educational organization. This may result in widespread consciousness of a common interest, which could be a major factor in developing a sense of identity among the Puerto Ricans. If this should occur, the schools may have contributed indirectly to the identity of the Puerto Ricans by creating the occasion for marshaling of community resources.

STATISTICAL EVIDENCE
OF THE PROBLEM

Serious and systematic attention was first given to the problem in *The Puerto Rican Study, 1953–57*,[3] an intensive study of the experience of Puerto Rican children in the public schools of New York City. The study documented the difficulties of Puerto Ricans particularly from two points of view—language handicaps and the relationship of the schools to Puerto Rican parents. It concluded with 23 recommendations to remedy the difficulties. In May 1968, Aspira conducted a nationwide conference on Puerto Rican education.[4] Eleven years after the Puerto Rican study, conference participants presented a discouraging picture of Puerto Rican education which indicated that, instead of being corrected, the problem was getting worse.

In 1964, in a proposal for a "Puerto Rican Community Development Project," the Puerto Rican Forum presented the most complete statistical description up to that time of the Puerto Rican community in New York City.[5] It demonstrated on the basis of 1960 census data that the Puerto

[3] *The Puerto Rican Study, 1953–57* (New York City: Board of Education, 1958).

[4] Aspira, *Hemos Trabajado Bien*, A Report on the First National Conference of Puerto Ricans, Mexican-Americans and Educators on "The Special Educational Needs of Puerto Rican Youth" (New York: Aspira, 1968).

[5] *The Puerto Rican Community Development Project*: A Proposal for a Self-help Project to Develop the Community by Strengthening the Family; Opening Opportunities for Youth and Making Full Use of Education (New York: Puerto Rican Forum, Inc., 1964).

Ricans are a very young population and that they had the lowest level of formal education in New York City. Both of these factors, youthfulness and low educational level, are symptomatic of the Puerto Rican educational crisis: more and more of their children are entering the school system, while those over 25 are experiencing the disadvantages of low educational levels in a society increasingly stratified on the basis of education.

The data of the 1960 census are out of date, and no comprehensive data are available about the present situation. As indicated in Chapter Two, the Puerto Rican migration continues at a high rate. The rate of return migration is increasing, creating a reverse school problem for Puerto Rican children from New York entering Island schools; the Puerto Rican population is increasing; and available evidence seems to indicate that the educational characteristics of the population remain largely the same. One important qualification is necessary here. There are evidences of considerable educational and occupational improvement among second generation Puerto Ricans. This will be discussed later. In the absence of up-to-date census data, the present chapter will focus on the current educational involvement of Puerto Ricans in the school system, current proportions, distributions, and educational achievement to the extent that data are available.

INVOLVEMENT IN
THE SCHOOL SYSTEM

Large numbers of Puerto Ricans are entering the New York Public Schools. Their numbers increased from 137,000 (14.2 per cent of the total registered) in all public schools in 1958 to 249,000 (22.2 per cent) in 1969. They are heavily overrepresented in the vocational schools, 31 per cent in 1969, and in special schools, 28 per cent in 1969; they are underrepresented in the academic high schools, only 14.2 per cent in 1969.[6] Since the academic high school has been the traditional route to college, the small representation of Puerto Ricans in these schools is not favorable. However, in the Autumn of 1969, the Board of Education announced that it was eliminating distinct diplomas; all graduates would receive the same diploma.[7] This, together with the beginning of the open admissions program in 1970, may modify the significance of the type of school a Puerto Rican attended. Up to the present, however, this has been a serious hand-

[6]Special Census of the School Population, Bureau of Educational Program Research and Statistics, Board of Education, New York City.
[7]*The New York Times*, October 10, 1969, p. 1.

icap. In 1963, of 21,000 academic diplomas granted, only 331, or 1.6 per cent, went to Puerto Ricans, while 7.4 per cent of the vocational diplomas went to Puerto Ricans.[8]

The reality of these handicaps on the high school level is reflected in the ethnic surveys of undergraduates in the City University of New York conducted in September of 1967 and 1968.[9] The latest figures for 1968 indicate that Puerto Rican matriculated (i.e., degree candidate) students constituted only 2.2 per cent of the senior college enrollment and 6.4 per cent of the community college enrollment. Puerto Rican nonmatriculated (generally part-time) students constituted only 2.7 per cent of the senior colleges and 5.3 per cent of the community colleges. On the basis of total student population, Puerto Ricans constituted 2.3 per cent of the enrollment in the senior colleges in Autumn 1968, but 5.9 per cent in the community colleges—over double the figure for the senior colleges. On the basis of matriculation status, they constituted 3.3 per cent of the matriculated students of the total university enrollment, but 3.9 per cent of the nonmatriculated students. The heavier concentration of Puerto Ricans in the community colleges and the large proportion enrolled on a nonmatriculated basis are indicative of the lower entrance standards of the community colleges and the lack of an academic high school diploma and low high school averages of many Puerto Ricans. There was practically no improvement in this situation between 1967 and 1968.

Recognition of the difficulties in college participation has evoked a positive response from the City University. In 1969 the Board of Higher Education approved a modified "open admissions" plan to make entrance into college available to larger numbers of Blacks and Puerto Ricans. Preliminary reports of the open admissions program indicate a sizable increase in number of Puerto Rican admissions. In 1970, 12.6 per cent of all admissions to the City University for freshman year were Puerto Ricans. This is considerably higher than the percentage in 1969, when 6.4 per cent of the entering freshmen were Puerto Rican.

Under-representation of Puerto Ricans in high schools and colleges in New York is generally taken as evidence of failure of the school system. This evidence is substantial, but one qualification must be kept in mind. No reliable demographic data are available which would permit an accurate analysis of the population profile among Puerto Ricans and the rest of the youthful population of the city; i.e., how many Puerto Rican

[8]Frank M. Cordasco, "The Puerto Rican Child in the American School," *Congressional Record*, Reprint 3, 195 (October 19, 1965).

[9]The following data were provided by the City University of New York, Office of the Vice Chancellor for the Executive Office.

youth of high school or college age are there in the total population in comparison to the number in the population as a whole, and how many Puerto Rican youth should be expected in the system? Until this figure is available, it is not possible to determine accurately to what extent the Puerto Ricans are underrepresented in the academic high schools and colleges.

ACHIEVEMENT TESTS

A second indication of serious failure on the part of the schools in the education of Puerto Ricans is the performance of Puerto Ricans on the Metropolitan and Iowa Achievement tests. Unfortunately the results of these tests are not reported according to ethnic group, but an indication of Puerto Rican performance is gained by examining the school districts which have the largest proportions of Puerto Ricans. The reading scores are given in Table 9–1. It is important to note that these tests are not given to children who have not reached a reasonable level of English speaking ability. For example, more than 16 per cent of the students in the schools (elementary through high school) were excluded from the tests in 1967.

TABLE 9–1

READING GRADE REPORT: NATIONWIDE NORMS, NEW YORK CITY MEAN, DISTRICT MEAN: APRIL 1968 METROPOLITAN ACHIEVEMENT READING TEST—FORM C

Grade	2	3	4	5	6	7	8	9
Normal average reading score (nationwide norms)	2.7	3.7	4.7	5.7	6.7	7.7	8.7	9.7
New York City mean reading grade report	2.7	3.7	4.7	5.7	6.8	7.1	8.1	8.9
District mean reading grade report:								
Districts								
15 (41.4% Puerto Rican)	2.3	3.1	4.1	5.0	5.7	6.0	6.8	7.4
2 (43.2%)	3.0	3.8	4.6	5.6	6.5	6.5	7.1	8.8
4 (43.9%)	2.5	3.2	4.1	5.0	5.8	6.1	6.7	7.6
1 (47.2%)	2.3	3.0	4.0	4.9	6.2	6.4	7.2	8.4
12 (52.5%)	2.2	3.0	3.9	4.8	5.7	5.6	6.4	7.2
14 (59.0%)	2.2	3.0	3.9	4.5	5.2	5.8	6.8	7.2
7 (61.2%)	2.3	2.8	3.8	4.4	5.1	5.5	6.4	6.9

SOURCE: Board of Education of The City of New York, Bureau of Educational Research.

At a quick glance, it is noted that in grade 2 the districts with large Puerto Rican enrollments are an average of 3 months behind the New York City mean; in grade 4 they fall an average of 6.4 months behind, 10.6 months behind in grade 6, and 13 months behind in grade 8. If the national norm were used, the discrepancy would become even greater in the seventh, eighth, and ninth grades. The disadvantage in the early grades becomes much worse as the Puerto Ricans pass through the school system.

It is not possible to say with certainty that the low mean district scores are the result of poor Puerto Rican performance. This would require examination of individual test reports. Nevertheless, the poorest of the seven scores are in the three districts with the largest percentage of Puerto Ricans.

The third grade scores on the Metropolitan Achievement Test, survey of arithmetic (Table 9–2), indicate that all but one district, District 2, fall below both the City mean for grade 3 (3.6) and the national norm (3.7). Furthermore, three of the seven districts already lag behind the nationwide norm by six months. The most serious problem, however,

TABLE 9–2

MEAN GRADE EQUIVALENT SCORES: NATIONWIDE NORMS,
NEW YORK CITY MEAN, DISTRICT MEAN:
APRIL 1968 METROPOLITAN PARTIAL BATTERY—
FORM C INTERMEDIATE AND ADVANCED LEVELS
SURVEY OF ARITHMETIC[a]

Grade	3	8
Normal average reading score (nationwide norms)	3.7	8.7
New York City mean grade equivalent scores	3.6	7.6
District mean grade equivalent scores:		
Districts		
15 (41.4% Puerto Rican)	3.3	6.5
2 (43.2%)	3.7	6.7
4 (43.9%)	3.3	6.1
1 (47.8%)	3.3	6.9
12 (52.5%)	3.1	6.1
14 (50.0%)	3.1	6.3
7 (61.2%)	3.1	6.0

SOURCE: Board of Education of The City of New York, Bureau of Educational Research.

[a]Problems and concepts score.

appears again in the eighth grade scores: The discrepancy between mean scores for the heavily Puerto Rican districts and those for the City and Nation widens. Evidently in arithmetic skills, as with reading, the Puerto Rican disadvantage increases rather than diminishes with years of school. Thus, in the eighth grade, all heavily Puerto Rican districts are below the city mean by an average of 12.3 months, and all but one are at least two years behind the national norm.

EDUCATION AND OCCUPATION

No reliable up-to-date information is available about the relationship between education and occupation, although there is a common awareness that poor educational experience and poor employment experience go together. The 1960 census data indicated clearly that the Puerto Ricans were lowest in the city in both education and occupation. The *Profile of the Bronx Economy*,[10] completed in 1967, indicated that there were high rates of unemployment among Puerto Ricans in the same areas where there were low rates of education. Most of these were Puerto Ricans born on the Island who migrated to New York after they were past school age. Of Puerto Ricans coming to the mainland between 1957 and 1961, 46 per cent were between 15–24 years of age; 53 per cent had had no previous work experience.

The significance of education for employment in New York City is clearly revealed in the report, *Labor Force Experience of the Puerto Rican Worker*.[11] The report presents the results of a Labor Department survey of April 1966 which indicated that an abundance of white collar jobs was available in the poverty areas of New York City, but the residents of these areas did not have the skills to fill them; jobs were not available on the lower skill levels which the residents possessed. The persons who suffered most from this skill gap were the Puerto Ricans, who are concentrated on the blue collar levels of occupation and have a much lower percentage (19 per cent of employed Puerto Ricans in 1960) of white collar workers than the nonwhites (30 per cent of employed nonwhites in 1960). The heavy concentration of Puerto Ricans on the blue collar levels is also evident in the data of a special survey of 1966 presented in Table 9–3.

[10]*A Profile of the Bronx Economy* (Bronx, N.Y.: Institute for Urban Studies, Fordham University, 1967), p. 35.

[11]*Labor Force Experience of the Puerto Rican Worker*, U.S. Department of Labor, Bureau of Labor Statistics, Regional Report, No. 9 (June 1968), Middle Atlantic Region, 341 Ninth Avenue, New York, N.Y., 10001, p. 13.

TABLE 9–3

OCCUPATIONAL DISTRIBUTION OF EMPLOYED RESIDENTS
BY ETHNIC GROUP, NEW YORK CITY, 1950 AND 1960,
AND THREE POVERTY AREAS[a], NOVEMBER 1966

| Occupational Group | Total | : Puerto Rican | Three Poverty Areas[a], November 1966 | | | | | |
| | | | White[b] | | Nonwhite[b] | | Puerto Rican | |
			1960 :	1950	1960 :	1950	1960 :	1950
Total employed								
Number (000's)	190	34	2,643	2,871	461	320	203	85
Per cent	100	100	100	100	100	100	100	100
White collar	28	21	58	54	30	20	19	16
Blue collar	44	57	32	36	40	42	65	64
Service	29	22	10	10	30	38	16	20

SOURCE: *Labor Force Experience of the Puerto Rican Worker*, U.S. Department of Labor, Bureau of Labor Statistics, Regional Report, No. 9 (June 1968), Middle Atlantic Region, Table 21, p. 28.

[a]Harlem, East Harlem, and Bedford-Stuyvesant.

[b]Other than Puerto Rican.

It is evident that educational advancement to the level of white collar skills is essential for Puerto Rican employment in the New York area to improve. In May 1968, The Center for the Study of the Unemployed at New York University held a conference on "Employment Problems of Puerto Ricans."[12] This was the most complete assessment in recent years of the employment situation of the Puerto Ricans. The conference touched every aspect of employment, but the particular need of educational preparation for available employment in New York City was emphasized at every moment.

The one favorable feature in the Puerto Rican employment picture is the impressive educational and occupational advancement of second generation Puerto Ricans over first generation Puerto Ricans. In 1960, for example, second generation Puerto Ricans had reached a much higher level of education than those of the first generation.[13] They were also far advanced in occupation: only 1.8 per cent of employed first generation Puerto Rican men were on the professional and technical level, but 7.4 per cent of the second generation were on this level. In the same year, 11.4 per cent of first generation Puerto Rican men were in clerical and sales positions, whereas 23.8 per cent of second generation men were on this level. On the other hand, 45.2 per cent of the first generation Puerto

[12]*Summary of Proceedings: Workshop on "Employment Problems of Puerto Ricans"* (New York: Center for Study of the Unemployed, Graduate School of Social Work, New York University, 1967).

[13]*Labor Force Experience of the Puerto Rican Worker, op. cit.*, Table 14, p. 20.

Rican men were operatives and kindred workers, while only 29 per cent of the second generation had this kind of job. The picture for second generation Puerto Rican women was even more favorable.[14] The only difficulty with these data is that relatively few Puerto Ricans were second generation in 1960. The census data of 1970 will be much more significant. Nevertheless, the second generation data present a favorable picture of steady advancement, and offer genuine hope for the future.

COMPENSATORY EDUCATION AND CULTURAL PLURALISM

The foregoing picture of failure with regard to academic performance and achievement of the Puerto Ricans has impressed upon the Puerto Rican community and upon educators the necessity of discovering causes and remedies. Much of their attention has found its expression in various programs of compensatory education.

"Compensatory education" is a term which has come increasingly into use since 1960 to refer to "those pedagogical efforts directed at overcoming or circumventing assumed deficiencies in the background, functioning, and current experiences of children from economically deprived, culturally isolated, and/or ethnically segregated families."[15] It has become an umbrella beneath which a variety of experimental programs have been sponsored by both government and private agencies and foundations.

The significance of the compensatory education programs as regards Puerto Ricans and their problem of identity rests in the emphasis on culture which has come to the fore in discussions of the Puerto Rican edu-

---

[14]U.S. Bureau of the Census, *U.S. Census of Population, 1960. Subject Reports. Puerto Ricans in the United States*. Final Report. PC(2)-1D (Washington, D.C.: U.S. Government Printing Office, 1963), Table 11. Reprinted above on p. 61.

[15]Edmund W. Gordon and Adelaide Jablonsky, "Compensatory Education in the Equalization of Education Opportunity: I and II," *The Journal of Negro Education*, XXXVII, 3 (Summer 1968), 268. The programs examined in Gordon and Jablonsky include a wide variety of elements: (1) enrichment and modification of curriculum; (2) enrichment of extracurricular activities; (3) modifications and selectivity in training, recruitment, and utilization of personnel; (4) remedial reading and language development; (5) expanded guidance services; (6) increased parental and peer involvement; (7) extended reciprocal involvement of school and community; and (8) extensions and additions to the school day and year. More specifically, the projects examined by Gordon and Jablonsky included Project Head Start; Title I and Title III Projects; Upward Bound; School Dropout Programs; Project 100,000, Department of Defense; Benneker Project of St. Louis, Missouri; More Effective Schools Program of New York City; Higher Horizons; Project Case II: MODEL (Motivationally Oriented Designs for an Ecology of Learning). They concluded their study with a rather critical comment: "it is obvious that compensatory education as presently practiced is either insufficient or irrelevant to the needs of disadvantaged young people."

cational problem. It has become increasingly clear that a major reason for the failure of the schools rests in cultural differences: the school system presupposes a cultural style and preparation which are different from those which characterize the Puerto Ricans. It is implied that the schools need to adjust the system of learning to the cultural characteristics of Puerto Rican children. If this should occur, the relationship of the schools to the cultural identity of the Puerto Ricans would shift considerably, and the process of adjustment of Puerto Ricans to New York could be quite different from that of former ethnic groups.

The first major attempt to address this problem was the *Puerto Rican Study, 1953–57*. Although the study began with the problem of language, it soon broadened its scope to include the equally important areas of community-orientation and acculturation. It recommended the strengthening or development of programs which would take account of the particular cultural style of the Puerto Rican parents and children. This concern for language and culture was largely as a means toward an end, namely, an improvement of communication which would enable the Puerto Rican children to achieve better in the established system.

A different perspective of the significance of culture and cultural differences in the schools began to appear in such books as Frank Reiss-man's.[16] Reissman noted the middle class bias of the term "culturally deprived," and urged recognition of the positive values in the culture of various ethnic and racial groups on lower socioeconomic levels. What Reissman urged for compensatory programs was use of the existing cultural contributions of the various ethnic and racial groups involved, and relating of these to other, wider cultural pursuits. He insisted that innovative programs should be designed not only in relation to the problems, handicaps, and poor conditions of the deprived person's life, but also in relation to its strengths and positive aspects. Use should be made of the different but impressive styles of art, language, and expression of the poor; their imaginativeness and initiative in finding ways to cope with their difficult situation; and the values which they express in quite different ways from those of the more affluent teachers and citizens.

This emphasis on the culture of the disadvantaged child was given more detailed attention by Martin Deutsch and his associates.[17] Deutsch

[16]Frank Riessman, *The Culturally Deprived Child* (New York: Harper & Row, Publishers, 1962).

[17]Martin Deutsch *et al.*, *The Disadvantaged Child: Studies of the Social Environment and the Learning Process* (New York: Basic Books, Inc., Publishers, 1967). Another important work, Mario D. Fantini and Gerald Weinstein, *The Disadvantaged: Challenge to Education* (New York: Harper & Row, Publishers, 1968), took a position quite different from that of Deutsch *et al.* Fantini and Weinstein believe there is no difference between the disadvantage of the poor and the affluent, and are inclined to find the real fault with the school for failing to educate either type of disadvantaged child.

recognizes that the achievement of the school system requires a set of attitudes and skills, a cognitive style, and a particular kind of motivation which depend on one type of socialization rather than another. The fact that children lack these necessary qualities to achieve in one particular system implies an unfavorable judgment about neither the school nor the family or culture from which the child comes. It simply means that if children are expected to achieve in the existing system in the United States, and are not culturally prepared for it, the cultural preparation must be provided by compensatory programs.

This insight into the role of culture and education is applied particularly to Puerto Ricans by Stella Chess and associates.[18] This is a study of child rearing practices and their effect on the performance of children in a task oriented society. The study sample used two groups of three year olds from stable families, one group of 136 children of native born, educated, middle class parents, and the other of 95 children of unskilled and semiskilled Puerto Rican working class families. The children were tested to determine if there were differential responses to demands for cognitive performance, and, if so, their relationship to the child rearing practices that characterized each group. The findings support the hypothesis that differential functioning in disadvantaged children is not necessarily a derivative of rejection by parents, or an indication of deficiency in the children. It may be a consequence of the total socializing practice in which the child was formed. Such acquired differential behavior patterns may nevertheless be a liability in a task oriented society.

A more important clarification of the role of culture in education is presented in a monograph by Lesser, Fifer, and Clark.[19] These authors distinguish *ethnic* (including racial and religious) group membership from social class membership on the basis of patterns and levels of educational ability. Using four groups as sample populations for the purpose of comparison—American Chinese, Jews, Negroes, and Puerto Ricans—they concluded that ethnic groups differ in *both* level and pattern of mental abilities, while social class (using the criteria of occupation, education, and neighborhood) affects level of ability but does not alter the basic patterns of mental ability associated with ethnicity.

In describing these findings in a later article,[20] Lesser pointed out their implications for defining and delimiting the concept "disadvan-

---

[18]Stella Chess et al., "Social Class and Child-rearing Practices," paper prepared for the American Psychological Association Divisional Meeting, November 17, 1967.

[19]G. S. Lesser, G. Fifer, and D. H. Clark, "Mental Abilities of Children from Different Social Class and Cultural Groups," *Monographs of the Society for Research in Child Development*, XXX, 4 (1965).

[20]Susan S. Stodolsky and Gerald Lesser, "Learning Patterns in the Disadvantaged," *Harvard Education Review*, XXXVII (Fall 1967), 546–593.

taged." According to him: "Defining the 'disadvantaged' as belonging to a particular ethnic group has one set of consequences for the development of intellectual skills. . . . Defining the term using the social-class criteria of occupation, education, and neighborhood leads to quite different consequences. . . ."[21] The strategies of compensatory education differ in each case. If "disadvantaged" is defined in terms of differences in social class position, it is possible to follow the strategy of giving the "have nots" what the "haves" possess. If, on the other hand, "disadvantaged" is defined to mean differences in ethnic group membership, it is no longer possible to follow that strategy; ethnicity cannot be changed through money, social decree, or compensatory programs. The strategy in this case must not be that of giving equal opportunity to all in order to *equalize* development, as was advocated in the Coleman report,[22] but that of giving equal opportunity to all ethnic groups in order to *maximize* their development, even if this means continuation of ethnic differences among the groups. This distinction between equalization (vis-à-vis social class) and maximization (vis-à-vis ethnicity) raises some important questions about compensatory programs and their relationship to the question of cultural pluralism.[23]

The issue of cultural pluralism around schooling, therefore, remains fundamental. Policy decisions concerning this issue will directly affect educational strategies, and educational experience will directly influence policy. Are there common cultural features which all people living in the United States must share if they are not going to be seriously deprived within this environment? If not, what educational policies must be adopted in order to enable people to retain their specific cultural background if they wish? If yes, what educational policies must be adopted to form school children in that culture, despite the different mental abilities and behavioral skills in which their families have already formed them? Compensatory education, to be effective, must be defined in relation to these major issues of policy and strategy, and the way the decisions are made will have a major influence on the identity of the Puerto Ricans.

This problem is faced immediately in a school system when it comes to the question of language. No one has ever questioned that mastery of English is essential to a child growing up in the mainland United States. But the relationship of language to learning in United States schools has been a source of difficulty, controversy, and experiment, and touches directly on the problem of the education of Puerto Ricans. Many

21*Ibid.*, 573.

22*The New York Times*, September 13, 1966, p. 72.

23Milton Gordon, *Assimilation in American Life* (New York: Oxford University Press, 1964).

programs in compensatory education for Puerto Ricans are now being built around this problem. In view of this, some detailed consideration of bilingualism will be helpful.

BILINGUALISM

The first section of this chapter has presented data indicating the below standard achievement levels of the Puerto Rican school districts. The selective character of these data was also noted, since a large number of children are excluded from the tests because they know little or no English. These facts make it clear that the language problem of Puerto Ricans in New York City schools is very serious. The problem is compounded by current social and economic conditions. As Glazer and Moynihan point out, when the Jewish and Italian immigrants were arriving in the city in large numbers, language was not so serious a problem because they could leave school at an earlier age, often as early as 12. "The children who could not learn English forty years ago got out before their problems became too noticeable."[24] The legal requirement for school attendance until 16 aggravates the problem of a child with poor English ability. Furthermore, the employment picture in New York City, as indicated earlier, shows an abundance of jobs on the white collar level and a scarcity of jobs on the blue collar level; English is essential for white collar employment. The complicated nature of government agencies and private industries and associations makes knowledge of English essential for anyone who wishes to deal effectively with these bureaucracies. Finally, the distressing experience of school dropouts makes a remedy imperative.

Other features of the contemporary situation also affect the problem. Puerto Ricans are native born citizens of the United States whose native language is Spanish. This has already been recognized in the change of New York State laws for voter registration. Since 1965 a literacy test in English is no longer required. In the continual movement back and forth between Puerto Rico and the mainland, loss of Spanish by a Puerto Rican leaves him handicapped in the land of his Fathers and his family. Furthermore, an increasing awareness of the value of bilingualism in any tongue and in any situations has led to a greater concern for helping a child to retain the language of his parents.

The entire question is now affected by the heated community and political environment in which Black Power, Puerto Rican Power, Stu-

---

[24]Nathan Glazer and Daniel P. Moynihan, *Beyond the Melting Pot* (Cambridge, Mass.: Harvard-M.I.T. Press, 1963), p. 127.

dent Power, and other social and political movements are demanding recognition and effective participation, and seeking symbols of identity. The Blacks find identity in color and heritage; the Puerto Ricans are likely to seek it in cultural background and language. If language becomes a symbol of identity in political struggles, the problem of bilingualism in the schools can be seriously complicated.

All of these influences and forces converge at the school, where both staff and students are faced with a dilemma about language. The question is no longer how to teach English and impose it as rapidly as possible, but rather how to teach English as a second language, or how best to bring a child to a mastery of both languages? Never before has the city been caught in the tension between a determination to teach English, and a desire to preserve Spanish.

The issue of bilingualism must be examined in a setting of two important background factors: the experience of bilingualism in Puerto Rico, and the relationship of New York Puerto Ricans to the Island. Some optimists believe that Puerto Rico is itself becoming bilingual, and therefore migrants in the near future will more easily slip into the American social structure because of their command over English. Ismael Rodriquez Bou and Ralph Long are more realistic in their appraisal of the status of bilingualism on the Island. Rodriquez Bou,[25] in a review of its historical development, describes the chaos which has characterized the educational system on the Island since American possession in 1898. The curriculum has been heavily loaded with linguistic studies—more a political than an educational policy. For years the teaching of English was associated with patriotic loyalty to the United States, as American educational principles were imposed on a culture poorly adapted to them. Finally, in 1949 English was formally put in its place as a second language. The current educational scene in Puerto Rico, however, is not without its problems. Ralph Long[26] describes them as a proliferation of demoralizing experimental programs, overcentralization, and lack of clear orientation. The general conclusion is, therefore, that "English has gained considerable ground in Puerto Rico and not at the expense of Spanish, but most Puerto Ricans are not really bilingual."[27]

The second important background factor is the relationship of New

[25]Ismael Rodriquez Bou, "Significant Factors in the Development of Education in Puerto Rico," in *Status of Puerto Rico: Selected Background Studies* (Washington, D.C.: United States-Puerto Rican Commission on the Status of Puerto Rico, 1966), 147–314.

[26]Ralph Long, "The Puerto Rican Experience in English as a Second Language," in Virginia French Allen, ed. *On Teaching English to Speakers of Other Languages* (Champaign, Ill.: National Council of Teachers of English, 1965), p. 26.

[27]*Ibid.*, p. 28.

York Puerto Ricans to the Island. The speed and low cost of air travel has resulted in constant movement between the Island and the mainland for vacations, family visits, and in response to job opportunities in one place or the other. Periodic employment on the Island and the mainland, and periodic schooling or long spans of residence in both places affect the problem of language learning. It is important that Puerto Ricans retain their knowledge of Spanish for purely practical reasons, but the movement back and forth makes it difficult for them to master English if they live periodically on the Island, or to retain their Spanish if they live periodically on the mainland.

Three final observations must be made. First, the Puerto Ricans are a heterogeneous community. Elena Padilla[28] distinguishes among at least three groups: older migrants, recent migrants, and those born and reared in New York. She found that each has a different reference group and, accordingly, a different espousal or denial of Spanish as a language to be maintained. The New York born and reared Puerto Rican, for example, identifies with American society and may feel insulted if a professional converses with him in Spanish. Newly arrived migrants, on the other hand, may actually exaggerate their use of Spanish and their Hispanic customs to compensate for a feeling of being lost on the mainland.

Second, the question of language is affected by the attitudes of militant students and by the agitation, both in Puerto Rico and the mainland, around the issue of Puerto Rican independence. People involved in either of these movements place a heavy emphasis on the retention and use of Spanish as a traditional mark of identity. It is not yet clear whether this influence will become widespread and effective, but it is very much on the youth scene at the present time.

Finally, language acquisition may upset the defined roles within the Puerto Rican family, i.e., male-female and parent-child. Situations in which poorly educated parents must depend on their children's greater knowledge of English may involve a painful role reversal. While bilingualism may lead to assimilation, or at least more facile upward mobility within the dominant society, the acquisition of a second language may be one more factor in the process of cultural assimilation which contributes to tension between the first and second generations, and may be a disorganizing factor in the home.

These background factors indicate the complicated way in which language is related to the process of migration and the problem of identity in Puerto Rico or in New York. They also describe the context in which the language issue has been played out within the New York City

28Elena Padilla, *Up from Puerto Rico* (New York: Columbia University Press, 1958).

school system. A brief review of the experience with the language problem will throw even more light on its complexity.

The existence of a Puerto Rican "problem" in the school system was recognized as early as 1948, when a report entitled *A Program of Education for Puerto Ricans in New York City* was published. This report by the Association of Assistant Superintendents was the first system-wide effort to deal with problems of children of Puerto Rican background.[29] In recognition of the fact that something had to be done for the Spanish speaking children, a Substitute Auxiliary Teacher (SAT) position was established for qualified bilingual persons. Most of the appointees were Puerto Rican. Their primary duty was to work with teachers and supervisors in helping Spanish-speaking pupils and their parents in school and community adjustment. Ten SAT's were hired in 1949. In 1961 this position was given regular status by the Board of Education; an Auxiliary Teacher's license for a bilingual person with a B.A. plus 12 additional credits was established. By 1965 there were 142 bilingual Auxiliary Teachers employed in the elementary grades, and in 1964 the position of Supervisor of Auxiliary Teachers was created to assist the coordination of this program.

Additionally in 1948, regularly licensed teachers from the city (OTP's—Other Teaching Position) were assigned to teach English to the Puerto Ricans. As of June 1955 there were 33 such positions, also referred to as Non-English Coordinators. As the number of Puerto Rican pupils increased, these OTP's concentrated on training classroom teachers in methods of teaching English as a second language. Bilingual teachers who were teaching English in the Junior High Schools were called Puerto Rican Coordinators. In 1967 these two programs (SAT and OTP), which had been joined together under "Education for the Non-English Speaking Child," were separated. The SAT's were transferred to the "Human Integration Relations Unit" and became "Bilingual Teachers (BT's) in School and Community Relations," focusing on the social adjustment of Spanish speaking children. The OTP's, left in the school as English teachers, became "Teachers of English as a Second Language," focusing on language training. Establishment of the BT as an official position in the educational system represents a strong step forward. The present role of the BT also reflects the shift in policy with reference to the Spanish language. The BT is a resource person providing background materials on Puerto Rican culture; he is a strategic link to the community at a time when sensitivity about language and ethnic identification is increasing. He also fulfills for the Puerto Rican parent the image of the school

29*Educating Students for Whom English Is a Second Language*, Board of Education, New York City, 1965, pp. 1–2.

teacher, common in Puerto Rico, as the person who is conveniently on hand to settle problems.

The Board of Education seemed to be guided in the early programs (1948–1954) by a policy of rapid Americanization. Initial use of the SAT's and OTP's seemed to be directed toward helping Puerto Rican children over the language gap until they could manage effectively in English, and as a means of communication between English speaking teachers and Puerto Rican children. The early programs were not inspired by a desire to preserve the child's command of Spanish. When it was found that Puerto Ricans were not learning English quickly enough, or were dropping out of school, the response was generally an increase and intensification of English instruction. The programs sometimes had other, unintended, consequences. In the early 1950's, for example, newly arrived Puerto Rican children were sometimes placed in orientation classes presumably for three months, but actually remained in them for much longer periods. Despite a great deal of good will on the part of those who inaugurated the early programs, they were far from adequate.

A second major move by the school system was a committee named in 1951 by the Division of Curriculum Development to conduct a study of the needs of Puerto Rican pupils. The results of this study gave concrete form to the best experiences and achievements of New York teachers as of 1953 and were published in a booklet.[30] This pamphlet indicates growing awareness of the importance of knowledge of the Puerto Ricans' cultural background, a recognition of the value of taking advantage of the child's knowledge of Spanish, and the need for some knowledge of Spanish on the part of the teacher. It is not clear how widely these principles were held, or how extensively the suggestions were implemented. The booklet, moreover, offered only "suggestions," not a program. More definite data and answers were needed. Consequently, *The Puerto Rican Study* was sponsored by the Board of Education from 1953 to 1957. The Study addressed itself to two major problems: teaching English as a second language to Puerto Rican pupils, and identifying techniques to promote a more rapid and effective adjustment of Puerto Rican parents and children to the community, and of the community to them.

The Study found that while all the teachers were committed to the "over-all goal of helping their pupils to communicate effectively in English and to use English effectively as a tool in learning,"[31] there was no single accepted method or any standard content. The result was the de-

---

[30] *Teaching Children of Puerto Rican Background in New York City Schools,* Board of Education, New York City, 1953.

[31] *The Puerto Rican Study,* 1953–1957, Board of Education, New York City, 1958, p. 18.

velopment of two series of related curriculum bulletins—*Resource Units* organized around themes and designed for all pupils, and a corresponding *Language Guide Series* which provides the content and methods for adapting the instruction to the needs of the individual or group learning English. The Study also led to a detailed description of the Puerto Rican pupils, a scale to rate English speaking ability, and in-service programs to train teachers.

A brief scanning of the *Resource Units* and *Language Guide Series* reveals an emphasis on experiential learning and the teacher-child relationship. The emphasis placed on the Puerto Rican culture is not as extensive as we would expect today. In general, with reference to bilingualism, *The Puerto Rican Study* reflected growing recognition of the significance of the culture of the Puerto Ricans, of the importance of knowing and respecting this culture, and of relating to it positively. But the emphasis on culture and Spanish language was seen as instrumental in helping the Puerto Ricans to adjust more rapidly to the American way of life.

Unfortunately, the implementation of the recommendations of *The Puerto Rican Study* has never been carefully evaluated. A brief review of subsequent programs, which is presented in another booklet,[32] emphasizes the various teacher training programs, such as exchange of teachers between New York and Puerto Rico, which developed since completion of the Study. There is a general impression, supported by the data presented earlier in this chapter, that, despite the good intentions, whatever has been done has been largely ineffective.

Meanwhile, the Puerto Rican community was increasing its complaints and demands for innovation. The First Citywide Conference of the Puerto Rican Community,[33] which took place in April 1967, expressed deep indignation about the education of Puerto Rican children and submitted 32 recommendations to the Mayor. Many of these were repetitions of recommendations from *The Puerto Rican Study*, but many others reflected the significant change which had taken place in community attitudes in the early 1960's. The Conference demanded bilingual programs, not simply as an instrument for learning English, but also for developing and preserving the knowledge of Spanish among Puerto Rican children; the introduction of courses in Puerto Rican culture, literature, and history; a much greater involvement of the Puerto Rican community in the

[32]*Educating Students for Whom English Is a Second Language, op. cit.*, Board of Education, New York City, 1965.
[33]*Puerto Ricans Confront Problems of the Complex Urban Society: A Design for Change*, Community Conference Proceedings, Office of the Mayor, New York City, 1968.

planning of school programs for Puerto Rican children; the use of Puerto Rican paraprofessionals as aids to teachers and staffs; and representation on the Board of Education.

The Aspira Conference of May 1968 reiterated many of the complaints and recommendations of the Community Conference, but in the meantime the controversy over decentralization had become the central issue of the educational system. This dispute has changed the entire climate of the city with reference to the education of Black and Puerto Rican children, and eventually will have a decisive impact on the question of bilingualism in the schools.

A major development around the issue of bilingual education took place on a national scale when Congress passed the Bilingual Education Act in January 1968. The Act is in essence part of the amendments to Title I of the Elementary and Secondary Education Act of 1965. Under Title VII, "in recognition of the special education needs of the large numbers of children of limited English speaking ability in the United States, Congress hereby declares it to be the policy of the United States to provide financial assistance to local educational agencies to develop and carry out new and imaginative elementary and secondary school programs designed to meet these special educational needs."[34] Fifteen million dollars was authorized for the first year. Activities provided for by the Act are very vague, since no specific programs are indicated. Some of the plans suggested in the Senate Hearings included: (1) teaching Spanish as the native language; (2) teaching English as the second language; (3) efforts to attract and retain as teachers promising individuals of Mexican or Puerto Rican descent; and (4) efforts to establish closer cooperation between the school and home.[35]

The Senate Hearings on the Bilingual Education Programs are concerned mainly with the Southwest. Two points of view are represented in them: one is that English is the language of the nation, and the Bilingual Act must be directed to cultivating it;[36] the other is the view pressed by Joshua Fishman that every effort must be made to preserve the native language of the newcomer as a great value to the nation while he is taught English.[37] Aside from purely political motivations, the values which were

[34]"Title VII—Bilingual Education Programs," Sec. 702, p. 34, in *Public Law*, 90–247, 90th Congress, H.R. 7819, January 2, 1968.

[35]*Bilingual Education*: Hearings, U.S. Senate, Committee on Labor and Public Welfare, Special Subcommittee on Bilingual Education, 90th Congress, 1st Session (Washington, D.C.: U.S. Government Printing Office, Part I (May 1967), Part II (June 1967).

[36]Senator Paul J. Fanin, *Hearings* before the Special Subcommittee on Bilingual Education of the Committee on Labor and Public Welfare, May 1967 (36).

[37]Joshua Fishman, *Language Loyalty in the United States* (The Hague: Mouton & Co., 1966).

expressed in the Hearings on bilingualism, and which eventually prevailed, are not those which stress the teaching of Spanish for the preservation of a culture, but as an instrument for learning English more effectively, and for more rapid assimilation to American life. The far more serious and radical issue of cultural pluralism raised by Professor Fishman was obscured by the preoccupation of Committee and witnesses with issues of practicality and power.

Some significant research on language and bilingualism has already been done.[38] A special study contained in the Coleman Report[39] concluded that, although children from non-English speaking homes enter school with a disadvantage, that disadvantage largely disappears during the period of schooling. Although the conclusions and data of this study have been frequently called into question, James Fennessey utilized it to study children in New York schools. He concluded that differences in scores seem attributable, not to language, but to general family characteristics.[40]

One further aspect of bilingualism remains to be discussed, namely, the potential of language as a unique characteristic of the Puerto Ricans about which they might build a sense of group identity and establish a power base. Elsewhere I have written that language "is an unusual public symbol of identity, of the solidarity of the Puerto Ricans in a group of their own kind . . . of the strength they can have if they remain together."[41] Findings of a study of 431 Puerto Rican individuals in a Jersey City neighborhood recently completed by Joshua Fishman, however, indicate that "the Spanish press does not serve a readership that actively seeks to maintain or to develop Hispanic culture in New York in any ideologically mobilized fashion."[42] Fishman also found that Puerto

[38] Anne Anastasi and Fernando Cordova, "Some Effects of Bilingualism Upon the Intelligence Test Performance of Puerto Rican Children in New York City," *J. Ed. Psychol.*, XLIV (January 1953), 1–17; Anne Anastasi and Cruz de Jesus, "Language Development and Nonverbal IQ of Puerto Rican Pre-school Children in New York City," *J. Abnorm. Soc. Psychol.*, XLVIII, 3 (1963), 357–366.

[39] James S. Coleman *et al. The Equality of Educational Opportunity* (Washington, D.C.: U.S. Government Printing Office, 1966).

[40] James Fennessey, "An Exploratory Study of Non-English Speaking Homes and Academic Performance" (Baltimore: Research and Development Center for the Study of Social Organization of Schools and the Learning Process, Johns Hopkins University, 1967). (On file at ERIC Information Retrieval Center on the Disadvantaged.)

[41] Joseph P. Fitzpatrick, "The Role of Language as a Factor of Strength for the Puerto Rican Community." Paper delivered at Conference on "The Puerto Rican Child in His Cultural Context," Barranquitas, Puerto Rico, 1965. For the publication of this paper in Spanish, see *Educación*, 19 (April 1966), Departamento de Instrucción Publica, Hato Rey, Puerto Rico.

[42] Joshua Fishman and Heriberto Casiano, "Puerto Ricans in Our Press," in Joshua Fishman, R. L. Cooper, and R. Ma, eds., *Bilingualism in the Barrio*. Final Report under Contract No. OEC-1-7-062817-0297. (New York: U.S. Department of Health, Education and Welfare, 1968), p. 96.

Ricans in New York are not yet language conscious or organized on behalf of language use and maintenance; language loyalty and purity are foreign ideologies and, even among the intellectuals, few are involved in maintenance efforts. The ordinary Puerto Rican "does not believe that Spanish is absolutely necessary to being Puerto Rican; he sees his being Puerto Rican as a simple fact of ascribed status; he sees no conflict between that ascription of birth and parentage and his attainment of Americanness."[43] In addition, the majority of Puerto Rican parents feel that transmission of Spanish to the children is their task, while only the intellectuals would rather place more responsibility on the schools.

Nevertheless, the schools have accepted the responsibility and it appears that the parents support it. In 1968 the first completely bilingual elementary school was started, kindergarten through fourth grade, with bilingual teachers and bilingual instruction for all subjects. A second school was started in 1969. Early experience encourages us that the children may be bilingual by the end of the fourth grade. Attempts at bilingual training on higher levels, especially on the college level, have met with difficulty. Fishman found that choice of English or Spanish depends upon the domain of interaction. "Use of Spanish was reported primarily in the domain of family, secondarily, for the domains of friendship and religion and least of all in those of education and employment, while the reverse held true for English."[44] Spanish is therefore more or less resistant to erosion according to the domain.

The implications of Fishman's findings for the theoretical position of language are related to the belief that, given the time and setting, if the Puerto Ricans are to overcome the disadvantages which they suffer, especially in education, they must become a political voice, an interest group pressuring for their own rights and interests. Formation of a political bloc is dependent upon two factors: establishment of a common identity and an issue about which to rally forces. Language could fulfill these two requirements. Spanish could foster a sense of identity, but this might be handicapped by the great heterogeneity within the Puerto Rican population found by Padilla, and also by the attitudes discovered by Fishman's study. Many more studies of the scope and depth of Fishman's are required to discover just how unified or divided the Puerto Ricans are over the issue of language maintenance. In any event, the literature reviewed in this chapter suggests that an extensive activation of language

43Joshua Fishman, "Puerto Rican Intellectuals in New York: Quantitative Analysis of Twenty Bilingual Interviews," in *ibid.*, p. 142.

44Lawrence Greenfield and Joshua Fishman, "Situational Measures of Language Use in Relation to Person, Place and Topic among Puerto Rican Bilinguals," in *ibid.*, p. 454.

consciousness would have to be undertaken by community leaders and the press if language is to be as powerful a symbol for the Puerto Ricans as color has become for the Negro.

Language could also provide the issue around which to rally a show of strength. The Bilingual Education Act has specified the legal right of Puerto Ricans to have their children bilingually educated. However, the extent to which the Puerto Ricans might demand certain curricula for their children is intimately bound up with the amount of control they obtain over their local schools in the entire decentralization-community control controversy.

THE COMMUNITY
AND EDUCATION

The issue of Puerto Rican education has been examined from an academic point of view in terms of learning and language. It is precisely this situation which provoked the demand for decentralization. The rise of the decentralization controversy and the awakening of Black and Puerto Rican communities around this issue have given a new perspective to the problems of language and learning. Failure of Puerto Rican children to learn is now being analyzed in terms of the organization of the school system and the exercise of power within it. Children are seen as not responsive to the system because the system has not been responsive to them. It has been described as too inflexible to adapt itself to the capacity of Puerto Rican children to learn if their creativity and style of expression do not fit into its standardized curriculum and methods. It has failed to win the support of Puerto Rican parents because they feel largely excluded from it. As a result, there has been wide acceptance of the theory that if the system is made more flexible by being decentralized, and made accountable to local communities, the response of children and of parents would be more favorable and productive. An extensive review of the complicated issue of decentralization and the history of the controversy around it is beyond the scope of this book, but the reaction of the Puerto Rican community to the controversy in New York City will be briefly described.

The decentralization issue is an assertion by local communities of their right to influence the education of their children through participation in and control of the structure and processes of the school system. A fundamental polarity between an educational ideal and the educational reality is involved. The educational ideal has been stated by the Bundy Report on the decentralization of the New York City public schools:

"The concept of local control of education is at the heart of the American public school system."[45] The educational reality consists of the fact that state and local governments have taken over the primary responsibility for educational matters. Theoretically the citizens control the educational system through school boards, but actually the system tends to create a bureaucratic structure designed to administer the educational enterprise, and the structure poses a serious block to the educational ideal of community decision-making.

The decentralization controversy has erupted in New York City because large numbers of scholars, officials, and citizens have decided that the educational reality cannot be adjusted to the educational ideal, and that reform will be achieved only if the political power of the citizens is exerted. Thus, while the issue is educational, the practical resolution is political. The community defines its activity not as a challenge to legitimate control, but as the reclamation of its own right to exercise legitimate control.

The more dramatic developments of the controversy erupted in the severe 1968–1969 school strike in New York City. Since that time a plan for moderate decentralization has been adopted by the New York State Legislature.[46]

The relationship of the Puerto Rican community to the decentralization controversy has been neither clear nor consistent. When the Bundy panel, set up by Mayor Lindsay to report on decentralization of the New York City schools, gave its recommendations in November 1967, the response of the Puerto Rican community was generally favorable. But there were dissenting voices, as indicated above on pp. 113–114. This opposition was not directed at the value of decentralization itself, but at the question of representation on the community level. What has emerged is a Puerto Rican community divided by an educational ideal and a political reality. Specifically, because the Puerto Rican community is dispersed throughout the city, its members are forced in many instances to share community programs, services, and leadership with other minority groups—particularly the Negro community. The association of Puerto Ricans and Negroes has not always been congenial, especially when questions of program leadership have been involved. In parts of the city where Puerto Ricans live in close proximity to large numbers of Negroes, the ability of the Puerto Ricans to adjust to the political realities of decentralization will be crucial to the feasibility of decentralization. United Bronx Par-

[45]Mayor's Advisory Panel on Decentralization of the New York City Schools, *Reconnections for Learning: A Community School System for New York City*, November 1967.

[46]*The New York Times*, May 1, 1969, p. 1.

ents, a predominantly Puerto Rican organization in the South Bronx, has played a particularly militant role in the area where the heaviest concentration of Puerto Rican school children is found; it apparently works effectively in collaboration with Blacks. Puerto Rican organization's in general have not been particularly aggressive or effective on the legislative front.

Beneath the conflicts and/or cooperation of the Puerto Ricans and Negroes there exists a fundamental dilemma for the Puerto Rican leadership. The philosophy of Aspira and other organizations committed to urging Puerto Rican students to take advantage of educational opportunities sees Puerto Ricans following in the steps of earlier ethnic groups. Glazer and Moynihan have observed: "Its identification is with the Jews or Italians of forty years ago, rather than with the Negroes of today. It has a rather hopeful outlook, which emphasizes the group's potential for achievement more than the prejudices and discrimination it meets."[47] In the realities of the decentralization and other issues, however, although Puerto Ricans may be uncertain about their identification with Negroes, they find that, because of their social, political, and geographic proximity, they must work with them. This can result in some serious tensions in terms of both mutual cooperation between the two groups and personal and community identity for the Puerto Ricans. The effectiveness of the Puerto Ricans as a community will greatly depend on their ability to organize cohesively and interact politically. Only in this way will they become a more viable political force in meeting the challenges and opportunities of today's urban educational experience.

A number of reasons can be suggested for the failure of the Puerto Rican community to organize and exercise its power more effectively in all areas of New York life. The confident exercise of any group's power depends on a strong sense of identity and solidarity. Many of the factors which contributed to a sense of identity and community among earlier immigrant groups have not been present in the experience of Puerto Ricans, so new sources of community solidarity and identification have to be found.

Thus, political power becomes a source of cohesion for the Puerto Rican community as well as a means of controlling its destiny. The potential for the development of political power around the decentralization issue, consequently, is great if the Puerto Ricans pursue it. As Richard J. Margolis has observed:

> No school system, no matter how humane its intentions, is likely to come up with a comprehensive program aimed at saving Puerto Rican children

[47]Glazer and Moynihan, *Beyond the Melting Pot, op. cit.*, pp. 128–129.

unless the community suggests one and presses for its enactment. The New York experience has already made this clear. In response to strong but non-specific pressures from the Puerto Rican community, the New York school system has "jumped on its horse and ridden off in all directions." It appears to be true that education is too important to be left entirely to the educators.[48]

The desire of Puerto Ricans for self-help and control over their own destiny, while still politically weak, is nevertheless genuine and becoming stronger with time. It may be that the issue of the schooling of their children will be the focus around which their strength and solidarity will crystallize.

[48]Richard J. Margolis, "The Losers," p. 14. Paper prepared for the First National Conference of Puerto Ricans, Mexican-Americans, and Educators on "The Special Educational Needs of Urban Puerto Rican Youth," May 14 and 15, 1968.

No book about the Puerto Ricans can overlook the problem of public welfare. The cause of the most widespread and hostile criticism against the Puerto Ricans, it is an ambiguous experience for Puerto Ricans themselves for which no ready explanation can be found. The experience of Puerto Ricans with public welfare, however, is an integral part of the problem of public welfare throughout the entire nation.[1] In that context, some comments can be made about it.

The category of public assistance which receives the sharpest criticism is Aid to Families with Dependent Children (AFDC). These are mother based families, for the most part, where no husband is present. Either he has abandoned the family, or the mother has had children by one or more men. In December 1965 there were 391,000 persons receiving AFDC benefits in New York City; by October 1968, three years later, the number had risen to 709,000. It is estimated that 40 per cent of the AFDC families are Puerto Rican.[2] If this is true, 283,600 Puerto Ricans are receiving AFDC benefits, which would be 35 per cent of the Puerto Rican population, if the estimates of a Puerto Rican population of 800,000 are at all accurate. This extraordinary number of welfare recipients is used as the basis for the bitter criticism that public welfare is promoting promiscuity and illegitimacy; the charge

Special Problems: Welfare

[1]An excellent discussion of the problem of public welfare appears in *The Public Interest*, 16 (Summer 1969), in the section "Poverty, Welfare, and Income Maintenance": David M. Gordon, "Income and Welfare in New York City," pp. 64–88; Edward Banfield, "Welfare: A Crisis without 'Solutions,'" pp. 89–101; Nathan Glazer, "Beyond Income Maintenance—A Note on Welfare in New York City," pp. 102–120.

[2]This estimate is based on a study of a sample of welfare families by Lawrence Podell, *Families on Welfare in New York City*, The Center for the Study of Urban Problems, Graduate Division, Bernard M. Baruch College, The City University of New York, 257 Park Avenue South, New York, N.Y., 10010, 1968. In November 1968, a report based largely on this study was submitted by Podell to the Joint Legislative Committee to Revise the Social Services Law of the State of New York, at Albany, New York. The report, entitled, "The Increase in Public Welfare in New York City: The Thirty Months from January, 1966 to June, 1968," was severely criticized by a group of social scientists called The Social Scientists' Committee on Welfare and Social Problems, c/o Professor S. M. Miller, School of Education, New York University, Washington Square, N.Y., 10003. The statement of the Committee was entitled: "Public Welfare in New York City: A Critique of the Podell Report." Podell prepared and issued a response to the criticism in May 1969.

is also made that it is creating a pattern of perpetual dependency among many welfare families.

The problem of abandoned children, or children with only the mother in the home, has been a difficulty in Puerto Rico for a long time. Poor families have developed methods of coping with it, and more recently public authorities have sought to provide adequate remedies.[3] But nothing in the Puerto Rican background can explain the extraordinary numbers of Puerto Ricans receiving AFDC benefits in New York City.

A 1956 analysis of the child welfare program of Puerto Rico showed that 102,000 children under 18 were receiving assistance. Of these, 34,000, or about one-third, were defined as abandoned children, abandoned for the most part by the father. Most of these children, 24,000, were born out of wedlock; the others, 10,000, were legitimate children whose fathers had left them. In other words, close to 10 per cent[4] of the child population under 18 was receiving public assistance, but only one-third of these children had been abandoned by a parent.[5]

Culturally, the Puerto Ricans have had a variety of ways of coping with abandonment. The family has always been the major resource. A girl who bears a child out of wedlock generally keeps the child, and it is raised in her home with the mother's parents or relatives. It is admirable to witness the generosity and thoughtfulness of many poor families in caring for the out-of-wedlock children of family members or friends. Mintz' study of poor families in Santa Isabel has some beautiful descriptions of this practice, even to the point of a woman caring dutifully for the children her husband has had by other women.

> I don't know if my father was married before. [He later recalls however, that his father had a mistress and had two sons by her. Taso knew his half-brothers, and they visited freely in his mother's house when he was a child.][6]

[3]Selenia Ponce de Leon Pratts, *El Abandono de Menores en Puerto Rico* Negociado de Bienestar de Niño, Departmento de Bienestar Publico, Departmento de Salud, San Juan, Puerto Rico, May 1961.

[4]This is based on an estimate of the child population under 18 for 1955. The assumption is that the percentage would not have changed noticeably in 1956. Even such a rough approximation is sufficient to indicate that 3 to 4 per cent of the child population consisted of abandoned children receiving public assistance. This is not a complete picture, since there were certainly many abandoned children not receiving assistance.

[5]Oficina de Estadisticas, Investigaciones Sociales y Educacion, Division de Bienestar Publico, Departmento de Salud, San Juan, Puerto Rico.

[6]Sidney Mintz, *Worker in the Cane* (New Haven: Yale University Press, 1960), p. 35.

Taso later describes the behavior of his sister Tomasa, whose husband, Cornelio, ran off with another woman, Nenita.

> But he [Cornelio] continued living at our home while my sister was alive. He would go away for two or three days—but he never gave up coming to the house. To such an extent that when Nenita began having his children, the children would come to our house—yes—and in the house—think of it— Tomasa after—after feeding them even dressed them up. They would eat, and then she would send them home.[7]

The institution of *compadrazgo*, a sense of responsibility for children abandoned by compadres; the functioning of informal family and friendship loyalties; and a widespread response among simple people to the elemental needs of the human family, especially children, have resulted in a set of cultural practices by which children are cared for. Oscar Lewis' description of the slum families of mothers "in the life" presents some vivid detail about the lives of children without fathers. Lewis' study was centered on a group of families in a well known slum area of San Juan which he calls "La Esmeralda."

> Over 50 percent of the marriages in La Esmeralda were of the consensual or free union type, a proportion much higher than that of the other slums studied. Almost seven out of ten family heads in La Esmeralda had had more than one union, legal or consensual. One of every five households in the slum was headed by a female, usually widowed or separated from her husband. This high incidence of mother-centered households was also found throughout the other slums.
>
> In La Esmeralda as in other slums, one out of five families was receiving relief in the form of money payments and surplus food allotments.[8]

The experience of the children as presented by Lewis was much harsher than that of the children described by Mintz. By the time Lewis did his study in the early 1960's, public welfare had entered the scene, and he found that 20 per cent of the slum families were receiving benefits from it.

Puerto Rican law has sought to provide benefits for abandoned children, and to identify their responsible fathers, in order to compel them to provide support. The latter effort has apparently not been very effective.

However, neither the cultural practices of Puerto Ricans in caring for abandoned children, nor the public welfare policies of Puerto Rico, are helpful in explaining the large numbers of Puerto Ricans receiving

[7]*Ibid.*, p. 50.

[8]Oscar Lewis, *La Vida: A Puerto Rican Family in the Culture of Poverty—San Juan and New York* (New York: Random House, Inc., 1965), p. xxxvi.

AFDC benefits in New York City. Out-of-wedlock births for Puerto Ricans in New York City in 1959 (11.4 per cent of Puerto Rican births) was higher than the rate for non-Puerto Rican whites (2.1 per cent) but lower than the rate for nonwhites (25 per cent).[9] Caution must always be exercised in calculating out-of-wedlock births for Puerto Ricans. The practice of consensual union makes it possible that children categorized as out-of-wedlock may be children of a stable union of parents who are not married.

With reference to the AFDC problem, it is important to note that Puerto Rican mothers of out-of-wedlock babies are much more likely to take their babies home with them and raise them in their own families than are other mothers in the city. Thus they are more likely to show up on AFDC rolls than on the rolls of institutions or in statistics on adopted children. Furthermore, Podell found that only 20 per cent of the mothers on welfare were unmarried; 40 per cent were separated from their husbands, and many of them had no children after the separation.

The large numbers of Puerto Rican AFDC cases in New York City must be examined in the context of the general problem of welfare in the city. In the first place, the Puerto Rican population in New York City is the poorest segment of the total population. David M. Gordon has pointed out that inflation has left the poor families in such a low financial condition that the enormous increase in welfare recipients between 1966 and 1968 can be explained by the simple fact that their incomes failed to keep pace with inflation. Rapidly increasing numbers of families slipped to the income level which entitles them to welfare. For example, in 1960, Puerto Ricans constituted only 18 per cent of the families under the poverty level in New York City; in 1968 they constituted 39 per cent of the poverty families. It is interesting to observe that the Puerto Ricans constitute the same per cent of persons on welfare (about 40 per cent) as they constitute families in poverty in the city (39 per cent).[10] Furthermore, New York City has very high payments for welfare recipients and (until the drastic cut by the State legislature in early 1969) continued to increase the level of welfare payments. Between 1962 and 1967, average wages in manufacturing in New York City rose 19 per cent; weekly earnings at minimum wage levels increased 30 per cent; but the budget allowance for a welfare family of four increased 45 per cent.[11]

Other factors have contributed to the increased numbers on welfare. The welfare rights movement has been active during the late 1960's, so

[9]Jean Pakter, Henry J. Rosner, Harold Jacobziner, and Frieda Greenstein, "Out-of-Wedlock Births in New York City," *American Journal of Public Health,* 51, 5 (May 1961), 683–696.
[10]Gordon, *"Income and Welfare," op. cit.,* 79.
[11]Glazer, *"Beyond Income Maintenance," op. cit.,* 103.

many families entitled to welfare but not receiving it were alerted to their rights and added to the rolls. The AFDC situation among Puerto Ricans is undoubtedly a mixture of genuine problems of poverty, problems of establishing levels of welfare payment in the city, political and social pressures for aid to the poor, and the organization of the poor themselves.

All of this contributes to the complexity of the issue. But 35 per cent of a total population on AFDC still represents an extremely serious social, political, and moral problem for the Puerto Ricans and for the city. The issue is twofold: To what extent does it reflect a traditional weakness in Puerto Rican families with a history of abandonment, and to what extent is a combination of poverty and the welfare system creating a problem of weakness for Puerto Rican families?

The possibility of the first should not be minimized. Traditional features of Puerto Rican culture (machismo, the practice of the mistress, consensual unions, the culture of poverty) have created a problem of abandonment in the past. In the process of migration, the cultural patterns whereby people sought to cope with the consequences of abandonment are easily lost. Furthermore, there is no doubt that the high welfare payments of New York City have attracted a disproportionate number of Puerto Rican poor, as they have attracted a disproportionate number of the poor of other groups. It is therefore understandable that large numbers of Puerto Ricans with a problem of abandonment would appear in New York City.

But the second possibility is certainly involved. The policies of public welfare lead inevitably to the practice of deceit, or the actual weakening of the family. Since Puerto Ricans are the poorest of New York's families, the pressures to find adequate income are severe. Although supplementary welfare payments can be arranged if a father's income is below a calculated minimum level, this supplement is small compared to the amount available if the mother can claim no support from a father in or out of the home. Thus the pressure for the father to vacate the home is very strong. He may continue to work, contribute to the family, visit the family regularly, and fulfill his role as father, while the mother represents her family as abandoned. This is what Puerto Ricans call "plaɟing the welfare business." The situation may prompt the father to leave the home so that both he and the family can live better, or it may put pressure on the mother to force the father out. The consequence may be continued separation and the breakup of the family. Either situation is unfortunate, and obviously contributes to family weakness.

This is not the moment for a lengthy discussion of alternatives to the present system of welfare. However, the situation has a direct relationship to the basic problem of the adjustment of Puerto Ricans to New York

City. The family is the fundamental basis for identity and community strength. Absence of a father and dependence of the family on welfare leave the family incapable of fulfilling both of these functions. The welfare check is hardly a substitute for the brother, cousin, compadre, or friend in the working out of those elemental loyalties which keep men aware of the bonds that link them in a common struggle for survival and achievement. There can be overromanticized longings to go back to a less organized, more intimate and familial life. It was not always pleasant. But in seeking to identify the challenge facing the Puerto Ricans, it is helpful to be aware that they do not have the strong support of traditional practices of mutual aid and generosity with which they formerly met the challenge of survival in Puerto Rico, and with which earlier immigrants met the challenge of survival in New York. The challenge to the Puerto Ricans is different. In the presence of organized systems of public welfare which tend to shake the traditional strengths of the Puerto Rican community, how can they retain a deep sense of family identity and community solidarity?

Perhaps efforts to organize community strength around issues of their right to public welfare may provide a basis for solidarity. The sense of political strength and security in achieving this goal could be a new basis for identity. But around this issue of family strength, the challenge to the Puerto Ricans continues. Family strength was the major factor in the adjustment and assimilation of earlier immigrants, and history has given no evidence of any adequate substitute in the United States. It is important to keep in mind, however, that this is not a particular problem of Puerto Ricans; it is simply a reflection in the experience of Puerto Ricans of the major challenges which affect the entire nation. As Puerto Ricans face it more sharply and directly than others are required to at the present time, they may contribute substantially to the ideas and methods which help the nation to meet the challenge on a larger scale.

The relationship of mental illness to migration has long been recognized.[1] It has been interpreted as the result of the shock of abrupt transition from a world in which the immigrant feels he belongs to a strange world of which he does not feel a part. The pain of the uprooting is a familiar theme in immigrant literature and folklore. Implied is the presumption that, if immigrants can retain their social solidarity and cultural identity, the danger of mental illness is lessened. Consequently, a discussion of identity among Puerto Ricans leads to an examination of the evidences of loss identity in the problem of mental illness. Rates of mental illness among Puerto Ricans are very high. Recent discussions of the problem, however, question whether these rates reflect the distress which accompanies migration, or whether they should not more accurately be interpreted as a flaw in the organization and functioning of the mental health enterprise in New York City.

Special Problems: Mental Illness

Rates of mental illness among Puerto Ricans were first studied by Benjamin Malzberg,[2] who found a high incidence of schizophrenia among Puerto Ricans in New York City during the period 1949–1951. Calculating the rate of first admissions for schizophrenia, the rate for Puerto Rican males was 105 per 100,000, in contrast to a rate of 45.4 per 100,000 for males in the general population; the rate for Puerto Rican females was 79.5, in contrast to 45.3 for females in the general population. In 1968 Fitzpatrick and Gould[3] replicated the Malz-

---

[1] The major features of mental disorder among refugees were described in a UNESCO study of refugees by H.B.M. Murphy, *Flight and Resettlement* (Paris: UNESCO, 1955). The experience of immigrants or migrants is generally not as abrupt or traumatic as that of refugees, but the stress of relocation is severe and is well described by Murphy. In a later publication, "Migration and the Major Mental Disorders," in Mildred B. Kantor (ed.), *Mobility and Mental Health* (Springfield, Ill.: Charles C Thomas, Publisher, 1965), pp. 5–29, Murphy presents an excellent position paper on the topic. V. Barnouw, *Culture and Personality* (New York: Richard D. Irwin, Inc.,

This chapter was prepared with the help of Robert E. Gould, M.D., Chief of Adolescent Services, Psychiatric Division, New York Bellevue Hospital, New York, and with Anthony Croce, William Contois, Natalie Hannan, and Joseph Polka, graduate research assistants. It is based on a task force paper, *Mental Health Needs of Spanish-speaking Children in the New York Area*, prepared for the Joint Commission on Mental Health for Children.

berg study and found that the differential in rates of schizophrenia between Puerto Ricans and the general population was greater than what Malzberg had noted. The rate of first admissions for schizophrenia for Puerto Rican males in New York State in 1967 was 122 per 100,000, whereas the rate for males in the general population was 36.6; for Puerto Rican females the rate was 84.2, while for females in the general population it was 32.6.

Malzberg could find no convincing explanation for the high rates among Puerto Ricans. He observed that the differential was related to the experience of migration, language difficulties, occupational problems, and the segregation of Puerto Ricans in areas of the city marked by a high incidence of physical and mental illness. Other explanations have been sought in factors in the culture of Puerto Rico which may induce schizophrenia; the effect of migration on mental health; and problems in the delivery of mental health services to poor Puerto Ricans. It is possible that in many cases Puerto Ricans are being treated for mental illness which they do not have.

PUERTO RICAN CULTURE
AND MENTAL ILLNESS

Surprisingly little study has been accomplished concerning mental illness in Puerto Rico. The first large scale systematic study was published in 1965 by Rogler and Hollingshead.[4] They found that schizophrenia was the most frequent illness among 1,500 patients at the only public mental hospital in Puerto Rico, and estimated that the rate for the Island must be unusually high. In an intensive study of 20 families in which either or both spouses were schizophrenic, and 20 families drawn from the same population who were not schizophrenic, they concluded:

---

and The Dorsey Press, 1963), also reviews the major literature. S. Parker and R. J. Kleiner, *Mental Illness in the Urban Negro Community* (New York: The Free Press, 1966), present a careful, critical analysis of studies of migration and mental illness. Uita S. Sommers, "The Impact of Dual-Cultural Membership on Identity," *Psychiatry,* 27 (1964), 232–241, and E. Brody, "Cultural Exclusion, Character and Illness," *Amer. J. of Psychiatry,* 122 (1966), 852–858, emphasize the unfavorable effects of migration into a hostile environment.

[2]Benjamin Malzberg, "Mental Disease among Puerto Ricans in New York City, 1949–51," *J. of Nervous and Mental Disease,* 123 (1956), 457–465.

[3]Joseph P. Fitzpatrick and Robert E. Gould, M.D., *Mental Health Needs of Spanish-speaking Children in the New York Area,* unpublished Task Force Paper prepared for the Joint Commission on Mental Health for Children, Institute for Social Research, Fordham University, Bronx, New York, 1968.

[4]Lloyd H. Rogler and August B. Hollingshead, *Trapped: Families and Schizophrenia* (New York: John Wiley & Sons, Inc., 1965).

Experiences in childhood and adolescence of schizophrenic persons do not differ noticeably from those of persons who are not afflicted with this illness. At an identifiable period in the life of the schizophrenic person, however, a set of interwoven, mutually reinforcing problems produces an onrush of symptoms which overwhelm the victim and prevent him from fulfilling the obligations associated with his accustomed social roles.[5]

Rogler and Hollingshead identified as contributing strains: (1) the cultural contradiction between the careful protection of the girl from sexual experience and the freedom given to the boy; (2) tensions created by the emphasis on submissiveness in the girl in her role as housewife in contrast to the emphasis on masculinity (*machismo*) which exerts pressures toward infidelity on the man; (3) tensions in the discrepancy between expected and achieved standard of living. The severe pressure of poverty emerges as a significant variable in the onset of mental illness.

A number of other studies touch directly or indirectly on mental illness among Puerto Ricans, and indicate cultural factors which seem related to it:

1. The contradiction in the values which govern the sexual behavior of the man and woman may lead to anxieties in the man about his masculinity, to a female martyr complex in the woman, or to excessive fear in the woman caused by cloistering.[6]
2. The close relationship between mother and son in Puerto Rican culture may lead to difficulties for the man in overcoming dependency on women or in establishing an adequate love relationship with a wife.[7]
3. As in many cultures, if strong authority patterns become excessive, they can provoke hostility against authority figures.[8]

[5]*Ibid.*, p. vii.

[6]H. B. Green, "Comparison of Nurturance and Independence Training in Jamaica and Puerto Rico, with Consideration of the Resulting Personality Structure and Transplanted Social Patterns," *J. of Soc. Psychiatry*, 51 (1960), 27–63. Green relates her analysis to the central role of *respeto* in the culture of Puerto Ricans which leads to an initial spontaneous personal relationship; to recognition of competence (*capacidad*) in adolescence which smooths the way into adulthood; and to involvement of the individual in a set of interpersonal relationships in which aggression is continually subject to control. She also notes the importance of fatalism in cushioning the shock of failure; failure can always be attributed to God's will.

[7]*Ibid.* David Landy, *Tropical Childhood: Cultural Transmission and Learning in a Rural Puerto Rican Village* (Chapel Hill: University of North Carolina Press, 1959), describes many of the same cultural and social traits as Rogler and Hollingshead. He finds a possible source of weakness in the inadequate development of the superego which results from a discontinuity in training between the first three years, during which the child's needs are continually satisfied, and the second three years, when proper behavior in the child was not rewarded by love, which Landy claims is needed for the development of a strong superego. Landy describes Puerto Rican children as remaining dependent on their parents.

[8]E. P. Maldonado Sierra and R. D. Trent, "The Sibling Relationship in Group Psychotherapy with Puerto Rican Schizophrenics," *Amer. J. of Psychiatry*, 117 (160), 239–243.

4. The keen sense of personal dignity (dignidad) and the emphasis on respect (respeto) may activate a potential for violence.[9]
5. The overwhelming burden of poverty and the accumulation of problems of the poor may make the difference between mental health and mental illness.[10]

A specific form of hysteria called "The Puerto Rican Syndrome" is widely recognized. Called the ataque by Puerto Ricans, it is a tendency to resort to a hyperkinetic seizure at a time of acute tension or anxiety.[11] Rogler and Hollingshead are the only ones who investigated the high incidence of mental illness in Puerto Rico. However, in the absence of comparable studies of other populations, it is not possible to determine whether the rates in Puerto Rico are unusually high for the kind of population studied.

MIGRATION

When attention is directed to mental illness among Puerto Ricans in New York, the experience of migration immediately enters the picture. The process of uprooting, of adjustment to a new and strange, possibly hostile, way of life, has always been noted as a cause of disorientation and mental disorder. The stress may become great enough to lead to a breaking point. Studies of migration and mental illness focus on three

[9]Green, "Comparison of Nurturance," op. cit. This is also a central theme of A. Lauria, "Respeto, Relajo and Interpersonal Relations in Puerto Rico," Anthro. Q., 37 (1964), 53–67; A. Rothenberg, "Puerto Rico and Aggression," Amer. J. of Psychiatry, 120 (1964), 962–970, finds the repression of aggression through the pattern of respeto a source of excessive violence when the repression fails.

[10]Oscar Lewis, La Vida: A Puerto Rican Family in the Culture of Poverty—San Juan and New York (New York: Random House, Inc., 1965), examines the day-to-day life of a family in what he defines as the "culture of poverty." Lewis found that the women of the family did not adhere to the submissive and cloistered role of other Puerto Rican women, nor did the men demonstrate an obsessive concern with machismo, and were more likely to be dependent on the women. To a greater extent than Rogler and Hollingshead, Lewis observed strengths among the people, such as spontaneity, less pathological sexual expression, more outlet for hostility in acts of violence, low aspiration level which cushioned the shock of discrepancy between their standard of living and that of others, and a general capacity for short range enjoyment. "The Rios family is closer to the expression of an unbridled id than any other people I have studied. They have an almost complete absence of internal conflict and of a sense of guilt [p. xxvi]." Nevertheless, long range goals are lacking to give stability through the full term of the life arc, and the prognosis is poor for the individual who manages to survive to later stages of the life cycle. One important insight is provided by the Lewis study; Many forms of behavior which middle class professionals would define as abnormal appear to be a routine part of the way of life of these people.

[11]Rothenberg, "Puerto Rico and Aggression," op. cit.; see also R. Fernandez Marina, "The Puerto Rican Syndrome: Its Dynamics and Cultural Determinants," Psychiatry, 24 (1961), 79–82.

hypotheses: (1) mental illness is a major factor in causing people to migrate—intense psychological distress prompts people to seek relief by moving; (2) stress due to migration causes mental illness in vulnerable persons; (3) mental illness is related to a nonessential association between migration and age, social class, or cultural conflict; in other words, since schizophrenia is an illness of the young, and since the great majority of migrants are young, youthfulness rather than migration may be the significant variable. The second hypothesis is the most widely accepted, and the one generally applied to explain the high rates of mental illness among Puerto Ricans. However, not a few practicing psychiatrists in New York City insist that the first hypothesis must be seriously considered.

No study comparable to the Rogler and Hollingshead has been carried on in New York. In the Midtown Manhattan Study,[12] Srole and associates studied 1,911 adults, 20–59 years of age, in a limited geographical area of New York City in an effort to explore the relationship between a selected number of social and cultural variables and the mental health or illness of the persons interviewed. There were 27 Puerto Ricans in the sample, and they came off far worse than any other ethnic group. Poverty was not found to be a significant factor; the study suggested the hypothesis of isolation. Puerto Ricans had a greater attachment to their place of birth than any other group, but the Puerto Ricans in the sample were living in isolation from the large concentrations of Puerto Ricans in the City.

Beatrice Berle,[13] in her study of 80 Puerto Rican families, was primarily interested in physical illness and its impact on the families, but in the course of her work she discovered a high incidence of personality disorder. She indicated that relevant factors in the personality disorders were largely unknown. However, she made two important observations: (1) disturbed persons are generally examined and treated away from the total context of everyday family life; and (2) many of the poor families displayed extraordinary capacity to cope with cases of personality disturbance. She emphasized the need for "the development of better local facilities for the management of mental defectives and disturbed individuals in their homes and neighborhoods." For example, after a lengthy description of the *ataque* (the Puerto Rican syndrome), Berle indicates that this is a culturally expected reaction to situations of serious stress, and that Puerto Ricans manage it as an ordinary occurrence. Someone

[12]L. Srole *et al., Mental Health in the Metropolis, The Midtown Manhattan Study* (New York: McGraw-Hill Book Company, 1962).

[13]Beatrice Berle, *Eighty Puerto Rican Families in New York City* (New York: Columbia University Press, 1959).

not familiar with the cultural background could interpret it as a symptom of more serious mental disturbance. Berle urged that the study of mental illness among Puerto Ricans be kept in a social and cultural perspective; if Puerto Rican behavior is not examined by someone who understands the culture of the people, there is danger of misdirected diagnosis.

Other studies of the Puerto Ricans, much more limited in scope, can be summarized briefly. The comparative studies of Malzberg and Srole *et al.*, based on statistical data, offer no satisfactory explanation of the unusually high rates of schizophrenia among Puerto Ricans. Cultural sources of mental illness among Puerto Ricans are indicated in some smaller studies. Strengths and weaknesses are revealed in the cultural traits of *respeto*, which is important in the process of socialization, and *machismo*, which is important in the role of the man in Puerto Rican culture. *Respeto* governs a wide range of interpersonal relationships and is instrumental in controlling hostility and maintaining tranquility. When thrown out of balance, *respeto* can lead to problems of violence through an excessive concern for *dignidad*, the dignity of the person, or as a consequence of continued repression of hostility through the practice of *respeto*. *Respeto* can also lead to problems with authority.[14]

Machismo in poorly defined situations, such as occur when people migrate to a strange culture, can lead to anxieties in men, and to fear and suspicion in women. Dependency of men on women appears as a source of ambiguity and tension.[15] Recourse to spiritualism and the Pentecostal sects can serve as a relief of anxiety. Family strengths are found in apparently disorganized situations. *Respeto* can lead to great confidence and security in interpersonal relationships; a sense of fatalism may act to spare a person a sense of guilt. A sense of authority provides strength against disintegrating forces. A central theme in all the above studies of mental illness among Puerto Ricans is cultural change due to migration, resulting in intergenerational conflict between parents and children, uncertainty caused by the new culture, and isolation within the new culture.[16]

[14]S. Minuchin *et al.*, *Families in the Slums* (New York: Basic Books, Inc., Publishers, 1967).

[15]*Ibid.*; M. K. Opler, *Culture and Social Psychiatry* (New York: Atherton Press, 1967); R. Fernandez-Marina, E. D. Maldonado-Sierra, and R. D. Trent, "Three Basic Themes in Mexican and Puerto Rican Family Values," *J. of Soc. Psych.*, 48 (1958), 167–181.

[16]E. C. Trautman, "Suicide Attempts of Puerto Rican Immigrants," *Psychiatric Q.*, 35 (1961), 544–554; J. M. Toolan, "Suicide and Suicidal Attempts in Children and Adolescents," *Amer. J. Psychiatry*, 118 (1962), 719–724; Fernandez-Marina *et al.*, *op. cit.*; S. L. Elam, "Acculturation and Learning Problems of Puerto Rican Children," in J. K. Robert (ed.), *School Children in the Urban Slum* (New York: The Free Press, 1965).

MENTAL HEALTH SERVICES
AND THE POOR

The attention of social scientists seeking to explain mental illness in recent years has been shifting from an emphasis on culture to an emphasis on social class. This raises the question as to whether the high incidence of schizophrenia among Puerto Ricans, or their high rate of admission to mental hospitals, may be related to their style of life as poor people rather than to their culture as Puerto Ricans.

For many years scholars and practitioners have been aware that officially defined mental illness is much more common among the poor than the affluent. The Hollingshead and Redlich[17] study is a landmark. They found that lower socioeconomic status is significant not only in the incidence of mental illness, especially schizophrenia, but also in the diagnosis (psychosis rather than neurosis) and treatment (organic and custodial treatment rather than psychotherapy). The meaning of this correlation has been challenged in recent years, partly on the basis of methodology, in an article by Dohrenwend,[18] but much more seriously in a wide range of publications, such as those collected by Frank Riessman and his associates,[19] which raise fundamental questions about the definition of mental illness and the institutional dislocation of mental health services in relation to the poor. Although the treatment of poor patients by affluent mental health professionals involves a cultural gap, the recent challenge to mental health services is directed more sharply to problems of organization, official definition of mental illness, and political management of mental health services.

In a classic article, Kingsley Davis[20] called attention to a serious bias in the mental health field in the treatment of the poor by middle and upper class professionals. He indicated that professionals defined the situation in their own terms and, according to their definitions, the poor were maladjusted. However, when seen from the viewpoint of the poor, much of their behavior was perceived as an understandable response to the life situations they had to face. Dohrenwend criticized the Midtown Manhattan Study for much the same reason. This study was particularly important because it studied untreated mental illness; residents were

17A. B. Hollingshead and F. C. Redlich, *Social Class and Mental Illness* (New York: John Wiley & Sons, Inc., 1958).

18B. P. Dohrenwend, "Social Status and Psychological Disorder: An Issue of Substance and an Issue of Method," *Amer. Sociol. Rev.*, 31 (1966), 14–34.

19F. Riessman, J. Cohen, and A. Pearl (eds.), *Mental Health of the Poor* (New York: The Free Press, 1964).

20K. Davis, "Mental Hygiene and the Class Structure," *Psychiatry*, 1 (1938), 55–65.

interviewed who had never been exposed to clinical diagnosis. As indicated above, indications of mental illness were found more frequently among Puerto Ricans than among any other group. Dohrenwend retested the instruments used in the Midtown Manhattan Study and discovered that differences noted in symptoms of mental illness may have been due to a bias built into the methodology. Differences in psychological symptomatology may reflect group differences in ways of expressing distress, and differences in cultural approval or disapproval of various kinds of behavior.

A much more abundant and outspoken literature has called attention to problems built into the class structure of our society. The extreme position is taken by Thomas Szasz,[21] who claims that definition of forms of behavior as symptoms of mental illness not only structures the population in terms of the definitions, but actually provokes an increase in the very kind of behavior it is trying to correct. In one cultural and conceptual framework, a form of behavior (e.g., hysteria) may make sense and win the sympathetic response of family and friends; in another framework, it may be defined as a symptom of mental illness and lead to confinement, treatment in a mental institution, and the labeling of a person as "crazy." In somewhat the same way, Bredemeier[22] sees mental health services as a vast institutional structure, established by professionals with the interests and definitions of professionals in mind. As Bredemeier describes it, the system is largely irrelevant to the fundamental problems of the poor. It meets them in artificial circumstances (the clinic or office), discusses their difficulty in a vocabulary and with a conceptual framework that have no relevance to their total world, and involves them in a treatment process which damages them by labeling them to themselves and their communities. In seeking to treat the "mental disorder" in isolation from other problems, the system may hopelessly complicate the life of the poor person. Within this process, from beginning (diagnosis) to end (treatment), the poor person comes off badly, is unable to protect himself, and sometimes ends up in a worse state than that in which he began. When the meaning of the high incidence of mental illness among the poor (and Puerto Ricans) is examined in this context, it takes on a different hue.

This kind of structural analysis of such problems as mental disorder (or education or delinquency) perceives the problem in a framework of social organization and the possession of means of access to strategic social,

[21]Thomas Szasz, *The Myth of Mental Illness* (New York: Harper & Row, Publishers, 1961).

[22]Harry C. Bredemeier, "The Socially Handicapped and the Agencies: A Market Analysis," in Riessman *et al., Mental Health of the Poor, op. cit.*, pp. 98–109.

economic, and political power. It sees many aspects of the way of life of the poor as legitimate alternatives in American society, or as imaginative and resourceful efforts to cope with difficulties which often result when a society functions in favor of the affluent. These forms of coping behavior are often defined as deviant, or as a symptom of mental disorder. Whether forms of behavior are legitimate alternatives, coping behavior, or actual indications of mental disorder, those in control of the mental health facilities determine the definitions, the methods, and conditions of treatment. They can confine those who are weak and segregate them for treatment. They can apply the system favorably to those they understand, and unfavorably to those they do not understand. What is crucial is that the poor have no access to strategic control. They cannot exert political power for the protection of forms of behavior which they consider legitimate; their coping behavior may bring them into conflict with the system; and they are helpless either to compel the system to operate in their favor, or to resist it when it operates to their disadvantage.

As a result, community action programs in recent years have sought to teach the poor to define their interests, to marshal the political strengths they possess, and to negotiate from a position of strength about the organization and conditions of such systems as mental health services. Forces already at work in the Puerto Rican community in New York are moving in a political direction.[23] They will ultimately affect the manner in which mental health services are related to the definition of mental health among Puerto Ricans and to the mental health needs of the Puerto Rican community.

The validity of the argument that high incidence rates of mental illness among Puerto Ricans are a consequence of the definition of mental illness and the structure of mental health services can be tested only over time during the years to come. Meanwhile, practical difficulties are very evident. Everyone in the mental health field laments the shortage of trained Spanish speaking personnel in mental health facilities. Lack of communication is a continual hazard to the Puerto Rican. Understaffing and overcrowding lead to too heavy case loads, too little time, rushed and routine diagnosis, and hasty treatment, thus adding to the danger of error in diagnosis and treatment. The response to this condition has generally been a call for more staff and more Spanish speaking personnel. But if the problem is misapplication of concepts of mental health and illness, the remedy will require more than personnel; it will require a redefinition of the whole situation. In that framework the meaning of the high rates of incidence may be understood more clearly.

23Joseph P. Fitzpatrick, "Puerto Ricans in Perspective: The Meaning of Migration to the Mainland," *The International Migration Review*, 11 (Spring 1965), 7–20.

One feature of New York life which is different from previous years, and which affects Puerto Rican migrants as it never affected earlier immigrants, is the problem of drug abuse. This is decidedly a New York problem which has become a problem for the Puerto Ricans because they have come to New York. Therefore, like welfare, it should really be discussed as a New York problem. But its impact on the Puerto Rican community has been widespread and tragic, and it will certainly have a significant influence on the adjustment of Puerto Ricans to New York. How it will relate to the question of identity is not clear. Whether a strong sense of community identity would protect the Puerto Ricans against it is not known, nor is it known whether it corrodes any sense of identity which already exists. For example, in his study of heroin addiction, Isadore Chein points out that 75 per cent of juvenile narcotics users lived in 15 per cent of the census tracts of New York City.[1] These tracts were the poorest, most crowded, and most dilapidated areas of the city. This is also evident from the data of the Narcotics Register Project of the Department of Health of the City of New York. Table 12–1 gives the data for newly reported heroin users by Health District. The extreme concentrations are in the poor areas of each of the boroughs, inhabited primarily by Blacks and Puerto Ricans. Chein found a high correlation among high levels of drug abuse, low levels of education, and high levels of family breakdown. In the Black and Puerto Rican residential areas which were less acute in their social and economic problems, he found low rates of drug abuse. This seems to indicate that drug abuse appears most frequently in areas which have characteristics of disorganization. But whether the rates of addiction have caused the disorganization, or are a result of it, is not clear. In either case, a description of the experience with drug abuse is essential to a study of Puerto Ricans in New York.

Special Problems: Drug Abuse

IDENTIFICATION OF THE PROBLEM

One major difficulty in a discussion of drug abuse is discovering

[1] Isadore Chein, *The Road to H* (New York: Basic Books, Inc., 1964), Chap. 2.

TABLE 12–1

PERCENTAGES OF NEWLY REPORTED HEROIN USE
BY HEALTH DISTRICT, 1968 AND CUMULATIVE,
1964–1968

Health District	1968	Total 1964–1968	New Reports 1968 % City	% Borough	Cumulative 1964–1968 % City	% Borough
Total New York City	11,926	40,634				
Total Manhattan	4,831	19,549	40.5	100.0	48.1	100.0
Central Harlem	1,619	6,784	13.6	33.5	16.7	34.7
East Harlem	810	2,877	6.8	16.8	7.1	14.7
Kips Bay-Yorkville	136	402	1.1	2.8	.9	2.1
Lower East Side	572	2,219	4.8	11.8	5.5	11.4
Lower West Side	494	2,384	4.1	10.2	5.8	12.2
Riverside	695	3,370	5.8	14.4	8.3	17.2
Washington Heights	437	1,445	3.7	9.0	3.6	7.4
District Unknown	68	68	.6	1.4	.2	.3
Total Bronx	3,166	9,059	26.5	100.0	22.3	100.0
Fordham-Riverside	146	405	1.2	4.6	1.0	4.5
Morrisania	1,039	3,064	8.7	32.8	7.5	33.8
Mott Haven	938	2,891	7.9	29.6	7.1	31.9
Pelham Bay	174	462	1.5	5.5	1.2	5.1
Tremont	560	1,494	4.7	17.7	3.7	16.5
Westchester	262	696	2.2	8.3	1.7	7.7
District Unknown	47	47	.4	1.5	.1	.5
Total Brooklyn	2,970	9,171	24.9	100.0	22.6	100.0
Bay Ridge	78	235	.7	2.6	.6	2.6
Bedford	595	1,815	5.0	20.0	4.5	19.8
Brownsville	477	1,405	4.0	16.1	3.5	15.3
Bushwick	399	1,106	3.3	13.4	2.7	12.1
Flatbush	174	549	1.5	5.9	1.4	6.0
Fort Greene	436	1,337	3.7	14.7	3.3	14.6
Gravesend	130	426	1.1	4.4	1.0	4.6
Red Hook-Gowanus	238	902	2.0	8.0	2.2	9.8
Sunset Park	149	437	1.2	5.0	1.1	4.7
Williamsburg-Greenpoint	276	941	2.3	9.3	2.3	10.3
District Unknown	18	18	.2	.6	—	.2
Total Queens	892	2,626	7.5	100.0	6.5	100.0
Astoria-Long Island City	97	392	.8	10.8	1.0	14.9
Corona	64	290	.5	7.2	.7	11.0
Flushing	124	351	1.0	13.9	.9	13.4
Jamaica East	335	873	2.8	37.6	2.1	33.2
Jamaica West	182	492	1.5	20.4	1.2	18.7
Maspeth-Forest Hills	61	199	.6	6.8	.5	7.6
District Unknown	29	29	.2	3.3	.1	1.1
Total Richmond	77	299	.6	100.0	.6	100.0

SOURCE: New York City Department of Health, Narcotics Register.

how extensive it is. The use of marijuana is so widespread that it is impossible to get any accurate information about its extent. Hallucenogenic drugs are more a college phenomenon than one involving the poor. For practical purposes, the problem can be reasonably described by identifying as clearly as possible addiction to heroin, which is the most serious and the one most likely to result in death.

According to the official information presented in Table 12–2, about 23 per cent of the persons reported to the Narcotics Register have been

TABLE 12–2

PERCENTAGE DISTRIBUTION OF ALL INDIVIDUALS
REPORTED TO THE NARCOTICS REGISTER, 1964–1968,
FOR ALL DRUG GROUPS, BY ETHNIC GROUP

Year	1964	1965	1966	1967	1968	Total
Total: Number	9,916	11,074	12,915	12,495	16,538	62,938
Per cent	100.0	100.0	100.0	100.0	100.0	100.0
White	26.9	29.6	28.3	29.9	28.2	28.6
Negro	48.1	44.4	45.8	45.9	45.7	46.0
Puerto Rican	21.5	23.8	24.3	23.5	22.1	23.0
Other	1.0	0.6	0.6	0.3	0.2	0.5
Unknown	2.5	1.6	1.0	0.4	3.8	1.9

SOURCE: New York City Department of Health, Narcotics Register.

Puerto Ricans. Of those reported as heroin addicts, about 24.64 per cent are Puerto Ricans. Since Puerto Ricans constitute about 15 per cent of the population of New York City, this percentage of drug users and heroin addicts is very high. Over the four year period, 1964–1968, 12,836 Puerto Ricans registered as heroin addicts. No one knows how many actual heroin users are never reported to the Narcotics Register, but the number of users is much higher than that reported. In any event, evidence indicates that drug abuse in the city is very high, and it strikes the Puerto Rican and Black populations particularly. The most convincing evidence of the seriousness of the drug problem is found in the statistics for deaths from drug abuse. In 1969, 119 Puerto Ricans died from drug abuse. This was 17.2 per cent of the 689 deaths from drug abuse during that year.[2]

More important than official information is the awareness on the part of the Puerto Rican community of the extent of the problem. Many Puerto Ricans returning to live on the Island have told the writer that

[2]Various categories are used for reporting deaths from drug abuse or causes related to drug abuse. The figures given above are those reported by the Bureau of Health Statistics and Analysis of the Department of Health of New York City. They represent simply, "Deaths due to drug abuse."

they were leaving the city because of their fear of drug abuse among their children. It is a central preoccupation of parents and one of the major concerns of the Puerto Rican community. Both youth and adults know the places where heroin is sold, and are generally bewildered why it cannot be stopped. Puerto Ricans generally see the problem as a social condition of New York which affects their children.[3] They have the impression that the children would be safe if public authorities really stopped the traffic. The situation was dramatically revealed in the newspaper publicity given to a 12-year-old Puerto Rican boy who was a heroin addict. The following is an excerpt from the report in *The New York Times.*

> The boy, Ralph de Jesus, told members of the [New York State] Joint Legislative Committee on Protection of Children and Youth and Drug Abuse . . . that he had been using drugs for almost a year.
> "I started mainlining[4] about six months ago. I learned how to do it in the street—in my neighborhood. I even sold drugs in my school for $2 a bag. I had a lot of customers.
> "I used to see my friends doing it and I didn't want to be left out. I started sniffing heroin, then skin-popping[5] and then mainlining."
> The frail 60-pound youth, about four feet tall, told the legislators that he had sold heroin to classmates in P.S. 60, . . . and had stolen to support his habit. . . .
> When asked if he had learned anything about what could happen to him if he continued with drugs, he answered: "Yes, I learned you could die from it.". . .
> His words that "nobody taught me, nobody forced me, but I didn't want to be left out when I saw my friends use drugs," had a reminiscent ring for many of the former drug users.
> Ralph said that while none of his six older brothers and sisters used drugs, "most of my friends use drugs and I wanted to be one of them."
> The youth said that he supported his habit by stealing pocketbooks, and by breaking into apartments and taking "anything I could find."[6]

CAUSES OF DRUG ADDICTION

No one has any convincing theory about the reasons for drug addiction. It is not confined to any social class, or to any ethnic or racial group.

[3]Return to Puerto Rico may offer little hope for escape. The Office of Investigations of the Department of the Treasury of Puerto Rico has an unofficial registration of drug addicts in Puerto Rico. This is considered reliable, but not complete information about drug abuse on the Island. The registration listed 19,000 heroin addicts on the Island as of the Fall of 1970. It is possible that the rate of heroin addiction on the Island may be as high as it is in New York. It is generally agreed that the drug problem in Puerto Rico is tied in with the problem in New York.

[4]Mainlining: injecting the heroin directly into the veins with a hypodermic needle.

[5]Skin-popping: injecting the heroin under the skin by a needle point.

[6]Reprinted from *The New York Times,* February 27, 1970, p. 1, by permission of the publisher. Copyright © 1970 by the New York Times Company.

Some theories seek an explanation in organic causes, in some physical condition of the human system.[7] Most theories stress personality factors as causes. The impressive rehabilitation programs of Synanon,[8] Daytop Village, and others find the cause in a personality weakness which leaves a person incapable of facing the reality of himself and his environment. Therapy based on this theory takes the form of a process of resocialization in the context of a therapeutic community. Through techniques of encounter, the addict is brought to confront himself and his environment; he develops a set of strong relationships with his companions in the therapeutic community, and, hopefully, is able to kick the habit.

A third theory looks at the character of the environment as the important variable in drug abuse.[9] After drugs infiltrate an area, a small-group culture begins to form around their use, and this group then expands. Economic interests form around the traffic in drugs and in the marketing of goods which addicts steal to support their habit; this in turn develops political ramifications. The whole structure of a neighborhood gradually begins to function around the narcotics habit. In Dan Wakefield's chapter, "Trip to the Moon," Pee-wee says: "If I wanted to live, I had to go on it [cocaine at school], everybody was on it."[10] Piri Thomas' vivid description of the drug subculture indicates that the pressures of the peer group are almost irresistible. In Elena Padilla's[11] description of drug use in Eastville, the young people often blame the habit on personality problems: "[drug addicts] are all mentally sick or emotionally disturbed." Sometimes they blame it on the environment: "I've always blamed my addiction on the environment. I've never been able to get away from it when I'm in the neighborhood."[12] Sometimes they blame it on the pressure of the peer group: "drug addicts in Eastville are defined by non-addicts as a group, and the addicts also speak of themselves as a distinct group."[13] Efren Ramirez, who founded an apparently successful rehabilitation program for addicts in Puerto Rico, was brought to New

[7]See the interview with Vincent Dole, "City and State to Join Disputed Narcotic Program," *The New York Times*, December 9, 1968, p. 1.

[8]Lewis Yablonsky, *The Tunnel Back: Synanon* (New York: The Macmillan Company, 1962), gives a detailed description of the Synanon method.

[9]Alfred R. Lindesmith, "A Sociological Theory of Drug Addiction," *Amer. J. Sociol.*, 43 (July 1938), 593–613. See also Solomon Kobrin and Harold Finestone, "Drug Addiction Among Young Persons in Chicago," in James F. Short, ed., *Gang Delinquency and Delinquent Sub-cultures* (New York: Harper & Row, Publishers, 1968).

[10]Dan Wakefield, *Island in the City* (Boston: Houghton Mifflin Company, 1959), p. 104.

[11]Elena Padilla, *Up From Puerto Rico* (New York: Columbia University Press, 1958), p. 248.

[12]*Ibid.*, p. 247.

[13]*Ibid.*, p. 237.

York by Mayor John Lindsay in 1967 to establish a similar program in the city. This later developed into the Addiction Services Agency, which administers the drug addiction prevention and rehabilitation programs conducted by the City of New York. Ramirez[14] always related the personal inadequacies responsible for drug abuse to large scale social problems in the area where the person lived. Residents fail to face the realities of their social, economic, and political situation, and so they cop out in various ways instead of confronting reality. Ramirez conceived the programs of addiction prevention as a method of bringing people, by means of encounter-confrontations, to face the reality of their own lives. In Ramirez' program, the preventive aspects involving social reform have been the least successful.

At present a wide variety of programs to prevent or correct drug abuse are being conducted by various segments of the Puerto Rican community, and wherever addiction prevention and rehabilitation programs are conducted in the City of New York, a large number of Puerto Ricans are involved in them. The largest addiction control program is the one conducted by the State of New York under the New York State Narcotic Addiction Control Commission. The central project of the Commission is a system of centers to which persons are committed for treatment after the courts have determined that they are addicts. Confinement may last for three years. The addicts receive medical care, personal counseling and group therapy in an effort to correct their addiction. During the period April 1, 1967, to March 31, 1968, 1,218, or 34.1 per cent of all certified admissions to the program, were Puerto Ricans.[15] The Commission also funds a large number of smaller projects conducted by public or private agencies.

New York City conducts a series of programs for addiction prevention and correction through the Addiction Services Agency. This agency manages a number of therapeutic communities called Phoenix Houses which operate generally on the model of the Synanon or Daytop Village programs. The ASA also funds a variety of programs conducted by public or private agencies. The largest one, called Horizon Project, is operated by funds provided by the National Institutes of Mental Health, and is located in the Lower East Side of Manhattan. This program seeks to rehabilitate addicts through a therapeutic community called Horizon House and a number of neighborhood clinics. It also has a preventive program which operates through a variety of community programs which

[14]For a popular article on the Ramirez program see Meriden Bennet, "The Concept: An Answer to Addiction?" *The Washington Monthly*, 1 (May 1969), 50–62.

[15]*First Annual Statistical Report, Fiscal Year ending March 31, 1968*, Narcotic Addiction Control Commission, State of New York, Albany, New York, p. 41.

hope to stimulate residents of high addiction neighborhoods to action
for improvement of the neighborhood and elimination of the drug traffic.
Horizon Project is located in a predominantly Puerto Rican area of the
city where the rate of addiction is high. According to Table 12–1, 11.4 per
cent of the addicts in Manhattan reported to the Narcotics Register during the years 1964–1968 were located in the Lower East Side. This area
includes the East Village, which has become the gathering center for drug
addicts from all over the country, thus complicating the effort to determine the relationship of drug addiction to the Puerto Rican residents.
Nevertheless, a considerable number of people on the Horizon Project
staff and in the programs have been Puerto Ricans, although complaints
have been raised that the Project is not sufficiently responsive to the needs
of the people in the area.

The danger of drug addiction is so serious on the Lower East Side
that all the community agencies have some kind of preventive or rehabil-
itative program. Nativity Mission Center, which has been a Puerto Rican
community center since the early 1950's, has had an active youth development and narcotics prevention program for years. The census tracts in
which the Center operates were indicated by the 1960 census to be the
poorest in the City of New York. Despite the continued efforts of the
Center, drug abuse in the area continues to increase at an alarming rate,
and the age at which it begins has been getting younger.

One of the early private programs for prevention of addiction
among Puerto Ricans is the program of the East Harlem Protestant
Parish.[16] This has been an important experimental parish center since
1948; since it is located in the heart of a densely populated Puerto Rican
area known as "The Barrio," most of its clientele have been Puerto
Ricans. The parish started a narcotics center in the mid-1950's which was
designed to be a place where anybody could come, no questions asked,
and be received by understanding people interested in helping him or
her. The center sought to cut through the complicated maze which generally faced the addict seeking assistance through the public agencies.
If an addict began to "kick the habit," he was brought into contact at
the center with other former addicts who were given responsibility for
helping him overcome the habit. The orientation was somewhat similar
to that which later became established at Synanon, but it has had the
advantage of being part of an existing community, of keeping the addicts
in the midst of their environment, and of linking the program to a series
of other activities which seek to improve the lives of the residents of the
area. The program has a formal religious aspect. This is not directed

16The beginnings of this program are described in Wakefield, *Island in the City*,
op. cit., pp. 106 ff.

toward conversion in the conventional mission style, but is designed rather to help the individual to increase in self-knowledge and arrive at the degree of self-mastery he needs to overcome his addiction. Although the directors of the program are cautious about claiming success, they have been sufficiently encouraged to continue.

Another program with a completely religious orientation has been conducted by the Damascus Christian Church (Pentecostal) in the Bronx under the direction of a Puerto Rican minister, the Reverenda Leoncia Rosado. This program, called The Christian Youth Crusade, was started in 1958. It is basically religious, with educational and recreational aspects, similar to the youth programs of other religious groups, but with an intensity of formation characteristic of the Pentecostal congregations. The program consists of a center in the Bronx to which the addicts can come and stay, and also a camp outside the city to which they can go. The approach to the addict is frankly and consistently religious, quite different from that of the therapeutic communities like Synanon. The guiding concept of the program is the belief that the addict is a sinner who must come to recognize his sinfulness and his need for help from God in order to master himself. Although medical help is sought when it seems necessary, the method of the Damascus Church program involves religious experience and conversion, bringing the individual to confront himself and God, and to seek divine help. It is the conviction of the Director that the addicts lack a purpose in life, and will develop a sense of purpose only through faith in God and religious practice. Reverenda Rosado is optimistic about her success. She estimates that, between 1958 and 1968, 250 to 300 addicts were rehabilitated through the program. Some have gone on to be ministers. One significant feature of the program is that it is a grass-roots Puerto Rican program which has sustained itself without public funds, and with the help and support of the Puerto Rican community.

How successful are the programs? No one really knows. Despite the enormous increase in resources for programs to correct the drug problem, it continues to grow worse. It is an increasing threat to the strength and stability of the Puerto Rican community in New York. When Dan Wakefield wrote his vivid description of drug addiction in East Harlem, many readers were shocked by the extent of addiction, the openness of the drug traffic, the futility of public efforts to correct the situation, and the tragic condition of a Puerto Rican community that seemed incapable of protecting its own children and had no public programs on which it could rely for effective support and protection. But since Wakefield's book was published in 1959, the problem has become a plague, and neither the Puerto Rican people nor the City of New York are any closer to a solution.

Therefore, one of the major factors which will affect the future of the Puerto Rican community, as it will affect the future of the City of New York, will be the problem of drug abuse. If the community can establish a strong basis for identity and develop the stability of a well organized segment of the New York population, this may be a major factor in its effort to resist the increase of drug abuse among its children. But this is a big "if," and there is no one in New York or in the nation who can prophesy what that future will be.

The preceding chapters have presented a number of aspects of the newest large migration to New York City. It is almost 25 years since the great wave of Puerto Rican migrants began to come to the mainland. An earlier and smaller wave had brought a substantial number to New York even before 1930. In any event, by this time Puerto Ricans have had a reasonably long and deep experience in the city. What can be said about it in terms of the problem of identity which is the central theme of this book?

In the perspective of the theories presented in Chapter Three, it is doubtful that Puerto Ricans will achieve a deep sense of identity through the development of a strong community on the model of earlier immigrant groups. In simple terms of residential settlement, the patterns of urban redevelopment and public housing make it impossible for them to cluster in strong, tightly knit communities. Their basis of strength will have to be sought elsewhere. Related to this is the difficulty of establishing a strong community on the basis of religious identification with the Puerto Rican parish. For the most part, the Puerto Rican parish does not exist. They are interspersed with other parishioners in "integrated" parishes. Although they have Spanish speaking priests, ceremonies and devotions in their traditional style, and many Spanish language societies, the parish is not "their parish" in the sense that it was the Italian, Polish, or Irish parish. The one religious experience which seems to be marked by the qualities of community, namely the Pentecostal sects and the storefront churches, appears to be an experience of the first generation which begins to fade away in the second or third.

The Meaning of Migration

The proximity of the Island and the ease of return seem to prompt the Puerto Ricans to find in the Island the sense of strength, support, and identity which former immigrants found in the clusters of their own kind in the immigrant communities of American cities. There is a great deal of truth in the comment that this is not a Puerto Rican migration, but a process of Puerto Rican commuting. Language, which could be the basis for identity, and which many of the young militants are asserting as such, does not seem to be holding at the present moment. The strong emphasis on bilingualism and the pressure of the youth may reverse this trend, but Fishman's studies indicate that Spanish will prob-

ably go the way of the language of every foreign group before. Furthermore, the rate of out-group marriage in the second generation indicates
that the romantic factor is as irresistible among Puerto Ricans as it was
with previous immigrant groups. The rate of out-group marriage is equal
to that of the immigrants of the early years of the century. Therefore,
strength of community on the basis of cultural background or cultural
ties does not seem to be the experience through which the Puerto Ricans
will establish their strength.

However, new developments have been taking place in recent years,
and a decided shift, from an emphasis on culture as the basis of community to an emphasis on power, begins to be apparent among the Puerto
Ricans. This is evident in the developments discussed in the chapters on
education and mental health, but it spreads out through other activities
of the Puerto Rican community.

This transition could best be expressed by a brief description of
the experience of the Puerto Rican Community Development Project.
As indicated in Chapter Five, this was a proposal, prepared by the Puerto
Rican Forum[1] and submitted to the Office of Economic Opportunity, for
a comprehensive, citywide coordinating agency which would promote,
integrate, and supervise a system of projects designed to assist Puerto
Ricans in New York. The explicit philosophy of this proposal was presented in a lengthy chapter entitled "Rationale for a Culturally Based
Project" which indicated the need to develop a project which would
enable the Puerto Ricans to develop a strong sense of identity and community. From this position of strength, they would be able to move more
securely toward integration with the larger society of New York City.
The proposal, in other words, reflected the theory of cultural pluralism,
current until recently, which stated that the preservation of traditional
cultures was the best basis for a strong sense of community among immigrants. This proposal was initially turned down for the reasons stated
above in Chapter Five. It was funded sometime later when city officials
expressed their confidence that it was in the hands of practical people
instead of impractical intellectuals. It has since taken a decidedly political
orientation, and illustrates the shift to an emphasis on power which has
become the central issue in relation to Puerto Ricans and all other racial
and ethnic minorities in the country.[2]

[1]Puerto Rican Forum, Inc., *The Puerto Rican Community Development Project*,
1964. Chap. 3 presents the rationale of the proposal.
[2]Internal political divisions troubled the Project during 1967–1968. In January
1968, the 15 top officials resigned in protest against the policies of the Board of Directors. See *The New York Times*, January 25, 1968, p. 24. It later became quite militant
in protests over funding (*The New York Times*, June 4, 1968), p. 32. More recently it
has been protesting the lack of support given to Puerto Rican Projects by the Council
Against Poverty.

This shift in emphasis from culture to power as the basis for community has resulted from a number of emphases which have been growing over the past 15 years—the politics of confrontation, the new strategies of protest, the community action programs of the antipoverty program, and a growing awareness on the part of the poor of the need to provoke substantial changes in the social structure. The theory underlying all these movements is that self-awareness, definition of community needs, marshaling forces to promote community interests, and maintaining a strong position to protect community interests all contribute to an increase in a sense of community and of identity which enable the poor to lead a more human existence. In this process, community strength comes to be promoted not by an emphasis on the preservation of culture, but in the organizing of resources around common interests.

This does not overlook the concern of power groups, particularly the Blacks, Puerto Ricans, and Mexicans, for the preservation of their culture, and their insistence on respect for their cultural background. Culture is recognized as an important element in identity, but the basis of strength is not the cultural background, but rather the organized power of the group. The theory of assimilation presented by Glazer and Moynihan, and summarized above in Chapter Three, leads one to expect this kind of development. Glazer and Moynihan indicated that, in the intermingling of people of many nationalities in a city like New York, the melting pot had never actually melted. In fact, they say, the ethnic group has not disappeared; it has become a new social form. Instead of people defining their interests around nationality background, as they did when they first came to the United States, they now define their interests around race or religion. The ethnic groups have become large scale interest groups. What the United States faces, according to Glazer and Moynihan, is not the assimilation of people of different cultural backgrounds into one predominant culture, but the accommodation of conflicting interests in a politically unified society. A basic theme in this analysis of immigrant experience is the strategic use of political and economic power by the ethnic groups to promote their interests in a democratic society. The significant theme is the achievement of identity by effective participation in the important decisions of the larger society.

Meanwhile, from quite a different perspective, scholars began to call attention to the culture of the poor, not so much as a traditional form which they should preserve in a pluralistic society, but as the focus of interest around which the poor should marshal their political strength. Walter B. Miller,[3] for example, insisted that the poor should not be

[3]Walter B. Miller, "Implications of Lower Class Culture for Social Work," *Social Service Rev.*, V, 33 (September 1959), 219–236.

looked upon as "deviant" from the dominant American way of life. It is important, Miller said, to view the behavior of the poor from within the context of their own lives. In this way, their culture or style of life can be seen as a positive thing, possessing its own strengths and values, and representing a creative response to the kinds of challenges they must face. Social service policy, therefore, should not take the form of trying to impose the dominant culture upon the poor, but of enabling them, within the context of their own strengths and values, to identify their needs, marshal their own resources, and create their own response and adaptation to American life and experience. Miller is not saying that the poor should never become part of the dominant culture; neither is he saying what the traditional position of the cultural pluralists implied. He is stating that the culture of the poor whom he studied in the Roxbury Community in Boston was, within their disadvantaged situation, an understandable creative response to the pressures of the dominant society in which their interests were not being served. Their culture, in other words, was their effort to create a system in which they pursued their own interests in the framework of a dominant society in which they were at a disadvantage. Although Miller never spells it out, his position implies that the culture of the poor reflects a massive conflict of interest between the poor and the more affluent members of their society; if they can organize and bargain from a position of strength about the accommodation of their interests, the cultural differences may begin to disappear. The preceding discussions about education and mental health indicated that this position may have important consequences in terms of political action by the Puerto Rican community around both these issues.

This type of thinking about culture was converted into a significant political force in the shift among the Black Americans from an emphasis on civil rights and integration to an emphasis on Black Power. Explicit in the movement for Black Power is the insistence that Black people must find a positive strength and value in the color that gives them their identity. They must define their interests as Black people, marshal their resources, and bargain from a position of strength about the conditions of the society in which they expect to live. Central to the movement is the remarkable development of a sense of pride in their color, but also important has been the creation of a sense of community solidarity out of their effort to organize their strength for the promotion of their own interests. Community identity and strength are not seen as something which emerged from the preservation of a cultural tradition, but from the political effort to press for a realization of their interests. As this emphasis on power has expressed itself in many areas of the lives of Black Americans, it has had an impact on the lives of Puerto Ricans.

In view of both the theory and practice described above, it would seem that, if Puerto Ricans can organize around an effort to promote their political interests, the achievement of identity and community strength may advance despite the problems which Puerto Ricans face on the Island or in New York. There is some indication that this may be taking place. The aggressiveness and success of the Black citizens in anti-poverty programs has resulted in a realization among Puerto Ricans that they must do likewise. As a result, a great deal of aggressiveness is appearing in areas where many Puerto Ricans are located; indeed, the activity in one area of the Bronx has provoked the intervention of city authorities to try to maintain some balance between Blacks and Puerto Ricans in a Community Corporation.[4] Furthermore, the Puerto Rican Community Development Project has been marked by the presence on its staff and Board of politically active people who see the need for political involvement if the Project is to remain strong.

It is not possible to predict what effect the present developments will have on the adjustment of Puerto Ricans to the City of New York. Their militancy about their interests in antipoverty programs, education, public welfare, and housing may enable them to develop a sense of identity and a community solidarity which they have thus far found it difficult to achieve. If this does take place, it will support the validity of the new theories of the adjustment of migrants to a new and strange city. They will integrate from a position of strength, but the strength will rest on the solidarity which results from organizing their efforts for the pursuit of group interests in the political arena.

Two tensions are evident among New York Puerto Ricans in this process. First, Puerto Ricans do have a rich cultural past and a deeply rooted style of life which they bring with them and seek to preserve. Much of this has been described in the chapter on the family. But many aspects of this cultural background are not well adapted to modern styles of confrontation, protest, and power. For example, the school in Puerto Rico is viewed as an extension of the home, and the teacher an extension of the family. The judge is likewise sought as a counselor rather than one who objectively enforces the law. These are seen as people with whom

[4] *The New York Times*, January 26, 1968, p. 19. This conflict of interests around the funding of antipoverty programs broke out again in November 1969. Protests came from Puerto Ricans involved in antipoverty programs (*The New York Times*, November 14, 1969, p. 51; November 15, 1969, p. 43), but they were later supported by a wide representation from the Puerto Rican community. Mayor Lindsay appointed a three man board, Herman Badillo, a Puerto Rican, Percy Sutton, a Black political leader, and Theodore Kheel, an experienced mediator, to mediate the conflicts between Blacks and Puerto Ricans in relation to antipoverty programs (*The New York Times*, November 26, 1969, p. 26).

one deals on a close personal basis rather than by protest or demonstration. Consequently, as the struggle for community power mounts, Puerto Ricans are sensitive to the danger of losing some of their treasured values through the very methods to which they must resort in an effort to defend them.

A second tension is evident between the growing number of young militant Puerto Ricans and the generation of their parents. Some of the former are college youth involved in militant activities on the campuses, demanding recognition of the needs of Puerto Rican Youth; others are young people outside the college system who are adopting the style of the aggressive and militant Blacks in pressing the demands of the Puerto Rican people. The Second Citywide Puerto Rican Conference of New York City, held in April 1969, was taken over by militant young Puerto Ricans. When some of them participated in the shutting down of City College in New York, there was evidence of considerable community support from other Puerto Ricans. But when a group of the young militants marched as a block in the Puerto Rican parade in June 1969, the response of the bystanders was not very favorable. This tension within the Puerto Rican community is similar to the tension between the young and the generation of their parents throughout the nation. What creates a particular problem for the Puerto Ricans is the danger that the militant action which may give the youth a sense of identity and unity behind a common cause may alienate many other people in the Puerto Rican community. This creates more serious complications for people in a period of transition in which they are trying to find themselves.

The adjustment of Puerto Ricans to New York City, therefore, is the continuation of an old experience among New Yorkers, but it is working itself out in very new ways. No particular theory of assimilation is adequate to analyze it. It is not yet clear what will become the basis of community strength which will enable the Puerto Ricans to move securely and confidently into full participation in the city's life. In the process, both New York City and Puerto Ricans will have changed. As New York becomes more Puerto Rican, and as Puerto Ricans become more intimately a part of New York, both can become enriched in the process. Toynbee says that the city without a challenge is a city which is dying. If that is true, New York and the Puerto Ricans are very much alive. If the history of New York City tells us anything, it tells us this: At the dark moments when people were convinced that the city was being destroyed, it was actually breaking through into a new and richer life. This may not be the basis for contentment and peace, but it is the basis for confidence and hope.

Index

DATE DUE

FEB 8 1972			
FEB 24 1972			
MT UNION			
FEB 1 9 1973			
ART UNION			
APR 24 1978			
UNIV ART			
FEB 1 0 1979			
JAN 29 1983			
APR 05 1983			
GAYLORD			